The Bender Gestalt Test
For Young Children

The Bender Gestalt Test
For Young Children

ELIZABETH MUNSTERBERG KOPPITZ, Ph.D.

Board of Cooperative Educational Services,
Bedford Hills, New York.

Grune & Stratton

A Subsidiary of Harcourt Brace Jovanovich, Publishers

New York   San Francisco   London

Grune & Stratton, Inc.
111 Fifth Avenue
New York, New York 10003

Distributed in the United Kingdom by
Academic Press, Inc. (London) Ltd.
24/28 Oval Road, London NW1

Library of Congress Catalog Card Number 63-19130
International Standard Book Number 0-8089-0239-3

Printed in the United States of America

Table of Contents

List of Tables

ACKNOWLEDGMENT

The work presented in this volume would not have been possible without the support and cooperation of numerous others. Above all I want to express my gratitude for the continued encouragement and help I received from my husband, Dr. Werner J. Koppitz. I am also deeply indebted to my former colleagues and collaborators at the Children's Mental Health Center· in Columbus, Ohio. These include especially, Mrs. Jenny Raduege, reading specialist, who first brought to my attention the usefulness of the Bender Gestalt Test for working with children who have learning and emotional problems, and John Sullivan and Dr. David Blyth, psychologists, who participated in the early stages of the Bender research and who shared with me their later research findings. Much appreciation is due to Mrs. Verdena Mardis, Thomas Stephens, Sam Bonham, and other school psychologists in Dayton and Montgomery County, Ohio, who collaborated on one of the research projects. I also want to give thanks to the school superintendents, principals, and class room teachers, too numerous to mention here by name, who generously gave of their time and cooperated in the Bender research projects, and to the 1500 boys and girls who contributed the Bender Test records upon which the studies presented here are based. My gratitude to Dr. Dan Jackson and Mrs. Anna Maher for their help in the preparation of the manuscript. And finally, my thanks to Dr. Lauretta Bender and the American Orthopsychiatric Association for their permission to reproduce Plate 1.

Elizabeth M. Koppitz

Preface

The studies presented in this volume developed gradually. They began with the search for a brief, meaningful test of visual-motor perception for young children. While working in a child guidance clinic the writer had become more and more impressed with the frequency and the severity of perceptual problems among youngsters with emotional and learning difficulties. Tentative explorations with the Bender Gestalt Test led to promising results but raised new questions and led to further investigations. The value of these studies seemed to be confirmed by the interest shown by other psychologists who either participated in the studies or who carried out their own studies with the Bender Gestalt Test. A series of related investigations was conducted and with each successive study the great potential of the Bender Gestalt Test for young children became more evident.

Most of the findings of the Bender research studies by the writer and her colleagues were published in the *Journal of Clinical Psychology,* the *Journal of Educational Psychology,* and the *Journal of Consulting Psychology.* The enthusiastic response to these articles demonstrated clearly, the need for more information on use of the Bender Gestalt Test with young children. It was therefore decided to integrate all research findings on the Bender Test for elementary school age children into one comprehensive volume. This book is the result of the effort.

The work presented here is a systematic exploration of the Bender Gestalt Test both as a perceptual test and as a projective test for *all* children, age 5 to 10 years, regardless of intelligence, neurological functioning, and emotional adjustment. The chief contributions of this work are probably the objective scoring systems which were standardized on more than 1200 public school children. The clinical application of the Bender Test data is illustrated by means of test protocols and case histories of clinic patients and of school children.

It is the writer's conviction that a meaningful psychological evaluation of a child should include an assessment of his interpersonal attitudes, as well as his intellectual and neurological functioning. Since the Bender Gestalt Test can be used both as a developmental test and as a projective test, it offers a maximum of information with a minimum of effort and time. The present volume has been written primarily for psychologists and therapists working with children in clinics, schools, and in private practice. It is hoped that it will prove to be a valuable aid in the diagnosing of learning problems, emotional disturbances, and neurological malfunctioning. It is also meant to assist in the screening of school beginners and in the prediction of achievement among elementary school pupils.

This book was designed to bring clarification and information to all those clinicians who have been using the Bender Gestalt Test in the past but who were uncertain how to interpret their findings. It is further intended to serve as an introduction to the Bender Gestalt Test for all those psychologists who have up to now been unfamiliar with the test or who have not been aware of its potential for use with children. The material presented here offers many findings and suggestions but it does not claim to have all the answers to all questions concerning the Bender Gestalt Test and its relationship to young children. It is therefore hoped that this book will also serve to stimulate further research in the field.

—E.M.K.

To the Memory of
Hugo Münsterberg

PART I. Introduction

The Bender Gestalt Test (Bender, 1938) needs little introduction. Twenty years after Bender published her monograph on *Visual motor Gestalt test and its clinical use*, it was rated among the most widely used clinical tests. Sundberg (1961) conducted a survey on the practices of psychological testing in clinical services. A total of 185 hospitals and agencies participated in this survey. Of these, 158 indicated that they use the Bender Gestalt Test to some extent. This places the Bender Test right after the Rorschach, the Draw-a-Person Test, and the Thematic Apperception Test in the order of frequency in which they were mentioned by the various clinical agencies and hospitals. The interest in the Bender Gestalt Test dates largely from the late 1940's. Between 1946, when an earlier survey was conducted, and 1958 the Bender Test jumped from the 54th place to the fourth place in the order of tests most frequently used by clinical psychologists.

Survey of the Literature

The Bender Gestalt Test consists of nine figures (Plate 1) which are presented one at a time and which the subject is asked to copy on a blank piece of paper. Wertheimer (1923) had used the designs originally in order to demonstrate the principles of Gestalt Psychology as related to perception. Bender adapted these figures and used them as a visual motor test. In doing so she applied the theory of Gestalt Psychology to the study of personality and to clinical practice. Bender (1938, p. 5) points out that the perception and the reproduction of the Gesalt figures are determined by biological principles of sensory motor action and vary depending on (a) the growth pattern and maturation level of an individual and (b) his pathological state either functionally or organically induced.

Bender describes in some detail the process of maturation of visual-motor perception in young children and presents a chart with illustrations of typical reproductions of the Gestalt figures by youngsters, age three to eleven years. The chart shows that most children are able to copy all nine Bender Gestalt designs without errors by the time they are eleven years old. Bender's work is mainly devoted to the clinical application of the Gestalt Test to various types of adult patients including those suffering from organic brain disease, schizophrenia, depressive psychosis, psychoneurosis and mental retardation. Bender uses a developmental approach in analyzing children's protocols and clinical evaluation in the assessment of test protocols of adult patients. Bender does not provide an objective scoring system for the test.

One of the advantages of the Bender Gestalt Test lies in the fact that it can be interpreted in several different ways. In addition to the developmental and clinical approach suggested by Bender, Hutt (1950, 1960) introduced another mode of analyzing Bender Test protocols. Hutt and his followers use the Bender Test as a projective test and interpret the drawings of Bender designs in accordance with psychoanalytic theory. Following this method,

1

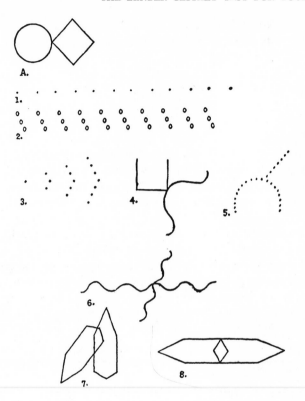

Plate 1. Nine Figures of the Bender Gestalt Test, adapted from Wertheimer. (Reproduced from Plate 1 of Research Monograph No. 3, "A Visual Motor Gestalt Test and its Clinical Use," published by the American Orthopsychiatric Association in 1938. Copyright, the American Orthopsychiatric Association, Inc. Reproduced by permission.)

Figure 8, for instance, becomes a phallic symbol and distortions on the drawing of this design suggest problems in the sexual area. This type of interpretation presupposes that the individual making the drawing has the ability to copy the Bender figures correctly and would do so if no emotional interference were present. Thus its usefulness is limited to older children and to adults whose visual-motor perception has fully matured.

Many psychologists use general clinical impressions when evaluating Bender Test protocols. The problem with this approach is, of course, that it is highly subjective. While some clinicians are extremely astute in their clinical judgments, others are not. Studies in this area have shown a lack of agreement and a low reliability between the clinical judgment of experts on the Bender Gestalt Test (Goldberg, 1959; Mehlman and Vatovec, 1956; Peek and Storms, 1958).

As the Bender Test was more widely used, many psychologists felt a great need for an objective scoring system that was both reliable and valid. Several attempts at developing such a scoring system have been made. Billingslea (1948) was the first to publish a rather elaborate scoring system for the Bender Test. Additional scoring systems for this test were developed by Gobetz (1953), Keller (1955), Kitay (1950), Peek and Quast (1951), and Stewart and

Cunningham (1958). These scoring systems are all designed for use with adult psychiatric patients or with retarded institutionalized children; they are not intended for use with young children of normal intelligence.

The most widely accepted scoring system for the Bender Test is that of Pascal and Suttell which was published in 1951. It was designed for adults, 15 to 50 years old, of normal intelligence who have the maturity and capacity to perceive and to reproduce the Bender Gestalt figures without error. Pascal and Suttell view the performance of a subject on the Bender Test as a reflection of his attitude toward reality. They see the ability to draw the Bender designs as a function of the individual's integrative capacity or his "ego strength." Thus Pascal and Suttell's scoring system for the Bender Test measures "ego strength" and is correlated with emotional adjustment, i.e., the higher the Bender score, the greater the likelihood that the individual is a patient of a psychiatrist. Pascal and Suttell further suggest that the magnitude of the Bender score is related to the severity of the emotional disturbance.

Pascal and Suttell recognize the effect of maturation on the performance of young children on the Bender Gestalt Test, but they discuss children's records primarily as a point of comparison for adult Bender records. Since their scoring system was developed for adults and from adult test data, Pascal and Suttell caution against using it with young children. For children under the age of nine they do not consider their scoring system very reliable. Bender protocols of youngsters below the age of six cannot be scored by the Pascal and Suttell method.

A general survey of the literature reveals that more than 130 books, studies and papers dealing with the Bender Gestalt Test have been published since the original Bender monograph appeared in 1938. A number of these papers are devoted to a general discussion of the Bender Test and to modifications in the administration and the execution of the test. About three-fourths of all publications on the Bender deal with its usefulness in differential diagnosis for adult psychiatric patients. A few additional studies are devoted to the diagnosis of brain pathology and to mental retardation in adult subjects. Some investigators have explored the effect of medication and of electroshock therapy on the drawing of Bender figures. And an attempt has also been made to relate the Bender Test to intelligence.

About one-fifth of all publications on the Bender Test, (i.e., 29 studies), are exclusively concerned with children. Most of these studies were published since 1955 showing the growing awareness of the value of the Bender Test for this age group. It is interesting to note that the Bender studies with children cover more areas of investigation than those using adults as subjects. Thus the Bender Test has been used with children to screen for school readiness (Baldwin, 1950; Harriman and Harriman, 1950; Koppitz, Mardis, and Stephens, 1961; Smith and Keogh, 1962), to predict school achievement (Koppitz, 1962a; Koppitz, Sullivan, Blyth and Shelton, 1959), to diagnose reading and learning problems (Koppitz, 1958a; Lachman, 1960), to evaluate emotional difficulties (Clawson, 1959, 1962; Koppitz, 1960a, 1960b; Simpson, 1958), to determine the need for psychotherapy (Byrd, 1956), to diagnose brain injury (Chorost, Spivack and Levine, 1959; Halpin, 1955; Hanvick, 1953; Koppitz, 1962b; Shaw and Cruickshank, 1956; Wewetzer, 1956, 1959), and to study mental retardation (Eber, 1958; Halpin, 1955; Keller, 1955). The Bender Test has also been employed as a test for differential diagnosis between young psychiatric patients (Goldberg, 1957) and between groups of juvenile delinquents (Corotto and Curmut, 1960), as a test of intelligence for school children (Armstrong & Hauck, 1960; Koppitz, 1958b), as a group test for school beginners (Keogh & Smith, 1961), and as a projective test (Greenbaum, 1955). All these studies will be discussed in more detail at a later time. They are mentioned here only to point out the diversity of the Bender Test studies with children.

❊   ❊   ❊

As was indicated earlier, most established scoring systems for the Bender Test are not suitable for use with young children. As a result, investigators studying children have had to develop or adapt their own methods for the evaluation and scoring of Bender protocols. The result has been a variety of Bender scoring systems and rating schemes, most of which are based on a very limited normative population and are designed for a particular group of children only, e.g., retarded children, emotionally disturbed children, etc. It is very difficult to compare the findings in the various Bender studies with children because of the variety of methods used in analyzing the test records.

Most of the Bender studies under discussion are well planned and carefully executed. But few investigators make an attempt to differentiate between the various types of distortions on the Bender Test. In the majority of studies, all kinds of deviations are scored equally regardless of whether they are primarily related to age and maturity, to perceptual problems, or whether they are manifestations of emotional attitudes. As a consequence, a given deviation on the Bender Test, e.g., rotation or failure to integrate parts of a figure, is considered by some investigators a sign of brain injury, by others a sign of emotional problems, and again by some a sign of immaturity. This situation is somewhat confusing. Can one deviation indicate all these things? And if this is so, how can one tell which interpretation is the correct one at a given time?

Up to this time no comprehensive work on the Bender Gestalt Test for children has been available. There is a great need to integrate all the research findings and to clarify objectively what level of performance can be expected from children at various ages. It is also essential to determine the significance of the different distortions and deviations on the Bender Test for children of different age levels. The present volume attempts to fill this gap.

Background and Purpose of This Book

Like a great many other psychologists, the author has used the Bender Test almost routinely when evaluating young children with emotional problems. It became apparent that most of the children with behavior problems also had learning problems and that most of them did very poorly on the Bender. Relying on her clinical judgment, the author concluded that poor Bender performance and learning problems were probably due to perceptual problems. However, when the writer studied Bender protocols of young school children without learning problems, she discovered that these too showed many deviations and distortions. A comparison of Bender records of clinic patients and school children revealed that no single distortion or deviation occurred exclusively in one group or the other.

This observation led to a systematic study of Bender records of school children, kindergarten through fourth grade, to discover what was "normal" and what was "abnormal" for Bender drawings at a given age. It was noted that children differ in the rate of maturation and in the sequence in which they learn the various visual-motor gestalt functions. Thus some children are able to reproduce the total Gestalt configuration of a design at a very early age but have difficulty drawing the details; others are excellent in reproducing details but require additional months or years before they are able to copy the figures in the correct horizontal or vertical positions; again others learn to draw correctly the detail and the direction of parts of the figures but only very gradually acquire the ability to integrate the parts into a whole Gestalt. It follows therefore that a meaningful interpretation of a Bender protocol of a young child should always include the total record rather than evaluating performance on individual figures.

A developmental scoring system for the Bender was constructed using composite scores for all nine figures. Normative data were collected from the Bender records of over 1100 school children, age 5 to 10 years. The scoring system was then applied to the Bender protocols of groups of exceptional children including those with emotional problems, brain injury, learning difficulties and mental retardation. In addition to the developmental approach, the Bender records were analyzed for indicators of emotional attitudes. A second scoring system was developed to measure emotional adjustment.

In the present volume the author attempts to differentiate between the distortions on the Bender which primarily reflect immaturity or perceptual malfunctioning, and those which are not related to age and perception but which reflect emotional factors and attitudes. The various deviations are divided into two separate scales which serve different functions. *Both* scales are used on any given Bender protocol. Bender suggested both a developmental and a clinical approach in the evaluation of test protocols, but she used only one *or* the other method on the record of a single patient. Most examiners interpret Bender protocols in only one way: they regard it as *either* a test of visual-motor perception *or* as a test of emotional adjustment and personality; they evaluate the subjects for intelligence or perceptual maturation *or* for "ego strength." To do this most investigators score *all* deviations found on a Bender record and add them up. Yet there is no evidence that all deviations measure the same thing nor is there any reason why a Bender protocol of a given child can only be interpreted in one way.

Many psychologists clamor for more and more tests; to gain a complete picture of a patient they administer a great many different tests, each of which tests only one dimension of the subject's functioning or personality. This is very time consuming and fatiguing for both the patient and the examiner. This writer believes that *the need is not so much for more tests as it is for a better and more complete utilization of existing tests.* It is suggested that each psychological test used, be analyzed and interpreted in at least two or possibly three different ways. By selecting two or three tests which lend themselves to a multidimensional interpretation, the time and energy required to evaluate a subject can be greatly curtailed and the efficiency can be increased. This also offers the advantage of greater flexibility. Psychological tests are designed to furnish valuable information each time they are used; however, examiners are well aware that there are occasions when a given test yields little or no important data for a specific subject. When a multidimensional approach is used, a test will rarely be unproductive, for even when one approach is not conclusive another one may be quite revealing. The Bender Gestalt Test is a test well suited for multiple interpretation according to different dimensions of personality.

The aim of this volume is to provide different ways of analyzing the Bender records of young children so that the examiner can evaluate their perceptual maturity, possible neurological impairment, and emotional adjustment from a single Bender Test protocol. The scoring methods presented are applicable to all children, age 5 to 10 years, regardless of their intelligence or the type of problems they present. All material in this book is based on published research findings of other investigators, on the author's clinical experience and on her own investigations. The findings presented apply only to the age levels indicated above with the exception of retarded subjects whose chronological age may range up to 16 years but whose mental age is 10 years or less. The scoring systems used are crude and are not meant to be used for older children or adults with fully matured visual-motor perception.

PART II. The Developmental Bender Scoring System for Young Children

INITIAL BENDER SCORING SYSTEM

The first step in the construction of a developmental scoring system for the Bender Test was to compile a list of twenty outstanding deviations and distortions found on Bender Test protocols of young children. These twenty deviations and distortions were used as the initial scoring categories in the evaluation of Bender records. Each scoring category was carefully defined. Since the scoring system was being designed for young children whose fine muscle coordination had not yet fully matured, the Bender records were scored for gross irregularities only. Minute deviations were deemed to be of little importance for this age group. For the same reason a simple dichotomous scoring method was employed; each item was scored as either present or absent.

The twenty initial scoring categories are listed below with abbreviated descriptions:

1) *Distortion of shape* (all 9 Figures): Disproportion of parts; incorrect number of dots; shape of design lost; lines instead of dots; lack of integration of parts.

2) *Rotation* (all 9 Figures): Rotation of figure or part of it by 45° or more.

3) *Erasures* (all 9 Figures): Erasures and redrawing of figure; extra lines.

4) *Part missing* (all 9 Figures): Omission of rows, columns, parts of figure.

5) *Confused order:* No discernible order in placing figures on the paper.

6) *Overlapping of figures:* Two or more figures overlap.

7) *Compression:* All figures placed in less than half of sheet of paper; all figures clinging to outer edge of paper.

8) *Second attempt:* Spontaneous attempt to draw a figure a second time.

9) *Perseveration* (Figures 1, 2, 6): More than 14 dots or columns; more than five sinusoidal curves.

10) *Circles or dashes for dots* (Figures 1, 3, 5): Two or more substitutes of circles or dashes for dots.

11) *Wavy line* (Figures 1, 2): Gross deviation from straight line.

12) *Shape of circles* (Figure 2): Three or more gross deviations from circle.

13) *Deviation in slant* (Figure 2): Two or more abrupt changes in slant.

14) *Dashes or dots for circles* (Figure 2): Substitutions for more than half of the number of circles.

15) *Blunting* (Figure 3): Point of arrow obliterated.

16) *Incorrect number of dots* (Figure 3): More or less than 16 dots.

17) *Square and curve not joined* (Figures A and 4): Corner of square and curve more than ⅛″ apart.

18) *Angles in curve* (Figure 6): Three or more distinct angles present.

19) *Extra or missing angles* (Figures 7 and 8): Incorrect number of angles.

20) *Boxes* (all 9 Figures): Box drawn around individual figure.

Subjects

Seventy-seven school children served as subjects for the initial evaluation of the Bender scoring items. Their age range was from 6 years 4 months to 10 years 8 months. All subjects were of at least average intelligence. They had been chosen from two first grades, two second grades, two third grades and one fourth grade in three different schools. Each classroom teacher had been asked to select from among her pupils the five or six with outstanding achievement and good overall adjustment and the five or six with poor achievement and poor overall adjustment. Forty-one of the subjects were good students, 36 were poor students. All pupils were divided into two groups according to grade placement. One group consisted of 43 first and second graders, while the other group included 34 third and fourth graders. The high and low achievers were equally distributed in both groups.

School achievement was selected as the criterion against which each Bender scoring item was to be validated. Most experts agree that a child has to reach a certain degree of maturity in visual-motor perception before he is able to learn reading, writing, and the comprehension of number concepts. A school beginner with well developed visual-motor perception is likely to be a good student in the elementary grades, whereas the child with immature visual-motor perception will have difficulty with his school work. The Bender Gestalt Test reflects maturity in visual-motor perception in school beginners.

The Bender Gestalt Test was administered to each child individually in school. The standard set of Bender Gestalt Test cards (Bender, 1946) was used for this and all subsequent studies presented in this volume. The instructions for the administration of the Bender Test are shown on page 15.

Reliability of Scoring

Another psychologist and the author scored 14 Bender Test protocols independently of each other on all twenty scoring categories. There was an agreement on 93 per cent of all items scored by the two examiners. Thereafter the author scored all Bender protocols "blindly," that is, without knowing what class a subject attended and whether he was a good or poor student.

Analysis of Data and Results

After the scoring was completed the Bender protocols were grouped according to grade level and according to high and low school achievement. Thereafter each scoring category was evaluated separately to determine how well it could differentiate between the good and the poor students. Twenty chi-square tests were computed comparing the number of subjects with high and with low achievement whose Bender records revealed the presence or the absence of a given scoring category. Seven of the twenty chi-squares were found to be significant at the five per cent level or better. The seven scoring categories which can differentiate between the high and low achievers are shown on *Table 1.*

These seven categories include: Distortion of shape, rotation, substitution of circles or dashes for dots, perseveration, failure to integrate the parts of a figure, substitution of angles for curves, and extra or missing angles.

Table 1. Initial Bender Scoring Categories Differentiating Good and Poor Students

Scoring Category	1st & 2nd Grades		3rd & 4th Grades		All 4 Grades	
	Chi-square	P	Chi-square	P	Chi-square	P
Distortion of shape	12.2	<.001	1.5	>.20	12.6	<.001
Rotation	2.8	<.10	9.2	<.01	20.2	<.001
Circles for dots	5.2	<.05	1.0	>.20	9.0	<.01
Perseveration	8.6	<.01	20.3	<.001	22.2	<.001
Integration of parts	2.9	<.10	4.1	<.05	6.1	<.02
Angles in curves	6.9	<.01	1.0	>.20	4.7	<.05
Incorrect angles	15.5	<.001	5.7	<.02	19.5	<.001

Thus it appears that school achievement in the elementary grades is related to three basic functions in visual-motor perception. Apparently a child must have achieved maturity in these areas before he can function well in school: 1) The ability to perceive a design as a limited whole and to be able to start and stop an action at will, e.g., he has to be able to follow simple instructions down to the last detail and must not expand the drawing of a limited series of dots into a long string of impulsive loops or dashes. He must not get carried away by an activity and must not repeat it over and over again, unable to stop himself from perseverating. He must be able to perceive and comprehend the beginning and the end of a word on a printed page. 2) The ability to perceive and to copy lines and shapes correctly in regard to direction and form, e.g., to be able to write letters correctly with all their angles and curves, and to be able to follow a written word from left to right. 3) The ability to integrate parts into a whole Gestalt, e.g., to be able to form whole words out of single letters and to understand that one and one make two.

A detailed analysis of the scoring category "distortion of shape" revealed that it was scored frequently for Figures A, 3, 5 and 7, and proved statistically significant for these Figures. However, it occurred only rarely on Figures 1, 2, 4, 6, and 8, and was not statistically significant for these Figures. For this reason, this scoring category is only used for Figures A, 3, 5, and 7 from here on in. Most of the seven significant scoring categories apply to more than one Bender figure. The seven scoring categories include a total of 31 different scoring items, all of which are mutually exclusive. These 31 scoring items form the Initial Bender Scoring System for Children. Each scoring item is scored as present or absent, that it, as 1 or 0. All scoring points are added for each subject into a composite score; thus a child can obtain a maximum composite score of 31.

The original list of scoring categories numbered 20 categories. Only seven of these are included in the Initial Bender Scoring System for Children. The remaining 13 scoring categories appear to be not related to school achievement in the elementary grades and by implication seem to be not related to maturity in visual-motor perception. But this does not mean that they are not related to other factors. A tentative analysis of the 13 scoring categories suggests that they fall into two main groups: 1) deviations primarily related to immaturity in fine muscle coordination and to poor planning ability in young children;

2) deviations reflecting primarily, emotional tension and attitudes which are not related to age and immaturity.

Bender deviations in the first group include: *poor organization of figures* on the sheet of paper including *overlap of designs, poor attention to details,* and the *omission of parts* while retaining the basic Gestalt of the figure, e.g., *wavy line, irregular shape of circles, deviation in slant, blunting* and *incorrect number of dots in Figure 3.* These deviations are apparently largely due to immature muscle coordination and a lack of knowledge of numbers (most second graders count dots carefully); they do not seem to be related to immature visual-motor perception. These deviations were found equally often on the Bender records of the good and the poor students in the first grade and decreased in frequency as the age of the subjects increased.

The second group of deviations concerns the quality and method of drawing and are also not related to visual-motor perception. These include: *Erasures* and the *redrawing of a figure,* a *spontaneous second attempt to draw a figure,* the *constriction* of all nine figures into less than half the sheet of paper, the *substitution of tense little dots or impulsive dashes for circles,* and the *boxing in of designs.* Interestingly enough all but the last of these deviations occurred more often among the good students than among the poor students, and more often among the older subjects than among the younger ones. But none of the differences were statistically significant. All these deviations seem to reflect tension and anxiety. Ours is a competitive society. It is quite probable that a certain degree of tension and anxiety may add to a child's motivation and effort for learning and may actually contribute to his achievement in the elementary grades. Without this drive a child will hardly achieve maximum performance. However, when the tension becomes excessive as in severely disturbed patients, then it paralyzes and interferes with achievement. This was the case with one subject who boxed in each of the nine Bender designs. This type of deviation occurs rarely and then most likely with psychotic or very disturbed children. Bender deviations which reflect emotional attitudes primarily will be explored more fully later on (see p. 123).

The Initial Bender Scoring System for Children, including 31 separate scoring items, was tested in its entirety on the original sample of 77 subjects (Koppitz, 1958). Composite scores were computed for each subject and from these the Bender mean scores were derived for the younger group and for the older group of children. Thereafter, chi-squares were used to determine how well the Bender composite scores could differentiate between the high and the low achievers. There was a comparison of the number of good and poor students whose Bender score was above or below the mean score for the age group under consideration. The results were statistically significant:

Grades	N	Chi-square	P
1st & 2nd	43	10.2	<.01
3rd & 4th	34	5.4	<.02
1st to 4th	77	15.9	<.001

These findings are not unexpected since the Initial Scoring System was developed from the records of these subjects. For this reason the Initial Scoring System was cross validated on a second group of subjects.

Crossvalidation of Initial Scoring System

The subjects for the crossvalidation were 51 young patients seen at a child guidance clinic. All were attending public school, grade one through four. Their age range was from 6 years 4 months to 10 years 8 months. The subjects were divided into two groups; one group included 31 children who were referred because of emotional problems *and* poor school achievement. The other group included 20 children whose school achievement was at least average. These children were referred primarily because of serious emotional disturbances. The Bender Test was administered to all subjects as part of a battery of psychological tests they were given during evaluation at the clinic. The procedure followed with this group of subjects was the same as with the original group of public school children.

All Bender protocols were scored according to the Initial Bender Scoring System. Thereafter the mean composite scores were determined for the first and second graders, the third and fourth graders, and for all subjects combined. Chi-squares were computed comparing the number of subjects with and without learning problems whose Bender scores were above or below the mean score for that particular grade level. All three chi-squares were statistically significant at the one per cent level:

Grades	N	Chi-square	P
1st & 2nd	25	11.7	$<.001$
3rd & 4th	26	9.1	$<.01$
1st to 4th	51	14.2	$<.001$

Thus it was demonstrated that the Initial Bender Scoring System can differentiate between students with and without learning problems.

Revision of the Initial Scoring System

Although the Initial Scoring System proved useful in working with young children, it became apparent that a few minor changes would improve it. Frequent reexamination of Bender protocols and the retesting of many children led to a revision of the Initial Scoring System in the fall of 1959. No basic changes were made, no significant scoring items were omitted or added. The revision represents primarily a sharpening of individual scoring items, e.g., on Figure 1 the addition of three or more extra dots was originally scored as perseveration. Careful study of Bender records showed that many well functioning six and seven year olds add two or three extra dots. Additions do not seem to become significant unless at least five or more dots are added. Thus the definition for perseveration on Figure 1 was changed from three to more than five extra dots. In similar fashion the scoring items for Figure 2 were changed so that not only an excessive number of columns was scored, but also an extra number of circles within the majority of columns, etc.

An item analysis was conducted evaluating each scoring item separately. The result of these reevaluations and modifications is the *Developmental Bender Scoring System for Young Children* which is used for most of the work presented in this volume.

THE DEVELOPMENTAL BENDER SCORING SYSTEM

The Developmental Bender Scoring System (see p. 15) consists of 30 mutually exclusive scoring items which are scored as either present or absent. All scorings are added into a composite score. Thus a child could theoretically receive a composite score of 30. Since the Bender Test is scored for errors, a high score indicates a poor performance while a low score reflects a good performance.

Each scoring item in the Developmental Scoring System was validated against first and second grade achievement as measured on the Metropolitan Achievement Test (Hildreth and Griffith, 1946). Only those items were included which were able to differentiate statistically between above and below average students in either the first *or* the second grade at the five per cent level or better, or which demonstrated a strong trend, i.e., significant at the 10 per cent level, in *both* the first and second grades.

The subjects for the item analysis of the Developmental Scoring System were 165 school children. Ninety-nine were first graders, of these 59 were above average and 40 were below average in their achievement on the Metropolitan Achievement Test. The remaining 66 subjects were second graders, 45 of these were good students and 21 were poor students. The subjects were selected from six different schools in urban, suburban and rural settings and represent a socioeconomic cross section of these areas.

Table 2 shows each scoring item of the Developmental Scoring System and its ability to differentiate between high and low achievers. The chi-square and P values are given for the first and second graders. Detailed definitions and examples of each scoring item are shown in the scoring manual on page 16.

Reliability of Developmental Bender Scoring System

Two aspects of the Developmental Scoring System must be considered in order to demonstrate its reliability: 1) The agreement among different scorers using the scoring system independently from each other and 2) the consistency of the test scores for individual subjects to whom the Bender Test has been administered more than once.

1) *Scorer reliability:* Miller, Loewenfeld, Lindner and Turner (1962) made a reliability study of the Developmental Bender Scoring System. They each scored independently, 30 Bender protocols from young clinic patients. Copies of the Bender records were also sent to the author for scoring purposes. Pearson product moment correlations were computed between the test scores of all five raters. All correlations were statistically highly significant and ranged from .88 to .96. The results were .94, .93, .93, .93, and .95 respectively when the correlations were converted into Z-scores and average inter-rater correlations were computed.

Table 2. Relationship Between Scoring Items of the Developmental Bender Scoring System and the Metropolitan Achievement Test for 1st and 2nd Graders

Bender Scoring Item	1st Grade Achievement		2nd Grade Achievement	
	Chi-square	P	Chi-square	P
Figure A				
1a. Distortion of shape	12.6	<.001	6.54	<.02
1b. Disproportion	trend		trend	
2. Rotation	14.99	<.001	12.85	<.001
3. Integration	10.06	<.01	trend	
Figure 1				
4. Circles for dots	4.94	<.05	trend	
5. Rotation	trend		4.42	<.05
6. Perseveration	trend		3.59	<.05
Figure 2				
7. Rotation	trend		6.73	<.01
8. Row added, omitted	35.73	<.001	18.15	<.001
9. Perseveration	trend		6.77	<.01
Figure 3				
10. Circles for dots	trend		trend	
11. Rotation	5.06	<.05	11.45	<.001
12a. Shape lost	26.02	<.001	trend	
12b. Lines for dots	trend (rare but very significant when present)			
Figure 4				
13. Rotation	5.28	<.05	6.63	<.01
14. Integration	10.23	<.01	trend	
Figure 5				
15. Circles for dots	trend		trend	
16. Rotation	trend		trend	
17a. Shape lost	trend		8.07	<.01
17b. Line for dots	12.15	<.001	trend	
Figure 6				
18a. Angles in curves	trend		trend	
18b. Straight line	14.60	<.001	4.42	<.05
19. Integration	trend		trend	
20. Perseveration	4.17	<.05	6.88	<.01
Figure 7				
21a. Disproportion	7.73	<.01	4.14	<.05
21b. Incorrect angles	21.48	<.001	4.24	<.05
22. Rotation	22.51	<.001	9.45	<.01
23. Integration	12.99	<.001	11.87	<.001
Figure 8				
24. Incorrect angles	14.91	<.001	6.84	<.01
25. Rotation	18.63	<.001	12.61	<.001

2) *Test score reliability:* The split-half method and the alternate form method are not appropriate for testing the reliability of the Bender Scoring System. This leaves the test-retest method. This method of testing for reliability presents some difficulties. Immediate retesting with the Bender would show the result of practice; while a long time interval between test administrations would reflect the effect of maturation in visual-motor perception in a young child. It is hoped that both practice effect and the effect of maturation have been minimized by selecting a time interval between the two test administrations that is neither very short nor very long. Each subject was retested with the Bender Test four months after the initial administration of the test.

Table 3. Reliability of Developmental Bender Scoring System

School	Grade	N	Tau	P
A	Kindergarten	34	.597	<.001
B	Kindergarten	26	.659	<.001
A	First	36	.547	<.001
B	First	16	.646	<.001

Two kindergarten classes and two first grade classes served as subjects for the reliability study. One kindergarten class and one first grade were taken from a school in a lower socioeconomic area (School A); the other two classes came from a middle class community (School B). All subjects were tested in school by the author. The Bender protocols were scored according to the Developmental Bender Scoring System for Young Children. Kendall's Rank Correlation Coefficient (Siegel, 1956, p. 213) was used to compute the reliability coefficient between the scores of the first and second administration of the Bender Test. The results are shown on *Table 3*. All correlations were found to be statistically significant at the .001 level. Thus it appears that the Developmental Scoring System is reliable and can be used with considerable confidence.

Scoring Manual for the
Developmental Bender Scoring System

A. Instructions for the Administration and Scoring
of the Bender Test

Seat the child comfortably at an uncluttered table on which two sheets of paper, size 8½″ by 11″, and a #2 pencil with an eraser have been placed. After rapport has been established show the stack of Bender cards (Bender, 1946) to the child and say: "I have nine cards here with designs on them for you to copy. Here is the first one. Now go ahead and make one just like it." After the child has adjusted the position of the paper to suit himself, place the first Bender card, Figure A, at the top of the blank paper in front of the child. No comments are made while observations and notes are made on the child's test behavior. There is no time limit for this test. When a child has finished drawing a figure, the card with the stimulus design is removed and the next card is put in front of him and so on. All nine cards are presented in this fashion in orderly sequence.

If a child asks questions concerning the number of dots or the size of the drawings, etc., he should be given a noncommittal answer like: "Make it look as much like the picture on the card as you can." He should be neither encouraged nor discouraged from erasing or making several attempts at drawing a design. It has been found practical to discourage the counting of dots on Figure 5 since this requires much time and adds little new information. The children who count dots on Figure 5 also tend to count dots and circles of Figures 1, 2, and 3. When a child begins counting dots on Figure 5 the examiner may say: "You do not have to count those dots, just make it look like the picture." If the child still persists in counting the dots, it then takes on diagnostic significance. The indications are that the child is most likely quite perfectionistic or compulsive. If the child has filled most of the sheet of paper and turns it sideways to fit Figure 8 into the remaining space, this should be noted on the protocol as this is not considered to be a rotation of design.

Each child is permitted to use as much or as little paper as he desires. If he asks for more than the two sheets of paper provided, he should be given additional paper without comment. Even though the test has no time limit, it is helpful to keep a record of the time needed to complete the test, as an extremely short or an unusually long period is diagnostically significant.

Care should be taken that the Bender Test is presented at the beginning of the testing session when the child is well rested as a fatigued child will not perform optimally. If it is felt that a child has been rather hasty in the execution of the test or if maximum performance has not been obtained, he may be asked to repeat the drawing of a Bender figure on another sheet of paper. If additional testing for maximum achievement seems indicated a notation to this effect should be made on the protocol.

All Bender scoring items are scored as one or zero, that is, as "present" or "absent." Only clearcut deviations are scored. In case of doubt an item is not scored. Since the Scoring System is designed for young children with as yet immature fine motor control, minor deviations are ignored. All scoring points are added into a composite score upon which the normative data are based.

B.   Bender Scoring Items with Definitions and Scoring Examples

The numbers under each scoring example refer to the scoring items which should be checked for that particular drawing.

Figure A.

1. *Distortion of Shape*

   a) Square or circle or both are excessively. flattened or misshapen; one axis of circle or square is twice as long as the other one.
   Examples:

   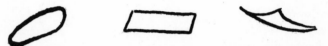

   If two sides of square do not meet at point of junction with circle then the shape of the square is evaluated *as if* the two sides did meet.
   Examples:

   scored   not scored

   Extra or missing angles (in case of doubt do not score).
   b) Disproportion between size of square and circle; one is twice as large as the other one.

2. *Rotation*

   Rotation of figure or any part of it by 45° or more; rotation of stimulus card even if then copied correctly in rotated position.
   Examples:

   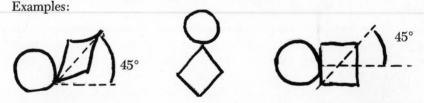

3. *Integration*

   Failure to join circle and square; curve and adjacent corner of square more than ⅛″ apart; this applies also to overlap.
   Examples:

   scored   not scored

Scoring Examples for Figure A.

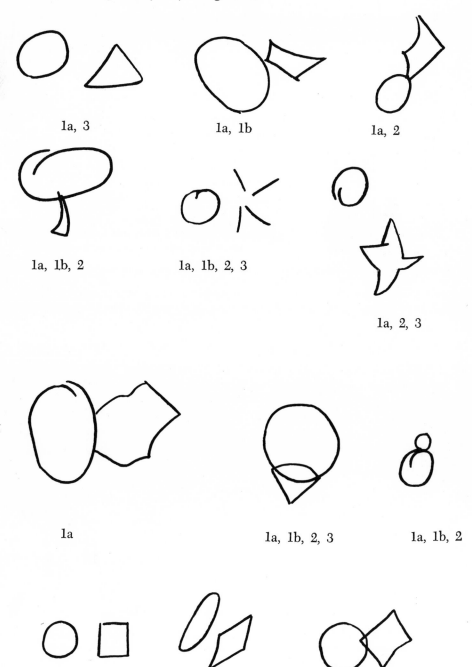

1a, 3   1a, 1b   1a, 2

1a, 1b, 2   1a, 1b, 2, 3

1a, 2, 3

1a   1a, 1b, 2, 3   1a, 1b, 2

2, 3   1a, 2, 3   no score

Figure 1.

4. *Distortion of Shape*

Five or more dots converted into circles; enlarged dots or partially filled circles *not* considered circles for scoring of this item—in case of doubt do not score; dashes *not* scored.

scored

not scored

5. *Rotation*

Rotation of figure by 45° or more; rotation of stimulus card even if then copied correctly as shown on rotated card.

6. *Perseveration*

More than 15 dots in a row.

Scoring Examples for Figure 1.

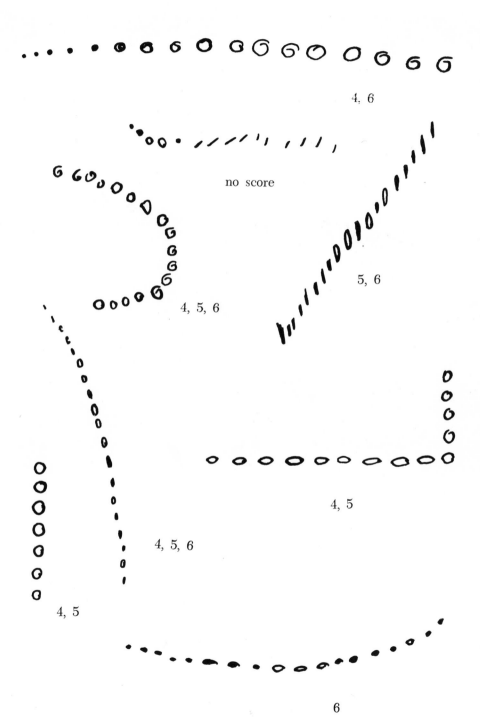

Figure 2.

7. *Rotation*

Rotation of figure by 45° or more; rotation of stimulus card even if then copied correctly as shown on rotated card.

8. *Integration*

One or two rows of circles omitted; row of dots of Figure 1 used as third row for Figure 2; four or more circles in the majority of columns; row of circles added.

9. *Perseveration*

More than 14 columns of circles in a row.

Scoring Examples for Figure 2.

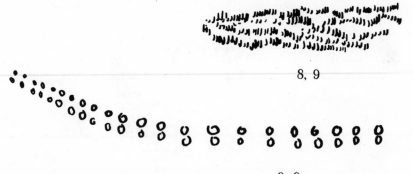

8, 9

8, 9

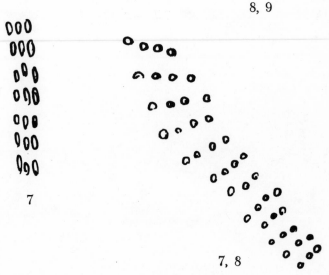

7

7, 8

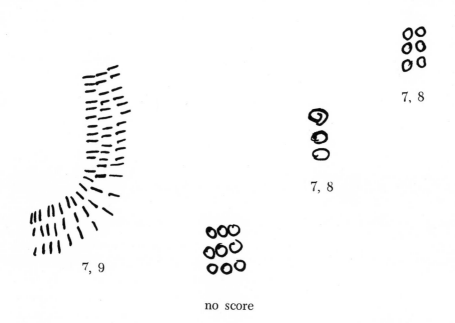

7, 8

7, 8

7, 9

no score

8

no score

Figure 3.

10. *Distortion of Shape*

   Five or more dots converted into circles; enlarged dots or partially filled-in circles *not* considered circles for this scoring item—in case of doubt do not score; dashes *not* scored.

11. *Rotation*

   Rotation of axis of figure by 45° or more; rotation of stimulus card even if then copied correctly as shown on rotated card;

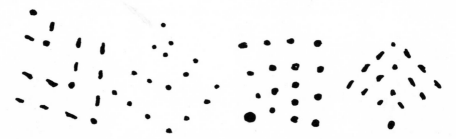

12. *Integration*

   a) Shape of design lost; failure to increase each successive row of dots; shape of arrow head not recognizable or reversed; conglomeration of dots; single row of dots; blunting or incorrect number of dots *not* scored.

   b) Continuous line insteaed of row of dots; line may be substituted for dots or may be addition to dots.

Scoring Examples for Figure 3.

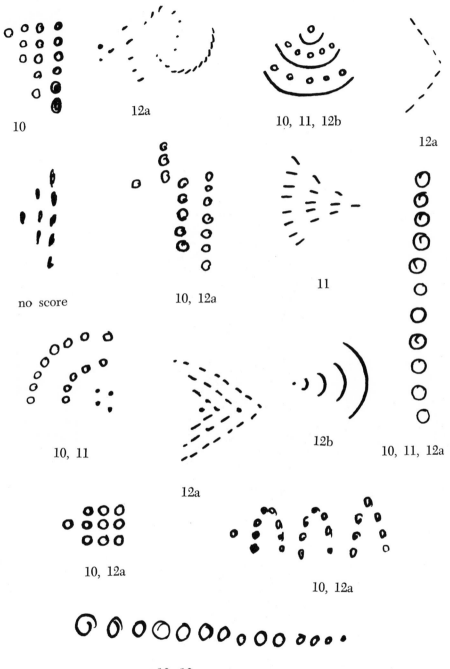

10

12a

10, 11, 12b

12a

no score

10, 12a

11

10, 11

12a

12b

10, 11, 12a

10, 12a

10, 12a

10, 12a

Figure 4.

13. *Rotation*

Rotation of figure or part of it by 45° or more; rotation of stimulus card even if then copied correctly as shown on rotated card:

14. *Integration*

Curve and adjacent corner more than ⅛″ apart, this applies also to overlap; curve touches both corners:

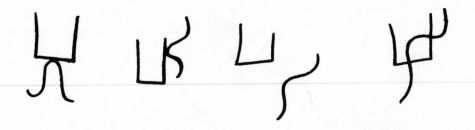

Scoring Examples for Figure 4.

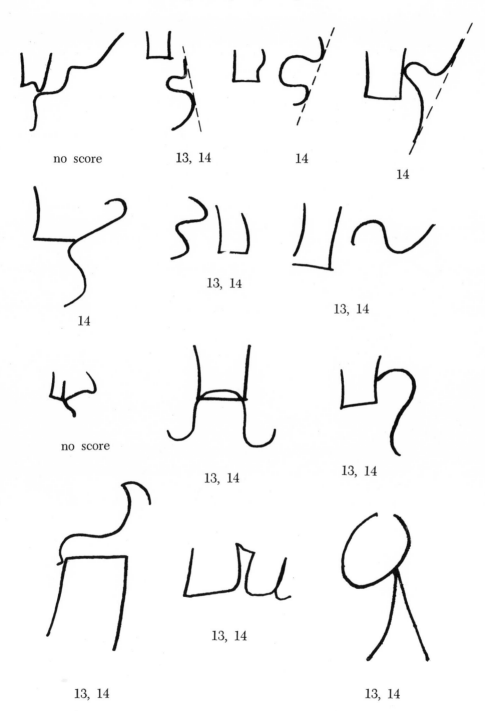

no score   13, 14   14

14

14   13, 14

13, 14

no score   13, 14   13, 14

13, 14   13, 14

13, 14   13, 14

Figure 5.

15. *Distortion of Shape*

Five or more dots converted into circles; enlarged dots or partially filled circles are *not* scored; dashes are *not* scored.

16. *Rotation*

Rotation of total figure by 45° or more; rotation of extension, e.g., extension points toward left side or extension begins left of center dot of arc; rotation is only scored once even if arc and extension are both rotated independently of each other.

Examples:

17. *Integration*

a) Shape of design is lost; conglomeration of dots; straight line or circle of dots instead of arc; extension cuts through arc; square or point instead of arc is *not* scored.

Examples

     scored   not scored

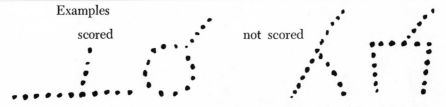

b) Continuous line instead of dots in either arc or extension or both.

Scoring Examples for Figure 5.

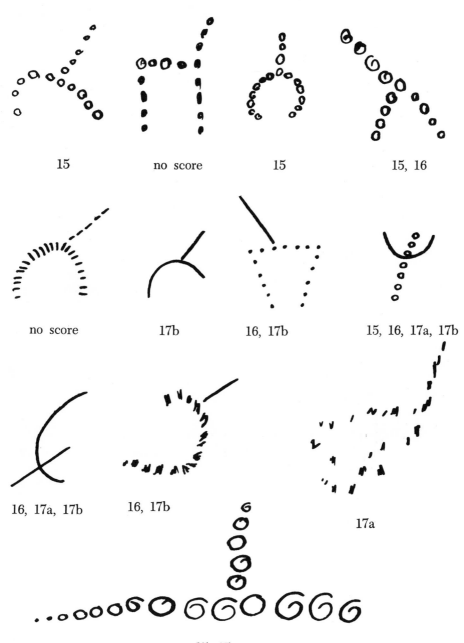

Figure 6.

18. *Distortion of Shape*

    a) Three or more distinct angles substituted for curves (in case of doubt do not score):

    b) No curve at all in one or both lines; straight line.

19. *Integration*

    Two lines not crossing or crossing at the extreme end of one or both lines; two wavy lines intervowen:

20. *Perseveration*

    Six or more complete sinusoidal curves in either direction.

Scoring Examples for Figure 6.

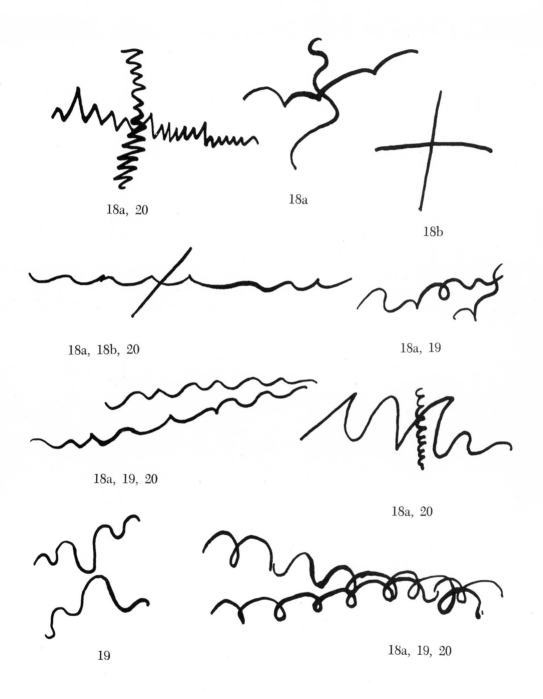

18a, 20

18a

18b

18a, 18b, 20

18a, 19

18a, 19, 20

18a, 20

19

18a, 19, 20

Figure 7.

21. *Distortion of Shape*

a) Disproportion between size of two hexagons; one must be at least twice as large as the other one.

b) Hexagons are excessively misshapen; extra or missing angles in one or both hexagons.

22. *Rotation*

Rotation of figure or any part of it by 45° or more; rotation of stimulus card even if then copied correctly as shown on rotated card.

Examples of Rotation:

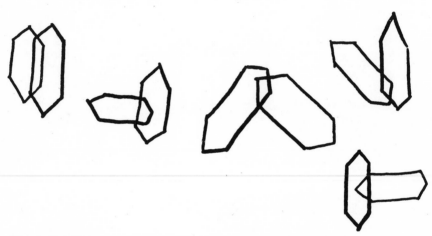

23. *Integration*

Hexagons do not overlap or overlap excessivly, that is, one hexagon completely penetrates through the other one.

Examples:

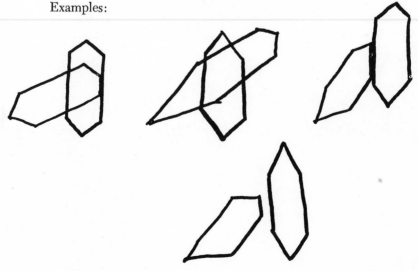

Scoring Examples for Figure 7.

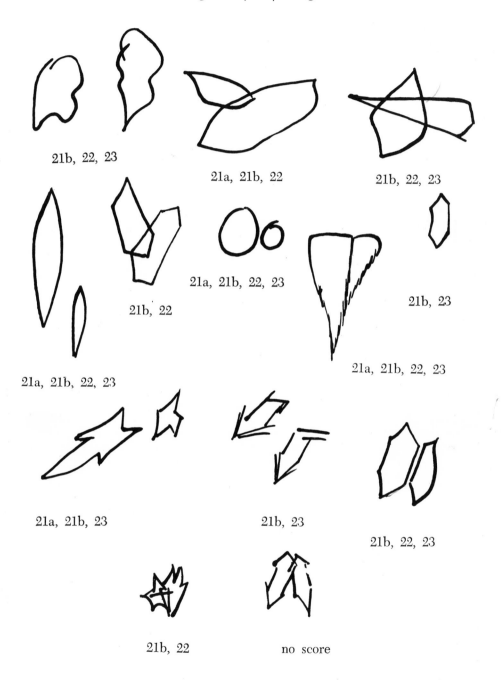

21b, 22, 23

21a, 21b, 22

21b, 22, 23

21b, 22

21a, 21b, 22, 23

21b, 23

21a, 21b, 22, 23

21a, 21b, 22, 23

21a, 21b, 23

21b, 23

21b, 22, 23

21b, 22

no score

Figure 8

24. *Distortion of Shape*

Hexagon or diamond excessively misshapen; extra or missing angles; diamond omitted.

25. *Rotation*

Rotation of figure by 45° or more; rotation of stimulus card even if then copied correctly as shown on rotated card (turning of paper in order to make most economical use of paper *not* scored and should be noted on the protocol).

Scoring Examples for Figure 8.

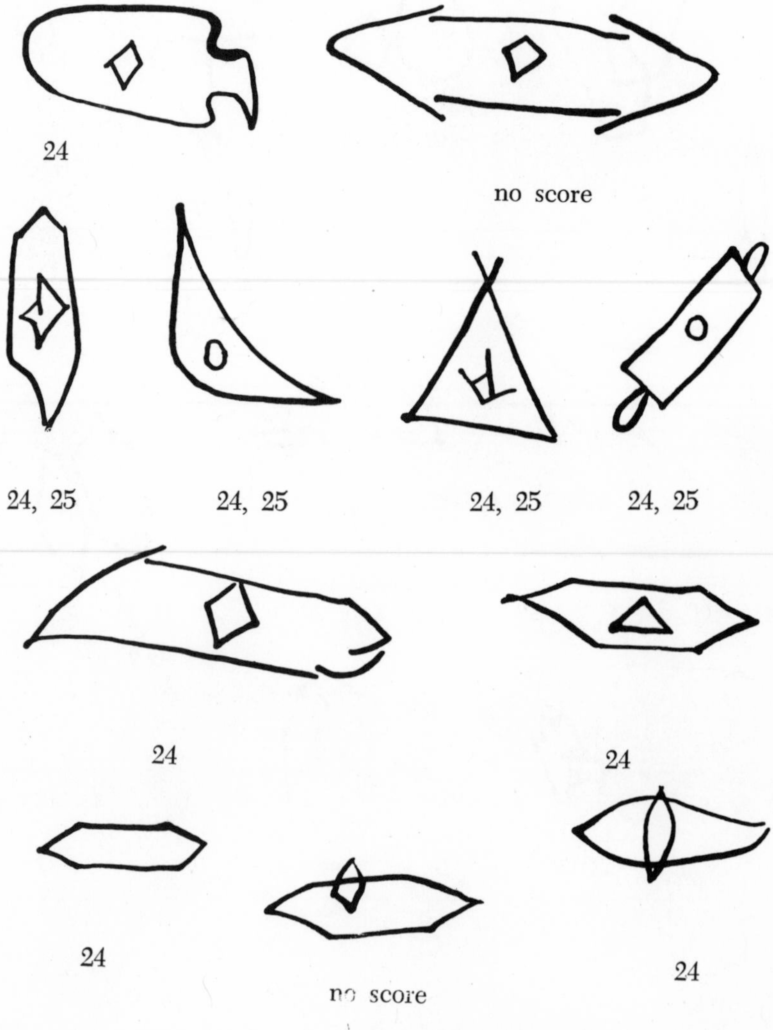

24

no score

24, 25   24, 25   24, 25   24, 25

24   24

24   no score   24

NORMATIVE DATA

Normative data for the Developmental Bender Scoring System for Children were derived from 1104 public school children representing 46 entire classes in twelve different schools located in rural, small town, suburban, and urban areas of the Midwest and Eastern States. Only those children were excluded from the normative population whose age was below 5 years or above 10 years and 11 months. The 46 classes included 10 kindergarten rooms, 13 first grades, 11 second grades, 5 each of the third and fourth grades, and two fifth grades. The distribution of the normative population by age and sex is shown on *Table 4*. The Bender Gestalt Test was administered individually to each child in

Table 4. Distribution of Normative Population by Age and Sex

Age	Boys	Girls	Total
5–0 to 5–5	37	44	81
5–6 to 5–11	81	47	128
6–0 to 6–5	89	66	155
6–6 to 6–11	103	77	180
7–0 to 7–5	95	61	156
7–6 to 7–11	62	48	110
8–0 to 8–5	39	23	62
8–6 to 8–11	37	23	60
9–0 to 9–5	32	33	65
9–6 to 9–11	28	21	49
10–0 to 10–5	15	12	27
10–6 to 10–11	19	12	31
Total	637	467	1104

school by a qualified psychologist; all Bender protocols were scored by the author according to the Developmental Bender Scoring System.

Mean Scores of Normative Population

The means of the Bender composite scores for the boys and the girls and for all children at each age level are presented on *Table 5*. The same data are shown on the graph on *Figure 1*. It can be seen that the Bender mean scores

Table 5. Bender Mean Scores by Age and Sex for Normative Population

Age	Boys	Girls	All Subjects
5	14.3	13.0	13.6
5½	10.0	9.3	9.8
6	8.3	8.6	8.4
6½	6.2	6.6	6.4
7	5.3	4.2	4.8
7½	4.9	4.4	4.7
8	3.9	3.6	3.7
8½	2.6	2.4	2.5
9	1.5	1.8	1.7
9½	1.6	1.5	1.6
10	1.5	1.7	1.6
10½	1.4	1.5	1.5

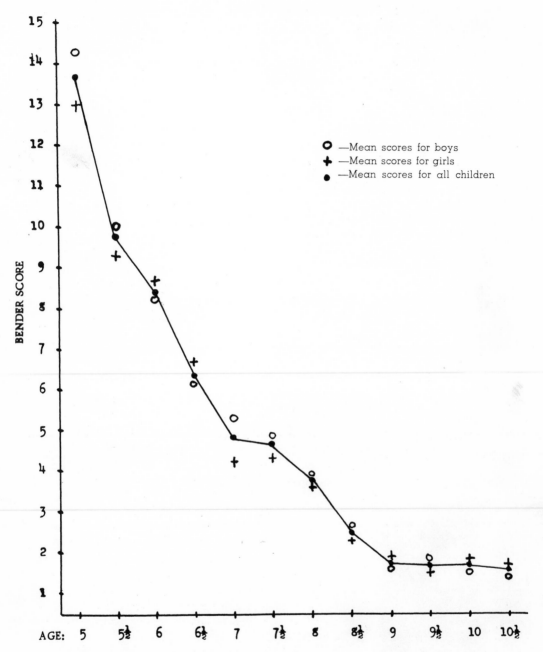

Fig. 1. Mean scores of normative population for the Developmental Bender Scoring System for Children.

for both boys and girls decrease steadily between the ages of 5 and 9 years thus reflecting the effect of maturation on visual-motor perception. At age 9 most children are able to execute the Bender Test without serious errors. Up to age 8, the Bender Test discriminates both those who are above average and those below average in test performance. After age 8, a Bender score of 0 or the absence of errors indicates nothing more than that the child's visual-motor perception is within the normal range for his age group. For children 7 years old and younger the Bender Test is useful for the identification of both immature and bright youngsters; for children 8 years old or older the Bender Test can only screen out those with immature or malfunctioning visual-motor perception.

At ages 5 and 7 girls appear to mature a little earlier than boys in visual-motor perception. However, at no age level were the differences between the Bender mean scores for boys and girls statistically significant. Thus the normative data for the Developmental Bender Scoring System for Children require only a single Bender mean score for all children of a given age level. The complete normative data are given on *Table 6;* included are the Bender mean scores and standard deviations for ages 5 through 10 years 11 months and for kindergarten through fourth grades.

Interpretation of Normative Data

The data presented on *Table 6** can be interpreted in three different ways, that is, a child's score on the Developmental Bender Scoring System can be compared with that of 1) other children of the same chronological age, 2) other children with the same level of maturation in visual-motor perception, and 3) other children at a given grade level.

For instance, if a child, age 5 years 8 months, has a Bender score of 5 it may be concluded that 1) compared to other 5-½ year olds this child's test performance on the Bender falls one standard deviation above the mean test score for this age group, that is, the level of his Bender score is above the 85th percentile for his age group and is in the bright average or possibly superior range; 2) the child's maturation in visual-motor perception as reflected on his Bender score is on the level of a seven year old child; 3) the Bender score of this 5-½ year old is similar to that of average beginning second grade students.

Another child, age 7 years 2 months, has a Bender score of 8. This means that 1) the youngsters' Bender score is one standard deviation below the mean score for other seven year old children, that is, his Bender score falls below the 16th percentile for his age group; 2) this child's maturation in visual-motor perception is on the level of a six year old child and is 3) similar to that of beginning first grade students.

A boy, age 9 years 7 months, obtained a Bender score of 2. According to the normative table this would indicate that 1) the boy's Bender score is slightly below the mean score for his age level is well within the normal range of scores for 9-½ year olds; 2) his maturation level in visual-motor perception is appropriate for his own age level; and 3) his Bender score is just below the mean score found in beginning fourth grade students.

And finally a girl, age 10 years 1 month, copied the Bender designs to perfection without a single error; her score is 0. Her test performance may be interpreted as follows: 1) The Bender score of 0 is above the mean score for

---

* See Appendix, page 188.

her age group but beyond that it is not possible to state whether the girl is average or outstanding compared to other 10 year olds; 2) the level of maturation in visual-motor perception shown by this child is appropriate for her age level; 3) the girl's Bender score is better than that of average beginning fourth graders and is most likely appropriate for fifth graders.

TIME STUDY OF THE BENDER TEST

While administering the Bender Gestalt Test the author observed that some children work with great ease and fairly rapidly, whereas others struggle laboriously and require a great deal of time to complete the test. Again others dash off the drawings of Bender designs in haste and work quite carelessly. The children who seem to have least difficulty with the Bender Test and who seem to do best, work at a steady but moderate pace. Since the time factor appeared to have some significance for the Bender performance, a study was conducted to determine the average time required by young children to complete the drawing of all nine Bender figures (Koppitz, 1960b). The subjects for this study were 339 children in 16 school classes. The children were unaware that their performance on the test was being timed. Each subject was clocked by the author from the moment he began drawing Figure A until the last stroke on Figure 8 was completed. The subjects came from four kindergarten classes, and from three classes of the first, second, third and fourth grades. *Table 7* shows the average time required for the completion of the Bender Test

Table 7. Time Required to Complete the Bender Gestalt Test

Age	N	Mean Time	Critical Time Limits*
5	58	5 min. 13 sec.	3 minutes to 10 minutes
5½	23	7 min. 0 sec.	4 minutes to 10 minutes
6	38	6 min. 20 sec.	4 minutes to 9 minutes
6½	40	6 min. 33 sec.	4 minutes to 9 minutes
7	27	6 min. 27 sec.	4 minutes to 9 minutes
7½	27	6 min. 53 sec.	4 minutes to 9 minutes
8	35	6 min. 45 sec.	4 minutes to 9 minutes
8½	30	6 min. 5 sec.	4 minutes to 9 minutes
9	37	6 min. 17 sec.	4 minutes to 8 minutes
9½	24	6 min. 30 sec.	4 minutes to 8 minutes
Total	339		

* Rounded off to full minutes.

and the critical time limits, i.e., plus-minus one standard deviation from the mean time, for each age level.

The findings indicate that girls tend to work a little faster than boys in the early grades. But at none of the age levels investigated was there a statistically significant difference in the time required to finish the Bender Test for boys and girls. There also appears to be little difference between the average time required to complete the test at different age levels, but the upper and lower limits at which time becomes important vary somewhat from one age level to the next. Thus it is not uncommon for five year olds to dash through the test in as little as three minutes or to struggle with it for as long as ten minutes.

Six to eight year old children tend to require at least four minutes to complete the Bender Test and rarely need more than 9 minutes to do so. By the time children are 9 years old, greater maturity in visual-motor perception usually enables them to execute the Bender Test in less than 8 minutes, but rarely can they finish the test in less than four minutes.

For practical consideration it is sufficient to state that the average time required to complete the Bender Gestalt Test for young children, age 5 to 9½ years, is 6 minutes and 30 seconds. Time appears to be significant only if a child finishes the Bender Test in more or less time than indicated by the critical time limits for each age level. It was found that a child who needs an excessively long time to copy the Bender figures tends to be either quite perfectionistic or he may be working hard to compensate for a problem in visual-motor perception or both. At times the Bender protocol of such a slow working child may be near perfect and without error, yet this child will have difficulty with school achievement since he requires such an exorbitant amount of time to complete his work.

Children who finish the Bender Test in unusually short time were found to be frequently impulsive and lacking in adequate concentration and/or effort to carry through the required task satisfactorily. Occasionally a very bright child may be able to complete the Bender Test without errors in less than four minutes. This is rare. In most cases a very short time needed for the test is associated with poor test performance and poor school achievement; it is most often found on the Bender records of children with neurological impairment (see p. 100). These findings suggest that the time required to complete the Bender Test is important and should be given consideration when evaluating a child's Bender record.

TEST-RETEST ON THE BENDER: LONGITUDINAL STUDIES

The mean scores on the Developmental Bender Scoring System for Children show a gradual decrease between the ages of five and nine (see *Table 6* and Figure 1) indicating a steady improvement in the ability to copy Bender designs with increasing age. However, these findings do not imply that every child matures at the same rate in visual-motor perception nor that the Bender scores of each individual child will necessarily correspond to the successive age group norms. The general rule of considerable individual differences of human characteristics and abilities holds also for the maturation process in visual-motor perception. A study was made by the author exploring the likelihood that a child who does well on the Bender Test at one age level will do equally well at a later age level and vice versa.

In this study the Bender Gestalt Test was administered more than once to 264 school children in regular classes and to 36 children in special classes. Five different groups of subjects were used: (a) One group of 91 kindergarten and first grade students was tested three times with four to six months intervals between test administrations. First they were seen at the end of the school year, then again at the beginning of the following school year and finally a third time at the end of that school year. (b) Forty-four additional children from the same population were tested twice; they were absent at either the first or the last of the three test administrations. (c) A third group of 129 youngsters was seen at the beginning of the first grade and again twelve months later at the beginning of the second grade. (d) And finally, 16 educable retarded children (IQ between 50 and 75) were tested at six month intervals, (e) as were 20 youngsters with medically diagnosed neurological impairment.

All Bender protocols were scored "blindly," that is, without any knowledge of the child's previous or later test score or his age. Thereafter, all Bender records were grouped according to the time interval between the first and second or third test and according to the children's age and grade placement. Comparisons were made between the Bender scores of the earlier and later test administrations after a time interval of six and of twelve months. Chi-squares were computed comparing the number of subjects whose Bender score was above or below the mean score for their respective age groups on the first and on the second, respectively third, test administration. A total of twelve chi-squares were computed. The results are shown on *Table 8*. Nine

Table 8. Test-Retest on the Bender Gestalt Test

N	First Testing	Second Testing	Chi-square	P
	Age	*Age*		
31	5½	6	5.86	< .02
62	6	6½	32.16	< .001
56	6½	7	2.19	> .10
46	7	7½	18.76	< .001
21	7½	8	3.24	< .10
35	5½	6½	8.57	< .01
62	6	7	1.2	> .20
67	6½	7½	11.49	< .001
25	7	8	17.63	< .001
129	Beginning 1st Grade	Beginning 2nd Grade	7.44	< .01
91	1st Testing	2nd Testing	18.54	< .001
91	1st Testing	3rd Testing	20.04	< .001

of the twelve chi-squares were statistically significant at the 2 per cent level or better; but even those chi-squares which were statistically not significant have important diagnostic implications.

A detailed analysis of the findings indicates that once a child has acquired sufficient maturity and skill to draw the Bender designs correctly he may be expected to maintain his good performance at a higher age level as well. It was found that children whose Bender performance is above average at age 5½ also do well at age 6 or 6½; those who do well at age 6 also do well on the Bender Test at age 6½ and 7, etc. The reverse, however, is not necessarily true. Only about one-half to two-thirds of the subjects with a poor Bender score on the first test did poorly again when they were retested. Particularly between the ages of 6½ and 7 was a marked improvement in visual-motor perception noticeable. Some children seem to mature at a somewhat slower rate than most youngsters but catch up with others by the time they are seven years old. Thus a child may produce an immature Bender performance at the beginning of the first grade but may mature sufficiently in visual-motor perception during the school year to do well on the Bender Test when retested at the end of the year.

*Plate 2** shows the Bender record of Jimmy, a six year two months old first grader. His Bender score is 10 which is below the average Bender performance for beginning first grade pupils. Jimmy was retested with the Bender at the beginning of the second grade and showed a marked improvement in his test performance. Jimmy's visual-motor perception had matured considerably, he obtained a Bender score of 1 which is better than the average score of second grade pupils. Jimmy's second grade protocol is shown on *Plate 3*. His school achievement at the end of the first grade and in the second grade was outstanding.

Failure to do well on both the first and the second administration of the Bender Test seems to indicate a general slowness or a serious malfunctioning in visual-motor perception and appears to be associated with poor school progress. The Bender protocol of Mike, another six year two months old first grader, is shown on *Plate 4*. Mike's Bender score is 10 or the same as Jimmy's. A year later at the beginning of the second grade Mike displayed no improvement on his Bender Test performance. In fact some of the Drawings of Bender designs appeared less mature on the second Bender record than on Mike's first Bender protocol, particularly Figures 3 and 5 (see p. 43). Mike obtained a Bender score of 9 on his second test protocol which is shown on *Plate 5*. Mike's school achievement was quite poor throughout the first and the second grades.

A study was made to test the hypothesis that among school beginners with below average Bender Test performance the rate of improvement on the Bender Test is related to school achievement in the first and second grades. The subjects for this study were 82 school children who were tested with the Bender Test first at the beginning of the first grade and then again at the beginning of the second grade. All subjects scored below average on the initial Bender Test performance for their respective age levels. The subjects were divided into two groups. In one group the subjects showed a marked improvement between the first and the second Bender Test score; in the other group the subjects showed little improvement between the first and the second test score. "Marked improvement" was defined as a decrease of five points or more on the Bender score or a move from below average to above average performance for each child's respective age level. School achievement was measured by means of the Metropolitan Achievement Test, Primary Battery, at the end of the first and the second grade respectively. Most of the subjects were included in the testing for both first and second grade achievement. However, about one-third of the children were absent either during the first or the second grade testing for achievement, or they dropped out of school during the second grade.

---

* The original plates were drawn on standard 8½″ x 11″ sheets, and have been reduced routinely by one-third. The individual drawings' relative size and position on the sheet have been preserved in all cases.

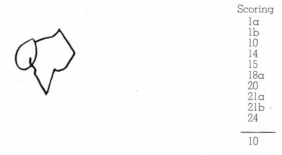

Scoring
1a
1b
10
14
15
18a
20
21a
21b
24
___
10

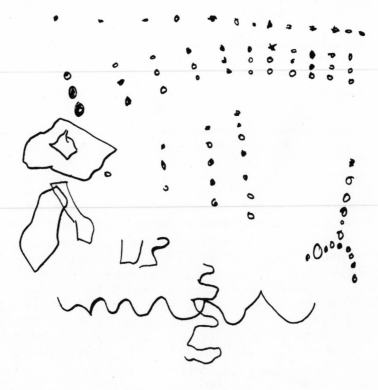

Plate 2. Jimmy, C. A. 6-2; beginning first grade.

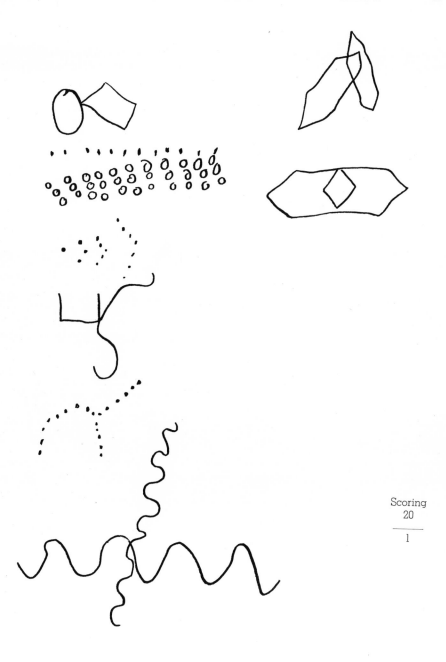

Scoring
20
—
1

Plate 3. Jimmy, C. A. 7-2; beginning second grade.

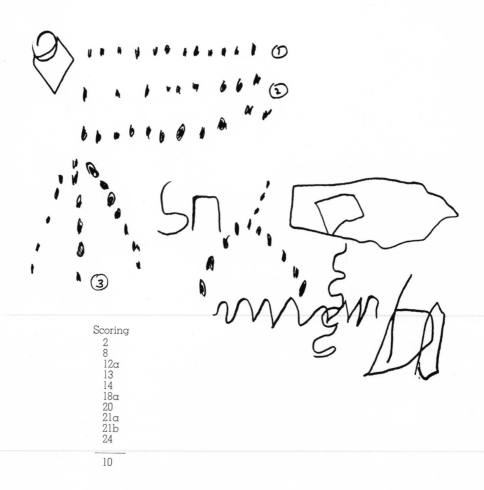

Scoring
2
8
12a
13
14
18a
20
21a
21b
24
___
10

Plate 4. Mike, C. A. 6-2; beginning first grade.

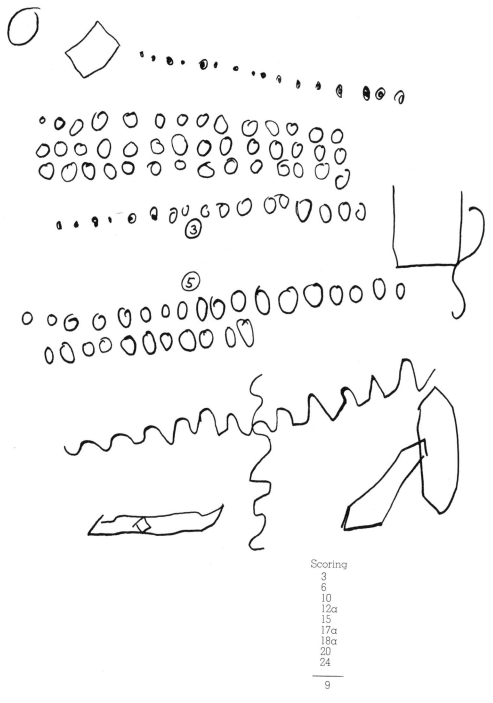

Scoring
3
6
10
12a
15
17a
18a
20
24

———
9

Plate 5. Mike, C. A. 7-2; beginning second grade.

Chi-squares were computed comparing the number of subjects with good and poor school achievement whose Bender performance showed improvement or did not show improvement between the first and second test administration. The results are shown on *Table 9*. Both chi-squares are significant at the .001

Table 9.   Relationship Between Improvement on Bender Scores and School Achievement

Bender Performance	Low Achievement	High Achievement	Chi-square	P
First Grade				
Improved	6	21		
Unimproved	30	9	17.76	< .001
Second Grade				
Improved	3	18		
Unimproved	22	6	17.31	< .001

level thus indicating that improving on the Bender Test is related to good school progress and vice versa. *It appears that good school achievement can be predicted with some assurance if a child does well on the Bender Test at the beginning of the first grade. If a child does poorly on this test he should be retested after a few months to assess his rate of maturation in visual-motor perception. If the rate of progress on the Bender performance is in keeping with the child's age then it may be expected that he will do satisfactory work in school.* His poor early test score may have reflected a somewhat slower rate of maturation in visual-motor perception but does not indicate any serious disturbances in this area. *If, however, a child's Bender performance remains poor and shows little improvement between the first and the second testing, then indications are that the youngster has serious problems in visual-motor perception or very modest endowment or both; his school achievement may be expected to be poor.*

This statement was given further support by the findings that educable retarded subjects did very poorly on the first administration of the Bender Test and revealed almost a complete lack of improvement on the second test administration (see p. 114). The results with neurologically impaired children of normal intelligence were similar. These subjects exhibited marked disturbances in visual-motor perception on both their first and their second Bender performances. The improvement between their earlier and their later Bender records was limited (see p. 95). Most brain injured children were also found to have poor school achievement (see p. 102).

PART III. Relationship of Bender Test to Intelligence and School Achievement

THE BENDER AS A TEST OF INTELLIGENCE

Psychologists are frequently asked to give a quick estimate of a child's intelligence, but most intelligence tests require a considerable amount of time to administer and score. There is a need for additional short tests of mental ability which can be quickly administered and easily scored for screening purposes. An exploration was therefore made of the usefulness of the Bender Test as a short intelligence test for young children.

Bender (1938, p. 112) pointed out that copying of Gestalt figures reflects the maturation level of visual-motor perception and that visual-motor perception is closely related to language ability and other functions associated with intelligence in young children. These include memory, visual perception, motor coordination, temporal and spatial concepts, organization and representation. Wewetzers' study (1959) supports this claim. He found significant relationships between the performance on the Bender Test and the Binet-Norden IQ scores for both his brain injured subjects and his control group. Wewetzer worked with children exclusively.

In contrast there appears to be no significant relationship between the intelligence of adults and their performance on the Bender Test. Pascal and Suttell (1951, p. 21) found that intelligence had little effect on the Bender Test score of adults of normal IQ. They also reported a lack of relationship between IQ scores and the Bender performance of children. However, it is felt that this finding reflects primarily, the inappropriateness of using the Bender scoring system of these two investigators with young children. Their scoring system was specifically designed for use with adults and was not meant to be used with young children. Peek and Olsen (1955) studied the ability of adult patients to draw the Bender figures from recall and found that the Bender recall scores were related to intellectual efficiency but not to intellectual ability. Peek and Storms (1958) further discovered that for adult psychiatric patients, intellectual ability cannot be reliably estimated from Bender Test protocols. Aaronson and Nelsons' study of adult V. A. patients (1953) had resulted in findings similar to those of Peek's. They too reported no significant relationship between Bender recall scores and the Shipley-Hartford IQ scores. But when using children and retarded epileptic patients as subjects, Aaronson (1957) obtained positive results between Bender recall scores and the Porteus Maze IQ scores.

It seems clear from the literature that the Bender Test is related to intelligence in children, but once visual-motor perception has fully matured the Bender Test can no longer serve as a measure of intellectual ability. Since age and maturation in visual-motor perception appear to be the determining factors in the Bender Test's usefulness as an intelligence test, a study was made by the author to see how well the scores on the Developmental Bender Scoring System correlate with intelligence test scores at various age levels.

45

In the present study the subjects were 239 children, age five years through ten years, who were seen at a child guidance clinic or by a school psychologist for evaluation because of emotional problems, learning difficulties, or both. In each case the Bender Test and the intelligence test were administered at the same testing session. The Bender Test always preceded the intelligence test. All Bender protocols were scored according to the Developmental Bender Scoring System. The IQ scores were derived from the Stanford-Binet Intelligence Scale, Form L (Terman and Merrill, 1937) or from the Wechsler Intelligence Scale for Children (hereafter: WISC) (Wechsler, 1949) depending on the child's age and ability. The WISC was used for all subjects who were at least seven years old and of normal intelligence, or who had a mental age of seven if they were retarded. The Stanford-Binet Scale was used for children less than seven years old and for subjects suspected of being mentally retarded with a mental age of less than seven years.

The subjects were divided into two groups. One group included 176 children with an IQ range from 75 to 149 and a mean IQ score of 98. The second group included 63 retarded children with an IQ range from 40 to 74 and a mean IQ score of 63. Pearson's product moment correlations were computed between the IQ scores and the Bender scores for the subjects of normal intelligence at each age level from 5 to 10 years and for the total group of retarded subjects. All correlations obtained are negative since the Bender Test is scored for errors and a high test score indicates poor performance on the Bender. The findings are shown on *Table 10*.

Table 10.   Correlations Between IQ and Bender Scores

Age	N	r	P
5	19	$-.79$*	$<.001$
6	15	$-.63$	$<.01$
7	36	$-.61$	$<.001$
8	37	$-.48$	$<.005$
9	44	$-.54$	$<.001$
10	25	$-.59$	$<.005$
	176		
Retarded	63	$-.44$	$<.001$

* All correlations are negative since the Bender Test is scored for errors.

All seven correlations were found to be statistically significant at the 1 per cent level. Thus it appears that the Bender Test can serve as a crude measure of intelligence for all children age 5 to 10 years. The highest single correlation was found at the five year old level which suggests that the Bender may be useful as a screening instrument for school beginners. The correlation between IQ scores and the Bender was also highly significant for the group of retarded subjects; however, further investigations revealed that the relationship between the Bender Test and the mental age of retarded children is even closer. The correlation between the Bender scores and the mental age of the 63 retarded subjects in this study was −.85 (see p. 110).

Both the Stanford-Binet Scale and the WISC consist of numerous subtests which are designed to measure different mental functions. The Bender Test consists of one short paper and pencil task which requires only the copying of nine designs. The question arises whether the Bender Test is related to specific subtests of the intelligence scales or whether the Bender scores are correlated primarily with the total IQ scores. A study was made (Koppitz, 1958b) to explore the relationship of the Bender Test and the WISC. This study was conducted prior to the standardization of the Developmental Bender Scoring System for Children. All Bender records in this study were scored according to the Initial Bender Scoring System (see p. 9). Unfortunately the author no longer has access to the Bender records and is therefore unable to rescore them with the Developmental Scoring System. However, it is not believed that the results of this study would be greatly altered if the Bender protocols had been scored with the Developmental Scoring System.

The subjects for this study were 90 elementary school children including:

—20 first graders

—20 second graders

—25 third graders

—25 fourth graders.

The subjects were divided into two groups. One group included the first and second graders, and the other group included the third and fourth graders. The age range of all subjects was from 6 years 7 months to 11 years 7 months. All subjects were clinic or private patients who had been seen for psychological evaluation because of emotional problems, learning difficulties, or both. The Bender Test and the WISC were administered to each subject at the same testing session. The range of the WISC Full Scale IQ scores was from 73 to 126 with a mean IQ score of 95.

Separate chi-squares were computed for each of nine WISC subtests comparing the number of subjects with above and below average Bender performance for their respective age levels, and with above and below average subtest scores. "Above average" was defined as a weighted subtest score of 10 or more, while " below average" was defined as a subtest score of 9 or less. Additional chi-squares were computed for the Verbal IQ and the Performance IQ. Here the number of subjects with above and below average Bender scores and above average and below average IQ scores were compared. In this case "above average" was defined as a weighted Verbal or Performance IQ score of 50 or more. A weighted score of 49 or less was considered to be "below average." And finally a chi-square was computed comparing the WISC Full Scale IQ scores and the Bender scores. In this instance, "above average" was defined as an IQ score of 100 or higher and "below average" was defined as an IQ score of 99 or less.

The results of this study are shown on *Table 11*. Chi-square and P values are given for the first two grades, for the third and fourth graders and for all subjects combined. The findings for the two age groups differ somewhat for the different Subtest and the IQ scores. A total of 36 chi-squares were computed, 18 of these were significant at the 5 per cent level or better.

It was found that the *WISC Full Scale IQ* is more closely related to the Bender performance of third and fourth graders than to that of first and

Table 11. Relationship Between Bender Test and WISC Scores

WISC	1st & 2nd Grades		3rd & 4th Grades		All 4 Grades	
	Chi-square	P	Chi-square	P	Chi-square	P
Full Scale IQ	3.0	<.10	4.4	<.05	7.3	<.01
Verbal IQ	5.9	<.02	2.1	>.10	7.4	<.01
Performance IQ	5.3	<.02	8.1	<.01	11.9	<.001
Subtests						
Information	not significant		not significant		not significant	
Comprehension	not significant		not significant		not significant	
Similarities	not significant		not significant		not significant	
Arithmetic	2.6	>.10	8.3	<.01	10.3	<.01
Picture Completion	4.9	<.05	2.1	>.10	6.8	<.01
Picture Arrangement	7.4	<.01	2.4	>.10	10.3	<.01
Block Design	2.6	>.10	3.9	<.05	7.3	<.01
Object Assembly	5.3	<.02	6.6	<.01	12.1	<.001
Coding	not significant		2.8	<.10	not significant	

second graders. These findings seem surprising, yet a glance at related research data shows that these results are not inconsistent with those of other studies. It appears that most children show considerable maturation in visual-motor perception between the ages of six and seven years. There are conspicuous individual differences in the rate of maturation in this area. For some children maturation is a gradual process, for others it seems to come about suddenly and rapidly. This results in unpredictable changes in the Bender scores of groups of six and seven year olds which in turn is reflected on the statistical data of this and other studies. Thus it was shown that the otherwise smooth normative curve for the Developmental Bender Scoring System for Children showed a marked irregularity between the six and a half and seven year levels (see Figure 1, p. 34), and it had been found that test-retest on the Bender is highly reliable for all age levels with the exception of ages six and seven (see *Table 8*, p. 38). Thus it can be stated that the Bender Test is closely related to general intelligence as measured on the *WISC Full Scale IQ* for children in the third and fourth grades and somewhat less so to the *WISC Full Scale IQ* of first and second graders.

The *Verbal IQ on the WISC* revealed a close relationship to the Bender performance of the younger group of subjects. This seems to support Bender's statement that the Bender Test is related to language ability in young children. As children grow older, tests of verbal intelligence demand not only factual information but also logical reasoning and social understanding. None of these bear a clear relationship to the copying of Gestalt figures. It is not surprising therefore that the chi-square comparing Verbal IQ and Bender performance of the third and fourth graders was not statistically significant.

As would be expected, the *Performance IQ* was found to be closely related to performance on the Bender Test for all subjects regardless of age. It is evident that the Bender Test measures many of the same functions as the WISC Performance Scale and that the Bender can be substituted for it with a considerable degree of confidence.

An analysis of the individual WISC Subtests and Bender performance shows that three verbal Subtests are not related to the latter test at any age level.

These tests include *Information, Comprehension,* and *Similarities.* These results could have been predicted.

Less obvious is the finding that *Arithmetic* on the WISC is closely related to the Bender performance of third and fourth graders and to a somewhat lesser degree to that of first and second graders. For the younger group, the *Arithmetic* Subtest consists mostly of counting wooden blocks and bears limited resemblance to the Bender. For the older children the *Arithmetic* test involves more part-whole relationships and number concepts which are also to be found in the Bender Test. Children have to analyze problems in their head and have to remember the principles involved. The present findings concur with the results of another study in which a high correlation was found between the Bender scores and arithmetic achievement scores (see p. 58).

Picture Completion was found to be significantly related to the Bender performance of the younger group of subjects but not to that of the older group. These results may reflect the subtle change which occurs in the nature of this Subtest as it progresses from easy to harder items. Thus the first items on *Picture Completion* represent relatively simple large objects which are familiar to most young children. A child who can perceive the picture will have no difficulty noticing the omissions on the drawings. As the series of drawings continues the pictures become more and more involved in detail and require social awareness on the part of the child. The Subtest changes from one of visual perception to one of reasoning and of awareness of the detail. It is interesting to note that *Picture Completion* is more highly correlated with the *Verbal IQ* score of the WISC than with the *Performance IQ* score (Wechsler, 1949, p. 10). The highest correlations between *Picture Completion* and other WISC Subtests occur with the *Comprehension* and *Vocabulary* Subtests.

The relationship between *Picture Arrangement* and the Bender Test performance for first and second graders was highly significant. This was not the case for third and fourth graders. These findings seem to reflect the nature of the *Picture Arrangement Subtest.* On the six and seven year level, the subjects are required to put parts of pictures together to form an integrated whole. This task is not too dissimilar from that required on the Bender. For subjects eight years old or older the *Picture Arrangement* Subtest changes from a test of visual perception to one of social understanding. Visual clues become less important than the content of the pictures. As a result, the relationship of this Subtest to the Bender Test performance diminishes greatly as the children get older.

Block Design was not as closely related to the Bender Test performance of the first and second graders as might have been expected. But it was significantly related to the Bender performance of the third and fourth grade subjects. The explanation for this may be found in the differing character of this Subtest for younger and older children. Six and seven year old children are asked to copy simple designs from actual blocks involving largely solid squares of color. Older subjects are required to perceive and analyze designs on pictures which involve few if any solid squares of color and have to reproduce them. This resembles the task presented by the Bender Test quite closely.

The *Block Design* Subtest differs from the Bender Test in one important aspect however; on the former test a slow child is penalized if he does not complete the assignment within a given time limit, on the Bender Test there is no time limit.

Of all WISC Performance Subtests *Object Assembly* was found to be most closely related to the performance on the Bender Test for all age levels tested. This is significant since *Object Assembly* is also the Subtest which Wechsler (1949, p. 10) reported as being most closely correlated with the WISC *Performance IQ* for seven and a half year old children. *Object Assembly* seems to require the ability to analyze and integrate parts into wholes and to reproduce figures, all of which also plays an important part in the Bender Test.

Coding was not found to be significantly related to performance on the Bender Test for either the younger or the older group of subjects. The task required by the *Coding* Subtest is relatively simple and very few children of normal intelligence have any difficulty with the requirement as such. This test seems to measure to a large extent, the child's ability to stick with a task for two minutes and to perform it at a high speed. The score on *Coding* is determined primarily by the child's speed. It was shown earlier that time has important diagnostic implications on the Bender Test (see p. 37) but these are not included in the Bender Test score. On the Bender Test, the time factor does not effect the test score. In the present study the WISC Subtests are compared only with the Bender scores derived from the Developmental Scoring System.

The results of this study show that the Bender Test is related in varying degrees, to five out of nine WISC Subtests, to the total *Full Scale IQ* score and to the *Verbal* and *Performance IQ* scores. *In general, it may be concluded that the Bender Test can be used with some confidence as a short nonverbal intelligence test for young children, particularly for screening purposes.*

No separate norms or cutoff scores are provided for use with the Bender Test when testing for mental ability. Since the Bender scores obtained with the Developmental Bender Scoring System for Children correlate highly with IQ scores (see *Table 10)* the normative data provided for the Developmental Scoring System can also be used as rough indicators of intelligence in young children. The interpretation of the Bender scores would be the same as was described earlier (see p. 35). For young children, maturity in visual-motor perception seems to be an indication of intelligence, unless the child has specific problems in visual-motor perception, or is highly verbal and develops somewhat slower in the visual perceptual area. To rule out these possibilities, it is suggested to use the Bender Test in combination with one or two brief verbal tests.

The author has found that the usefulness of the Bender Test as a measure of intelligence is greatly enhanced when it is combined with one of the Verbal Subtests of the WISC. The combination of the Bender Test and the *Information* or *Comprehension* Subtests has proven highly successful since these verbal tests measure areas not tapped by the Bender Test. The short verbal test is helpful in revealing youngsters with outstanding verbal ability whose good mental capacity might be overlooked because of somewhat immature performance on the Bender. On the other hand, a child with a very good Bender score may reveal serious speech problems or may do very poorly on the verbal test. Discrepancies between the Bender and the verbal test are always significant. When a verbal test cannot be used because of speech or hearing problems, the Bender Test then takes on added importance. The instructions for the Bender Test are so simple that they can be easily pantomimed if necessary. A child's Bender performance is in no way affected by speech or hearing.

In clinical and school settings psychologists are constantly faced with the problem of how to use their limited time most economically. A full scale intelligence test usually requires so much time that only a brief period is left for other tests or an interview. The author has used the Bender Test frequently with young children of normal intelligence who primarily seemed to show emotional problems and revealed no learning difficulties. The Bender Test not only gives the examiner a rough measure of the youngsters' intellectual ability, but also serves as a nonthreatening introduction to the interview. Children tend to enjoy copying the Bender designs, and in some cases the Bender figures evoke associations and spontaneous comments which can lead to further discussions. In most cases the Bender Test will suffice to rule out mental retardation or serious perceptual problems associated with neurological impairment (see p. 71) and the examiner can use most of his time for projective tests and an interview rather than spending it on a lengthy intelligence test which offers little insight into the dynamics of the child's emotional problems.

While no psychological test is entirely "culture free", the Bender Test comes close to it when scored according to the Developmental Bender Scoring System for Children. Thus it was found that some socially deprived children who scored poorly on the WISC or the Stanford-Binet Scale did well on the Bender Test and also did well in school. It appears that these children had good intellectual potential which had not been stimulated and developed at home. With special attention and help in school, these children were able to use their basic ability which was reflected on their Bender performance. Most intelligence test scores are influenced to a considerable degree by the child's cultural and social environment. The Bender Test has been found useful as a measure of young childrens' basic intellectual potential. It is well known that children from lower socioeconomic areas tend to test lower on IQ tests than children from more privileged areas. Yet Knoblauch and Pasamanik (1961) have shown that the difference in intellectual potential between infants of various social and racial groups is not significant. Many youngsters from deprived homes appear to be much more limited than they basically are.

On the other hand, many children appear alert and bright but test low on standard intelligence tests. Very frequently the psychologists will say that the test scores are not valid because the child had "a mental block", was upset, or the like. It will be inferred that he really *could* do much better if conditions were right. The author has found that appearances often deceive and that a child who scores low on the full scale intelligence tests *and* on the Bender Test usually *cannot* do much better, and that the test scores are valid. The Bender Test has proven a useful test to use when the validity of other intelligence test scores is in doubt.

THE BENDER AS A TEST OF SCHOOL READINESS

There is a growing interest in the screening of school beginners to help determine their readiness for academic work, especially reading. It is also believed that screening can help in detecting children who, because of their potential emotional and learning problems may require extra attention or more time before starting school in order to prevent serious difficulties from arising later on.

Brenner (1957) has emphasized that readiness for school is a function of maturation in perception and in the ability to analyze and integrate that which has been perceived. Brenner developed the New Gestalt Test (1959) to help assess a youngster's readiness for school. This test includes many of the same basic principles as the Bender Gestalt Test. Brenner's test appears to have merit, but the Bender Test seems to be no less promising in this area.

More than a decade ago Harriman and Harriman (1950) attempted to use the Bender Test as a measure of school readiness. The ideas they present are challenging; however, their findings proved to be neither valid nor reliable. Baldwin (1950) seems justified in criticizing the methodology used by Harriman and Harriman. Their study does not explore fully the usefulness of the Bender Test as a screening tool for school readiness.

Two recent studies (Koppitz, Mardis and Stephens, 1961; Smith and Keogh, 1962) offer strong evidence that the Bender Test is indeed a very useful instrument for the screening of school beginners. Smith and Keogh administered the Bender Test and the Lee-Clark Reading Readiness Test (Lee and Clark, 1951) to 149 kindergarten children and compared the results with the reading achievement of the subjects at the end of the first grade. Koppitz, Mardis and Stephens administered the Bender and readiness tests at the beginning of the first grade and compared the findings with total achievement of the subjects at the end of the first grade. Despite these variations in the time of test administration and in the measures of achievement, the results obtained in both studies are quite similar and are statistically significant. All correlations between the Bender Test scores and readiness test scores, and between these two tests and first grade achievement scores were found to be significant at the .01 level or better. Of particular interest in the Smith and Keogh study, is their method of administering the Bender Test.

In an earlier study Keogh and Smith (1961) had demonstrated that the *Bender Test can be administered successfully as a group test to school beginners.* They compared performance on the Bender Test using two different types of group administration and individual administration. They obtained no statistically significant differences in Bender Test scores between the various methods of administration. The correlations between the Bender Test scores and reading achievement were actually somewhat higher when the Bender was administered as a group test rather than as an individual test. The most effective method of group administration according to Keogh and Smith is to present each individual Bender design on a large card at the front of the room and to ask the subjects to copy it on a blank page of a booklet.

Group administration would overcome the biggest handicap in using the Bender as a screening test for large numbers of school beginners. In most school settings the time required for individual test administration is deemed as yet prohibitive. In time, it is hoped that an individual screening test for perceptual maturity in children about to enter school will be considered just as important as tests of visual and auditory acuity and as a general health checkup. At the present time, group administration of the Bender Test is essential for large scale screening of kindergarten children. In those cases where special problems are suspected or where the results on the Bender record are inconclusive, individual testing with the Bender Test may then be added later on.

It is of course obvious that group administration of the Bender Test has both advantages and disadvantages. As a time-saving device it is valuable, but there is a disadvanatge in that it deprives the examiner of the opportunity to observe the individual child at close range, and to study his work habits. By asking the children to copy each Bender design on a separate sheet of paper and by controlling the speed of presenting the stimulus cards, the examiner relinquishes the possibility of analyzing the child's organization of all nine Bender figures on a single sheet of paper (see p. 127) and he cannot inquire into the child's ability to perceive his own errors (see p. 95). Furthermore he cannot examine the child's use of time and space in executing the Bender Test (see p. 100). A Bender protocol can yield more than just a single test score. It is debatable whether it is in the long run more economical to administer the Bender Test to ten children in a group and to obtain less information from each one, or to administer the Bender to each child individually and to obtain maximum information from each test protocol. It is certainly of great value to have different methods for administering the Bender Test available for use in different situations.

Keogh and Smith developed a simple five category rating scale for scoring the Bender performance of kindergarten children which appears to be both valid and reliable. Koppitz, Mardis and Stephens used the Koppitz Bender Scoring System in their study. Both methods of test analysis yielded very similar results and there seems to be considerable merit in both scoring methods for use with school beginners. The one advantage of the Koppitz method may be that it has been standardized for children age five through ten years and that it can be used not only for screening school beginners but also for the prediction of long range school achievement (see p. 57), for the study of specific learning problems (see p. 61), as a rough measure of intelligence (see p. 45), as a diagnostic indicator of neurological impairment (see p. 71), and in the assessment of mental retardation (see p. 107).

The following is a detailed description of the study by the author and her associates on the relationship of the Bender Test, the Lee-Clark Reading Readiness Test, and the Metropolitan Readiness Test. The subjects for this study were 272 first grade students from 11 classes in seven different schools. None of the subjects were repeating the first grade. The schools selected for this study represent a socioeconomic cross section and are located in rural, semi-rural, suburban, and urban areas. During the first six weeks of the school year, the teachers administered the Lee-Clark Reading Readiness Test to eight of the classes, while three teachers gave the Metropolitan Readiness Test (Hildreth and Griffith, 1949) to their groups. During this same period each child was seen individually by a qualified school psychologist who administered the Bender Test. The Readiness Tests were scored following standard procedure. All Bender protocols were scored according to the Initial Bender Scoring System for Children (see p. 9). The three investigators scored each test used in this study "blindly," i.e., without knowing the scores of the other tests. Thereafter, the first grade achievement of each subject was predicted by means of the Readiness Test and the Bender Test. Predictive scores were derived from the grade equivalent scores on the two Readiness Tests and from the standard deviation scores on the Bender Test.

At the end of the school year all teachers administered the Metropolitan Achievement Test, Primary I Battery: Form R (Hildreth, 1946) to their classes. The three psychologists scored this test according to standard procedure. Actual achievement of each child as measured on the Total Average Achievement score of the Metropolitan Achievement Test was then compared with the predicted achievement on each of the screening tests. Pearson product moment correlations were computed between the Readiness Tests and the Bender and between the three screening tests and the Metropolitan Achievement Test. The results are shown on *Table 12*. All correlations between the

Table 12. Correlations Between Bender[1], Readiness and Achievement Tests

School	N	Lee-Clark & Met. Ach. T.	Bender & Met. Ach. T.	Bender & Lee-Clark
A	53	.67**	−.67**	−.64**
B	56	.42**	−.37**	−.30*
C	40	.54**	−.41**	−.21
D	26	.40*	−.58**	−.33
E	34	.67**	−.61**	−.54**
Total	199	.66**	−.68**	−.61**

		Met. Readiness & Met. Ach. T.	Bender & Met. Ach. T.	Met. Readiness & Bender
F	31	.63**	−.71**	−.73**
G	42	.66**	−.29	−.41
Total	73	.59**	−.58**	−.59**

[1] All Bender correlations are negative since it is scored for errors.
 * Correlation significant at .05 level.
 ** Correlation significant at .01 level.

various tests are quite similar in magnitude and all are statistically significant with one exception. Thus it appears that in general, the Bender Test can be used as effectively as the Lee-Clark Reading Readiness Test or the Metropolitan Readiness Test for screening school beginners. Of course, it is realized that the Lee-Clark Reading Readiness Test was specifically designed to test readiness for reading and was not meant to screen for overall achievement. However, in discussing the validity of the Reading Readiness Test, Lee and Clark quote Henig (1949) who compared the Readiness Test scores with actual reading grades at the end of the school year. He obtained a correlation of .59 between the Readiness Test scores and reading grades, which is similar to the results of the present study.

In six of the seven schools involved in the present study the correlations between the Bender scores and the Metropolitan Achievement Test scores were statistically significant. The exception was school G which is located in a high socioeconomic suburban area. In general, it was found that the children in this school were of above average intelligence and had outstanding verbal ability. They lived in a cultural environment which stressed academic achievement. High motivation for learning and good verbal skills enabled these children to do well in the first grade even though their visual-motor perception, as measured on the Bender Test, was not above average. These children were also furthered by an outstanding school system which offered them many opportunities not usually found in public schools.

When the predicted achievement from the three screening tests was compared with the actual achievement of each subject, it was found that the Bender Test had predicted too high an achievement for 33 children, was correct in its predictions for 128 children, and was too low in its prediction for 28 children. "Too high" was defined as predicting achievement three months or more above the actual achievement, "correct" was defined as predicting within three months from the actual achievement, and "too low" was defined as predicting three months or more below the actual achievement. Predictions on the Lee-Clark were too high for 77 children, correct for 103 children and too low for 19 children. It appears that the Lee-Clark tends to predict more often, too high achievement, while the Bender tends to underestimate achievement more often. The Bender tends to be more often correct in its predictions than the Lee-Clark. The Metropolitan Readiness Test resembled the Bender quite closely in its predictive ability. It also showed a tendency to underestimate achievement more often than the Lee-Clark Test.

An attempt was made to analyze some of the factors contributing to large discrepancies, i.e., 5 months or more, between the predicted and the actual achievement of individual subjects, and between the predicted achievement by means of the Lee-Clark Readiness Test and the Bender Test. Twenty-five of the subjects and their teachers were interviewed at the beginning of the following school year to obtain further information. The sample is small and the data obtained are at best sketchy and incomplete, but some tentative impressions can be gained. The findings are listed below:

Actual achievement as predicted on Lee-Clark Test, Bender prediction was too low (6 subjects):

3 subjects: high socioeconomic status, high verbal ability, poor visual-motor perception.

3 subjects: high socioeconomic status, excessive parental pressure to excel.

Actual achievement as predicted on Bender Test, Lee-Clark prediction was too low (2 subjects):

1 subject: deprived home background.

1 subject: lagging language development.

Actual achievement as predicted on Bender Test, Lee-Clark prediction too high (3 subjects):

1 subject: hyperactive in class, visual-motor disturbance.
2 subjects: unexplained.

Actual achievement below predictions on Bender and Lee-Clark (11 subjects):

1 subject: negativistic attitude, rebellion against parental pressure.
2 subjects: serious speech defect.
2 subjects: withdrawn behavior, emotional problems.
1 subject: slow compulsive performer.
1 subject: developed encephalitis during the school year.
1 subject: poor vision which may have become worse during the school year, achievement improved in second grade after corrective lenses were provided.
1 subject: excessively immature, overly dependent on teacher.
2 subjects: unexplained.

Actual achievement above predictions on Bender and Lee-Clark (3 subjects):

1 subject: anxious, tense child who relaxed as the school year progressed.
1 subject: allergies, compulsive behavior, parental pressure.
1 subject: unexplained.

The Bender Test tends to underestimate more often the school readiness of children from high socioeconomic areas, while it fairly accurately assesses the readiness of children in middle class and lower class communities. The Lee-Clark Test on the other hand tends to underestimate children from deprived backgrounds more easily. The findings suggest that the Bender is relatively "culture free" and is not unduly influenced by social and cultural factors. It measures maturation in visual-motor perception in young children regardless of the child's environment. The Lee-Clark reflects to a much greater degree, the social and cultural factors of the environment.

Some children develop outstanding verbal skills early but are a little slower in their maturation of visual-motor perception. In these cases, the Bender Test may underestimate the child's readiness. On the other hand the Bender Test is a good indicator of a child's maturity in visual-motor perception when immature speech or a serious speech defect may make him appear more immature than he actually is. At the beginning of elementary school, visual-motor perception seems to be more important for good school achievement than verbal skills unless the latter are outstanding, and exceptional motivation for learning is present. First and second grade achievement was found to be, in general, more closely related to the WISC Performance IQ than to the WISC Verbal IQ (Koppitz, 1958b).

When a child's school achievement is poor despite good scores on the Lee-Clark Readiness Test and the Bender Test, and if hearing and visual problems have been ruled out, then further investigations for emotional difficulties seem to be in order. Emotional problems tend to have a depressing effect on a child's school achievement. The same is true of prolonged or serious illnesses.

Once emotional or physical difficulties have been resolved or corrected, the child's academic achievement will improve rapidly if his basic potential is as good as indicated on the screening tests.

It has been shown that the Bender Test alone, is a useful screening tool for school readiness but its effectiveness is greatly enhanced when it is used in combination with one of the other standardized readiness tests. Especially when the status of a child is not clear, the Bender can offer valuable information to supplement the regular group screening tests that are often routinely administered in schools. The agreement or discrepancy between the Bender and another screening test can often determine whether a child is still too immature in his perceptual development for school and formal learning or whether his behavior is primarily the result of social and emotional factors. The Bender Test can also be of great value in the screening of children with exceptional ability who would profit from an enriched or accelerated program for school beginners.

THE BENDER TEST AS A PREDICTOR
OF SCHOOL ACHIEVEMENT

School achievement appears to be relatively stable during the first few years of school attendance. The grade averages and achievement test scores of first grade pupils were found to be significantly correlated with third grade and sixth grade achievement (Sullivan, Blyth and Koppitz, 1958). The correlations obtained were .61 and .71 respectively. It may be expected therefore that a test which is related to first grade achievement would be able to predict school achievement in the subsequent years of elementary school. Since the Developmental Bender Scoring System for Children (p. 12) was validated against achievement in the first two grades, it may be anticipated that Bender scores can predict not only achievement in the first two grades but also in other grades. This hypothesis was tested by means of three investigations which were conducted with three different samples of school children.

1) The first study (Koppitz, Mardis and Stephens, 1961) was reported earlier (see p. 54) as part of the investigation of school readiness. Mardis and Stephens tested 199 first graders with the Bender Test at the beginning of the school year and obtained Metropolitan Achievement Test scores at the end of the school year. The correlation between the Bender Test and first grade achievement was −.68 which is significant at the .001 level (*Table 12* and *Table 13*). (As mentioned before, all Bender correlations are negative since the Bender is scored for errors.) The data for this particular study were collected and scored independently by the above named psychologists. The results of this study are very similar to those found in another investigation by the author and her associate (1959). This similarity seems to indicate good reliability and validity of the Developmental Bender Scoring System.

2) The study by Koppitz, Sullivan, Blyth and Shelton (1959) was carried out with 145 first grade students from six classrooms in five different schools. These youngsters were first seen at the beginning of the school year when the Bender was administered by the psychologists. The Metropolitan Achieve-

ment Test was administered at the end of the school year by the classroom teachers. The findings for this group of subjects, based on the Initial Bender Scoring System (see p. 9) were published in 1959 in the Journal of Clinical Psychology. Since that time all Bender protocols have been rescored with the Developmental Bender Scoring System. The same group of subjects, with a few omissions and new additions, was again tested with the Bender at the beginning of the second grade and with the Metropolitan Achievement Test at the end of the second and third grades. All second and third grade data are reproduced from an unpublished paper by Sullivan and Blyth (1961) on long term achievement patterns predicted with the Bender Test. *Table 13* shows a summary of their findings. Twelve different correlations are given, all of which are statistically significant at the .001 level.

Table 13.   Correlations Between Bender[1] and Achievement Test Scores

N	Met. Reading Ach. & Bender Scores	Met. Number Ach. & Bender Scores	Met. Ave. Ach. & Bender Scores
	First Grade Bender and First Grade Achievement		
199	—	—	−.68*
145	−.54*	−.57*	−.64*
	Second Grade Bender and Second Grade Achievement		
141	−.53*	−.75*	−.59*
	Bender and Long Term Achievement		
	1st Gr. Bender & 1st Gr. Ach.	1st Gr. Bender & 2nd Gr. Ach.	1st Gr. Bender & 3rd Gr. Ach.
88	−.60*	−.49*	−.54*
		2nd Gr. Bender & 2nd Gr. Ach.	2nd Gr. Bender & 3rd Gr. Ach.
73		−.46*	−.50*

[1] All correlations are negative since the Bender is scored for errors.
* Correlation is significant at the .001 level.

It was found that Bender scores obtained at the beginning of the first grade correlate equally well with first grade Reading and Arithmetic Achievement on the Metropolitan Achievement Test. The correlation between the Total Average Achievement on the Metropolitan Test and the first grade Bender scores was maintained throughout the first three grades of elementary school. It is interesting to note that the correlation for the third grade is actually a little higher than that for the second grade achievement and the Bender. Bender Test scores obtained at the beginning of the second grade correlate as well with second grade Reading and Arithmetic Achievement as the first grade Bender scores correlate with first grade achievement. In fact, the single highest correlation found in the entire study was obtained between the second grade Bender scores and the second grade Arithmetic Achievement scores. This correlation is −.75 which corresponds well to findings reported earlier (see p. 49) in connection with the relationship between the WISC Arithmetic Subtest and the Bender scores.

Table 13 shows that second and third grade Average Achievement scores on the Metropolitan Test can be equally well predicted by Bender scores obtained at the beginning of the first and the second grades. The results of this study offer support for the hypothesis that achievement in the first three grades of elementary school can be predicted from Bender scores derived with the Developmental Scoring System for Children. The findings are enhanced in their significance by the small number of subjects in the third grade. Many of the poorest students had failed in the first and second grades. Each child who failed had a very poor Bender score at the beginning of the first grade, failure could have been accurately predicted at that time.

3) The following study, conducted by the author, deals with the relationship of Bender scores to teacher judgement of students' achievement. The grades on a pupil's report card are determined less by objective achievement scores than by the teacher's judgment. Objective scores and subjective assessment by teachers may or may not correspond. Some children get nervous when taking group tests while others are very good at guessing answers on objective tests. Teachers in turn are not only influenced by the child's actual achievement but also by his personality and behavior in the classroom. Teachers, of course, differ in their ability to appraise a child.

The subjects for this study were 197 children representing 14 different classes in two schools. Two classes were on the kindergarten level, and three each on the level of first, second, third and fourth grades. At the beginning of the school year the author administered the Bender to all children in these classes. All Bender records were scored according to the Developmental Scoring System. At the end of the school year each teacher was asked to name seven very good students and seven poor students in her room. In some instances the teachers felt that they did not have seven very good or seven poor students in their classrooms. Other teachers named more than seven children who they felt should be included in one or the other category. Because of this the number of children rated as good students and as poor students is not equal. Chi-squares were computed comparing the number of students with high and low teacher ratings whose Bender scores were above or below the normative mean score for their respective age levels.

Table 14. Relationship of Bender Scores and Teacher Judgement

Grade	High Teacher Rating		Low Teacher Rating		Chi-square	P
	Good Bender	Poor Bender	Good Bender	Poor Bender		
K	7	7	2	12	2.48	>.10
1	20	4	7	12	7.96	<.01
2	15	2	6	11	7.97	<.01
3	21	6	7	14	7.86	<.01
4	17	7	10	10	1.78	>.10

The results are shown on *Table 14.* They indicate that there is considerable agreement between the Bender scores and teacher ratings for first, second and third grade students. This corresponds well to the findings of the study reported above. In general, it appears that about three out of four students in the first, second and third grades with above average Bender scores at the beginning of the school year will be rated as high achievers by their teachers at the end of the school year. While about three out of four students with below average Bender scores at the beginning of the school year will be rated as low achievers by their teachers at the end of the school year.

The situation differs somewhat in kindergarten. Of the children who obtained a good Bender score at the beginning of kindergarten about four out of five were rated as good students by their teachers at the end of the school year. Of those with below average Bender scores at the beginning of the school year about two out of three were rated by their teachers as poor students. These findings are quite similar to those of an earlier study on test-retest of the Bender Test (see p. 37). In that study it was found that a poor Bender score among very young children may reflect *either* a slow but normal rate of development in visual-motor perception *or* a malfunctioning or retardation in visual-motor perception. In the former case the children will most likely mature sufficiently in visual-motor perception during the course of the school year to do well despite their poor initial Bender score. In the latter case the children's Bender score is likely to remain poor and their slow progress in maturation will be reflected in poor school achievement. It appears therefore that a single good Bender score at the beginning of kindergarten can predict good achievement as rated by the teacher at the end of the school year. But a below average Bender score at the beginning of kindergarten will require a second test administration three or four months later to assess the child's rate of maturation before school achievement can be predicted with any degree of confidence. If this is not feasible, the accuracy of prediction with the Bender Test can be enhanced by analyzing the deviations on the Bender record for indications of neurological impairment (see p. 75) or by supplementing the Bender with the Human Figure Drawing Test which reflects the child's emotional adjustment and his intellectual ability, both of which effect his functioning in school to a considerable extent (Koppitz, 1962a; Koppitz, Sullivan, Blyth and Shelton, 1959; Clark, 1962).

On the fourth grade level the Bender scores obtained at the beginning of the school year showed no significant relationship to school achievement as rated by the teachers at the end of the school year. This is not unexpected since the normative study for the Developmental Bender Scoring System (see p. 35) indicated that Bender scores lose their ability to differentiate between good and poor students beyond the age of nine. At this age level, the spread of Bender scores is quite limited; the majority of children score 0, 1, 2, or 3, with a mean score of 1.7. Only the exceptional child will score more than three. In the fourth grade, most students are able to reproduce the Bender designs without serious error and those with perceptual problems have usually learned by this time to compensate for their difficulties. Other factors besides visual-motor perception determine fourth grade achievement. Among the fourth grade students rated as outstanding by their teachers at the end of the year, about one in three had a below average Bender score, i.e., a score of 2 or 3, at the beginning of the school year, while half of the students rated as poor achievers by their teachers had a good Bender score at the beginning of the school year. It appears therefore that a Bender score obtained at the beginning of the fourth grade is not a good indicator of fourth grade achievement.

In summary it can be stated that Bender Test scores obtained at the *beginning of the first grade* can predict a child's first, second and third grade achievement as measured on the Metropolitan Achievement Test and also correlate highly with the teacher's rating of the child's achievement at the end of the first grade. Bender scores obtained at the *beginning of the second grade* correlate highly with achievement test scores in the second and third grades and with the teacher's rating of the child at the end of the second grade. *Third grade* Bender scores correlate with achievement rating by the teacher at the end of the third grade. *Fourth grade* Bender scores are poor indicators of achievement as rated by the fourth grade teachers. Bender scores obtained at the *beginning of kindergarten* are fairly reliable in picking out those youngsters who will be rated highly by their teachers at the end of the year. A second test administration of the Bender, an analysis of individual errors on the Bender, or a supplementary test such as the Human Figure Drawing Test is necessary to predict accurately how well kindergarten children with poor Bender scores will do in the course of the school year. Since visual-motor perception undergoes considerable maturation at the kindergarten level, a single Bender Test administration at the beginning of kindergarten is not sufficient for predictive purposes unless the child is above average in his Bender performance.

THE BENDER TEST AND ITS RELATIONSHIP TO PROBLEMS IN READING AND ARITHMETIC

In the present section the relationship between Bender scores and reading and arithmetic will be more fully explored. A certain degree of maturity in visual-motor perception is necessary before a child can learn to read. An essential part of the complex reading process is the perception of patterns, spatial relationships and the organization of configurations. Similar skills are involved in arithmetic. Since the Bender Test reflects the maturation level of visual-motor perception in young children, it stands to reason that Bender scores derived from the Developmental Scoring System for Children would be closely related to reading and arithmetic. That this is so was shown in the previous section (*Table 13*, p. 58). It was demonstrated that the Reading Achievement scores and the Number Achievement scores on the Metropolitan Achievement Test are significantly correlated with the Bender scores of first and second graders.

The following investigation by the author was especially designed to discover whether any particular sign or deviation on the Bender Test is associated with problems in reading or arithmetic. The subjects for this study were first and second grade pupils with exceptionally high or very poor Reading and Number Achievement on the Metropolitan Achievement Test. The Bender Test was administered to all subjects in school by a qualified psychologist. All Bender protocols were scored according to the Developmental Scoring System for Children. The subjects were divided into four groups which are described below. Several of the subjects are included in more than one group. The four groups of subjects are made up as follows:

Group I included 45 subjects to whom the Bender Test was administered at the *beginning of the first grade.* At the *end of the third grade* 29 of the subjects were reading on the Metropolitan Achievement Test at the 5.3 grade level or higher ("High Reading Achievement") and 16 subjects were reading at the 3.5 grade level or less ("Low Reading Achievement").

Group II included 29 subjects to whom the Bender Test was administered at the *beginning of the first grade.* At the *end of the third grade* 16 of the subjects were doing arithmetic on the Metropolitan Achievement Test at the 4.6 grade level or above ("High Number Achievement") and 13 subjects were doing arithmetic at the 3.6 grade level or below ("Low Number Achievement").

Group III included 49 subjects to whom the Bender Test was administered at the *beginning of the second grade.* At the *end of the second grade* 28 subjects were reading on the Metropolitan Achievement Test at the 4.0 grade level or above ("High Reading Achievement") and 21 subjects were reading at the 2.3 grade level or below ("Low Reading Achievement").

Group IV included 51 subjects to whom the Bender Test was administered at the *beginning of the second grade.* At the *end of the second grade* 29 subjects were doing arithmetic on the Metropolitan Achievement Test at the 3.6 grade level or better ("High Number Achievement") and 22 subjects were doing arithmetic at the 2.3 grade level or less ("Low Number Achievement").

Chi-squares were computed comparing the "High" and "Low" achievers in the four groups of subjects whose total Bender score was above or below the normative Bender score for their respective age level. Additional chi-squares were computed comparing the subjects on each of the 30 individual scoring items of the Developmental Bender Scoring System for Children. The total Bender score as well as 22 of the 30 individual Bender scoring items showed statistically significant relationships to achievement in reading and arithmetic on the second and third grade level. However, *no single scoring item on the Bender Test appeared to be exclusively related to reading and number problems.* The same scoring items were found to be for the most part significant for both reading and arithmetic achievement and the statistical results obtained were quite similar to those shown on *Table 2* (see p. 13). In addition, it was found that the total Bender score was consistently more closely related to reading and number achievement than any one single Bender scoring item. The results for the total Bender score as shown on *Table 15* are consistent with the earlier findings (see p. 58) that the total Bender Test score is more closely associated with arithmetic than with reading achievement.

It appears that attention to detail is particularly important for good reading and arithmetic achievement. The separate units and parts of the Bender Gestalt designs seem to have similar functions as letters and numbers which a child must not only perceive but must also be able to integrate into words and sums if he is to become a good student. Particularly significant seems to be the perception and reproduction of the correct number and shapes of angles, curves, dots and rows on Figures A, 1, 2, 3, 6, 7, and 8. Equally important appears to be the correct perception of the part-whole relationship of Figures

Table 15. Relationship Between The Bender Test and Achievement
in Reading and Arithmetic

Group	Achievement	Good Bender	Poor Bender	Chi-square	P
I	High Reading	18	11	8.39	< .01
	Low Reading	2	14		
II	High Arithmetic	12	4	10.64	< .01
	Low Arithmetic	1	12		
III	High Reading	22	6	12.46	< .001
	Low Reading	5	16		
IV	High Arithmetic	23	6	22.00	< .001
	Low Arithmetic	2	20		

A, 4, and 7. Both the integration of parts and the directionality of these three Figures showed a significant relationship with reading and arithmetic. These findings concur with those of Clawson (1959) and Lachman (1960).

An analysis of the research findings presented on *Table 15* shows that children with above average Bender Test scores are unlikely to have difficulty in reading if other conditions are favorable. Of the 47 subjects with good Bender scores in Groups I and III, 40 showed outstanding reading achievement. An investigation was made of the seven subjects whose reading achievement was poor despite a good Bender score. Two of these children were found to be seriously emotionally disturbed. They had above average intelligence but were so preoccupied with their anxieties and emotional problems that they were unable to concentrate on their school work. Two other subjects in the second grade were of low average ability and showed poor verbal ability; they appeared to be slow maturing youngsters. In both cases their first grade Bender performance had been extremely poor while their second grade Bender score showed a marked improvement. It is quite possible that the reading achievement of these children will improve as their perception improves. They may require a bit more time than most children to complete their work in school, but may be able to catch up with their classmates later on. No third grade achievement scores were available for these two subjects. But another subject could be followed through the third grade and may serve as an example of this kind of development.

This particular child had a very poor first grade Bender score; his first grade achievement was equally poor. By the beginning of the second grade his visual-motor perception had matured considerably and he was able to draw the Bender figures without serious errors. But despite a good second grade Bender score his achievement lagged behind. He had to make up for all he failed to learn in the first grade. By the end of the third grade he had not only caught up with his classmates but was in the top reading group in his room.

The remaining two children with poor reading achievement and good Bender Test scores were of dull normal intelligence and came from culturally deprived, unstable home backgrounds. It was felt that the poor scholastic achievement of these children reflected to a large extent their poor social and emotional environment, while the good Bender Test score indicated the potential ability of these children which was not being fully stimulated and developed.

The seven subjects discussed here point up the well established fact that poor reading ability may result from many different factors. Reading difficulties may be due to emotional problems, modest endowment, developmental lag, social and cultural deprivation, or problems in visual-motor perception. Since 30 of the 37 subjects in Groups I and III who were poor readers also had below average Bender scores it appears that perceptual problems may be the single most important factor contributing to poor reading ability. The Bender Test has been found very useful in diagnosing the etiology of children's reading difficulties and planning treatment programs for them.

If a child with reading problems reveals perceptual immaturity or malfunctioning on his Bender record then two possibilities suggest themselves. The child may be somewhat slow in his perceptual development and of limited intelligence. In this case his immature Bender performance may be in keeping with his total development, and his poor achievement may be due to requirements beyond his capacity. This youngster may require more time for maturation and would profit from easier assignments. He may need to repeat a grade. Extremely slow children may need placement in special classes for slow learners. The children in this group rarely need remedial reading. They require above all class placement in keeping with their ability.

If a child of normal intelligence shows reading problems and has a very poor Bender performance then a different course of action is indicated. It is suggested that the child receive a thorough examination by an ophthalmologist to see if perceptual problems exist which can be partially corrected with lenses. Such an examination is recommended even if the record shows that the child's visual acuity is within the normal range. In addition, the child with specific problems in visual-motor perception may require special training in visual perception and would profit from remedial reading lessons. He has to learn to compensate for his problems and to use channels of perception and learning which are open to him. A child of superior intelligence is often able to achieve this by himself if given time and encouragement. A less capable child will need help if he is to overcome his perceptual handicap. Strauss and Lethinen (1947), de Hirsch (1952, 1957), and others have described specific techniques for helping children with reading problems due to perceptual malfunctioning. It is believed that emotional problems usually develop in these children secondarily to the perceptual problems. These children tend to be quite vulnerable and are easily frustrated when they cannot learn as successfully as other children. The situation is often intensified by the fact that parents and teachers do not recognize the child's specific perceptual problems and consider him lazy or stubborn for not doing satisfactory work in school despite adequate intelligence.

On the other hand, if a child of average or better intelligence with a good Bender Test score shows poor reading achievement after hearing difficulties and poor auditory perception have been ruled out, then emotional problems should be investigated. An emotionally upset child tends to show little interest in learning and his academic progress is usually poor. Such a child will benefit more from guidance and psychotherapy than from remedial reading. This is not to say that remedial help is harmful or of no help, but the benefit to the child will be derived primarily from the close personal contact with the accepting remedial reading teacher and not from the special reading techniques she has to offer. A conference with the parents and guidance for them may result in a lessening of excessive pressure for achievement and in more encouragement for the child which in turn may change the child's attitude toward school. As a child's emotional adjustment at home and in school improves, his scholastic achievement also tends to improve. A happy child who feels loved and appreciated wants to please his parents and teachers by working hard in school, and he derives pleasure from learning and progressing academically.

Perhaps the most difficult situation to remedy is the poor reading achievement of severely deprived, dull normal children with somewhat immature visual-motor perception who live in an environment which places little value on school achievement or reading. The odds against these children are so overwhelming that they may simply give up and not even try to learn. As time goes by, they will appear more and more retarded despite potentially normal endowment. Lacking motivation and opportunity for intellectual growth, they may become belligerent and may develop serious behavior problems. Neither a therapist nor a remedial reading teacher can bring about lasting changes in these youngsters unless the total situation is changed. Nothing short of a total program involving all aspects of the child's environment and education can save these children from the appalling human waste that exists in many underprivileged slum areas. What can be accomplished in this regard has been demonstrated in the Higher Horizons program of New York City's East Harlem.

The various factors contributing to poor reading achievement have been discussed here separately, however, it is obvious that these factors rarely occur in isolation; more often they will be combined with others. A child with reading problems is likely to have not only poor visual-motor perception, but will also show signs of emotional problems; in addition, he may be somewhat slow in his development. The opposite is also true. Outstanding visual-motor perception in young children may well be the primary contributing factor for high reading achievement in the early elementary school grades, but it is by no means the only contributing factor. It was found that 57 subjects in Groups I and III had high reading achievement. Of these, 40 subjects had above average Bender Test scores while 17 subjects had below average Bender Test scores.

It can be assumed that good visual-motor perception accounted to a large extent for the good reading ability of 40 subjects. An investigation was conducted to explain the high reading achievement of the 17 subjects with below average Bender scores. Since three of these subjects, one in Group I and two in Group III, had moved out of the area no further information was available on them. The remaining 14 subjects had one thing in common: they were all of high average or superior intelligence. It was found that the Bender Test scores of 10 subjects in Group I were poor at the beginning of the first grade, but that the second grade Bender Test scores for these children showed a marked improvement and were all above average. All of these subjects were endowed with exceptional verbal ability and it is likely that their early verbal maturation resulted in a somewhat slower maturation of visual-motor perception. A child rarely matures simultaneously in the various higher mental functions. These findings are in agreement with those reported earlier in relation to the test-retest on the Bender (see p. 37).

Four subjects in Group III with high reading achievement had below average Bender scores at the beginning of the second grade. This does not necessarily mean that their Bender performance was very poor. In fact all four subjects had Bender scores that were just one point from the normative Bender score for their respective age groups. It was discovered that these same children had scored above average on the Bender Test at the beginning of the first grade. It had been pointed out earlier (p. 38) that a good Bender score indicates maturity in visual-motor perception and once maturation has been achieved, it persists even though a child may obtain one or two scoring points less when retested later on. Being familiar with the test, the child may be careless or may not put forth as much effort as the first time. The first grade Bender scores in these cases were better measures of the four subjects' perceptual maturity than the second grade Bender scores. Minor fluctuations in Bender scores are unimportant. A gross deterioration of performance on the Bender Test is highly significant and reason for concern. Such a change may reflect a serious mental or organic deterioration and should be further investigated at once.

The discussion so far has dealt primarily with reading achievement. The findings also seem to apply to number achievement since many of the same children were included among the subjects with high reading achievement and with high number achievement. The overlap of subjects in Group I and II and in Group III and IV was considerable. A separate discussion of Bender performance and arithmetic problems seems superfluous. There are however some differences between the Bender records of subjects with reading problems and those with poor achievement in arithmetic.

Children with reading problems tend to have difficulty in discriminating between dots and circles and between curves and angles. They also exhibit more incidents of rotation on their drawings of Bender designs (see *Plate 6*). *It appears that good reading ability is related to the correct perception of the direction and the shape of forms and designs.* Children with problems in arithmetic tend to have difficulty in drawing the correct number of dots and circles on the Bender designs. They also tend to perseverate more often. Their Bender records more often reveal failure to integrate the parts of the designs into a whole Gestalt (see *Plate 7*). *Number achievement seems to be closely related to the correct perception and reproduction of the number of units in a Bender design and in the part-whole relationship of these configurations.* But no deviation occurred exclusively on the Bender records of children with either reading or number problems.

Plate 6 shows the Bender record of Don, a 10 years 6 months old boy with reading problems. Because of neurological impairment Don is still reading on the fourth grade level despite average intelligence and several years of remedial reading help. He obtained a Bender score of 4 on the Developmental Scoring System which is more than one standard deviation from the mean normative

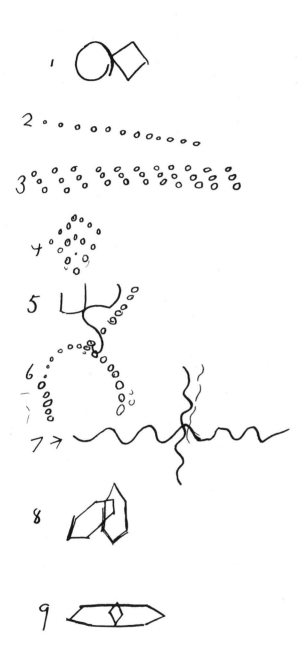

Plate 6. Don, C. A. 10-6; reading problem.

Scoring
1a
1b
2
3
8
11
13
14
16
17a
19
20
21b
23
24
25
_____
16

Plate 7. Jeff, C. A. 8-4; serious problem with arithmetic.

Bender score for his age group. The scoring points he received were for substituting circles for dots on Figures 1, 3 and 5 and for rotating Figure 3. It was stated above that these particular deviations on the Bender are closely related to reading difficulties.

The Bender record of Jeff is shown on *Plate 7*. Jeff is an 8 years 4 months old boy with a severe disability in dealing with number concepts. His intelligence is in the dull normal range and Jeff shows evidence of neurological impairment. His social understanding is fairly adequate but abstract reasoning in any form is hard for this youngster, particularly when numbers are involved. Jeff is unable to even count nine blocks or to add two and three. His Bender protocol reveals serious malfunctioning in visual-motor perception. He obtained a Bender score of 16 which is similar to that of an immature five year old child. Most outstanding is Jeff's failure to integrate the parts of Figures A, 4, 5, and 7. On Figure 6 the two lines cross three times instead of only once. Jeff also tends toward perseveration on Figure 6 and Figure 2. On Figure 2 he draws more circles than requested on most of the columns. None of the Bender figures show the correct number of units, be they dots, circles, curves or angles. It was indicated earlier that these particular Bender deviations are closely related to problems in arithmetic. Jeff's record illustrates this point.

A child's motivation and achievement in reading seem to be greatly influenced by his parents' attitude toward books and reading as well as by his cultural environment. Such differences were not evident in the achievement in arithmetic. Thus the discrepancy in reading achievement between children from high and low socioeconomic areas is much greater than the difference between these dissimilar groups in arithmetic achievement. This may explain in part, why the Bender Test scores are more closely related to arithmetic than to reading. Both the Bender and arithmetic achievement are relatively little influenced by cultural factors.

The study presented above concerns first and second graders and their second and third grade achievement. But every now and then one hears of preschool children who are able to read before they enter the first grade. Usually the proud teacher or parent claims that this accomplishment is the result of his special training. Our own observation tends to suggest that such youngsters are not only of superior intelligence but also have achieved a high degree of maturation in visual-motor perception. Thus being "ready" for school, they will acquire academic skills if given the opportunity and encouragement to do so. Inherent curiosity and a desire for learning seem to be the mark of a gifted child.

The author had the opportunity to test three little girls who were referred by their kindergarten teachers when it was discovered that they could read on the third and fourth grade level and were able to do second grade arithmetic. The teachers wanted help in planning a special program for these children. All three girls were physically well developed and mentally alert. The two five year olds were outgoing and preferred playing with children one or two years older than themselves; they were leaders in their group. The third child was just six years old, she was quiet and shy but well liked by her peers.

All three had outstanding Bender scores of five, six, and two respectively. This means their visual-motor perception was on the level of six and a half to eight year old children. All three children had stable, intelligent parents who had neither pushed nor drilled their youngsters at home. The two outgoing, five year old girls had attended a "school" of sorts since their older sisters delighted in playing school with them and had taught them everything they themselves had learned in their classrooms. Both older sisters were attending the third grade. The third child lived on an isolated farm. Her parents were too busy to spend much time with her and her only playmate was a twelve year old girl. The child had many books and amused herself by reading a great deal. She taught herself to read at age three by asking the names of letters and words and by memorizing the words on television commercials.

The history of the three little girls suggests that children of superior intelligence who have matured in visual-motor perception to the level of a six year old child are ready to learn to read regardless of their chronological age. It would appear that the Bender Test could be used to screen kindergarten children who could begin with reading and who would profit from an enriched school program. There seems little virtue in keeping children back at the kindergarten level when they have reached the mental, perceptual and social maturity required of a first grade student. In many school systems children are accelerated later on or are given enriched programs at the third grade level or higher up. There seems to be no reason why such acceleration or enrichment cannot start at an earlier age so that a child need not skip any part of the school curriculum and can benefit from a maximum of additional work. The Bender seems to offer much promise as one of several screening instruments for gifted children at the kindergarten level.

PART IV. The Bender as a Test for Diagnosing Brain Injury

Survey of the Literature

It appears to be generally accepted that the Bender Gestalt Test is a valuable aid in the diagnosing of neurological impairment. About one-fourth of all studies devoted to the Bender Test deal with the differentiation of psychiatric patients with organic and functional disorders or with the discrimination between individuals with endogenous or familial retardation and exogenous or organic retardation. In all but three of these studies, the subjects used were adults or mixed groups of adults and children. Only Hanvick (1953), Shaw and Cruickshank (1956), and Wewetzer (1956, 1959) investigated the Bender Test's relationship to brain injury in children exclusively. There appears to be a good deal of agreement regarding the usefulness of the Bender Test in diagnosing brain injury at all age levels even though the function of the Bender Test differs somewhat for adults and children.

Investigators concur that the Bender protocols of groups of brain injured individuals, regardless of age and intelligence, differ significantly from those of non-brain injured individuals who are not psychiatric patients (Barkley, 1949; Baroff, 1957; Beck, 1959; Bensberg, 1952; Feldman, 1953; Hanvick, 1953; McGuire, 1960; Niebuhr and Cohen, 1956; Shaw and Cruickshank, 1956; Wewetzer, 1959). There also appears to be a consensus that the Bender records of brain injured persons tend to show more immaturity and more primitive features than those of non-brain injured persons.

In discussing the effect of brain lesions, Bender points out (1938, p. 75) that visual-motor perception is an integrative function of the Personality-as-a-whole which is controlled by the cerebral cortex. Any disturbance in this highest center of integration would modify the integrative function of the individual to a lower and more primitive level. The effect of brain injury would depend on the interaction of several factors including: the locus and the extent of the brain lesion, the maturation level of the person prior to receiving the brain injury, and the emotional and social adjustment of the individual.

Wewetzer's (1959) intensive study of children with neurological impairment employed a variety of psychological tests including the Bender Gestalt Test. He found specifically that brain injured subjects had much difficulty joining the parts of Figures A, 4 and 7 into a total configuration for their perception of part-whole relationships was poor. He also reported that the performance of these children on the Bender Test reflected their emotional attitude in general which was not the case for his non-brain injured control subjects. Wewetzer cautions against using any one "sign" on the Bender as a diagnostic indicator of brain injury since each type of deviation and distortion recorded on the Bender Test was found among both the brain injured and the control group. Wewetzer stresses that the entire Bender protocol should be evaluated when analyzing a child's test performance. However, other investigators mention specific indicators which they found to correlate highly with brain injury.

71

The following Bender deviations have been mentioned as being diagnostically significant for brain injury: *Rotation* or the disorientation of the whole figure or part of it on the background was suggested by Bensberg (1952) and Hanvick (1953). *Perseveration* or the repetition of the whole figure or part of it is considered significant by Barnes (1950), Bensberg, and Feldman (1953). *Distortion* of figures is cited by Barnes, Baroff (1957), and Beck (1959). *Fragmentation* or the missing of parts of a figure as well as *poor integration* or the failure to cross lines on Figures 6 and 7 are reported by Feldman. *Substitution of lines for dots* was another deviation mentioned by Bensberg. And *difficulty in placing parts of Figures A and 4 at correct angles* was recorded by Shapiro, Field and Post (1957).

All the findings reported above concern persons suffering from permanent brain injury. Similar deviations on the Bender Test protocols can be observed in patients suffering from temporary brain diseases or from acute confusional states regardless of etiology (Abramson, 1955; Bender, 1938, p. 76; Murray and Roberts, 1956). As a patient recovers from the brain disease or from the confusional state he will again return to a higher level of integrative functioning passing through successive developmental stages of maturation in the process. Thus it would appear that the Bender Test reflects not only permanent brain injury, but it is sensitive to cortical malfunctioning, be it temporary or permanent.

As mentioned above, the Bender Test is frequently employed in differential diagnosis between groups of psychiatric patients. The findings in this area are not nearly as clear cut as between brain injured patients and non-brain injured individuals who are not psychiatric patients. In fact, little significant differences have been found between the Bender records of functional and organic patients (Goldberg, 1959; Halpern, 1951; Mehlman and Vatovec, 1956; Nadler, Fink, Shantz, and Brink, 1959; Olin, 1958; Pascal and Suttell, 1951). Many of the so-called "organic signs," e.g., rotation, fragmentation, primitivization, were also found to occur frequently among patients with functional disorders. The only exception to this ambiguity was found in the Bender records of patients with severe brain injury whose grossly distorted Bender protocols explain the obvious. In these cases the patients' behavior and their case history hardly require additional information from the Bender for adequate diagnosis. Less severely brain injured adult patients of normal intelligence cannot be easily distinguished from psychotic patients on the basis of their Bender performance.

Pascal and Suttell (1951, p. 62-66) point out that a Bender protocol can only indicate the presence of neurological impairment if the brain lesion effects the ability to reproduce the Bender Gestalt Figures. That is, if the integrative functioning of the brain injured individual has regressed or has failed to mature to or beyond the level of a nine year old child. Since most nine year old children can draw the Bender designs without error, it may be assumed that a brain injured person who is functioning in visual-motor perception at or above the nine year old level, can reproduce the Bender figures without deviations or errors. For this reason it is not possible to differentiate between organic and functional disorders of adult patients of normal intelligence unless the brain injury is very severe. Pascal and Suttell conclude that there may be present in adolescents or adults, types of brain injury which cannot be diagnosed by means of the Bender Test.

Bender (1938, p. 57) has discussed the effect of the locus of the brain lesion on the Bender Test performance. Hirschenfang's study (1960) seems to support her hypothesis. He found that right hemiplegics did considerably better on the Bender Test than did left hemiplegics. There also appears to be some indication that epileptic children show less disturbance on their Bender records than do children with other kinds of brain disease (Shaw and Cruickshank, 1956; Wewetzer, 1959).

RESEARCH STUDIES

Most of the studies discussed so far in this section are primarily concerned with adult psychiatric patients and with retarded individuals. It is felt that these studies offer valuable hypotheses for the study of the Bender Test and its relationship to brain injury in young school children of normal intelligence, but the findings cannot be accepted as valid for young subjects without further exploration. Therefore, a study (Koppitz, 1962b) was designed to determine whether the Bender Test as a whole or in part can differentiate between brain injured and non-brain injured school children, age 5 to 10 years, and whether the results obtained vary depending on the children's age and intelligence. No mentally retarded children were included in this study.

The subjects for the following study were 384 elementary school students. Of these, 103 subjects had been diagnosed as brain injured while the remaining 281 subjects, with no known history of brain injury, served as controls. All subjects were attending public school classes, kindergarten through fifth grade, with the exception of 16 children with neurological impairment who were in special public school classes for children with brain injury. None of the subjects had any serious physical defects or motor impairment, although two children with very mild cerebral palsy and two youngsters with partial hearing loss were included. *Table 16* shows the distribution of all subjects by age and sex.

Table 16. Distribution of Subjects by Age and Sex

Age	Brain Injured			Controls		
	Boys	Girls	Total	Boys	Girls	Total
5 & 6	10	0	10	30	0	30
7	22	4	26	62	12	74
8	25	5	30	60	20	80
9	19	4	23	47	16	63
10	11	3	14	25	9	34
All	87	16	103	224	57	281

The brain injured subjects had all been referred to a child guidance clinic or to the school psychologist for evaluation because of behavior problems, learning problems, or both. All brain injured children were diagnosed as suffering from neurological impairment by means other than psychological tests. The diagnosis was based on medical and developmental data including any one or several of the following: traumatic prenatal history, traumatic birth history, "blue baby," severe illness including meningitis, encephalitis, measles or whooping cough with very high fever during infancy, history of convulsions in early childhood, serious accidents involving skull fracture or prolonged unconsciousness, a positive EEG, brain tumor, or a positive neurological examination by a qualified neurologist.

The IQ scores for the brain injured group ranged from 75 to 122 with a mean IQ of 90. All IQ scores were derived from the Wechsler Intelligence Scale for Children or the Stanford-Binet Intelligence Scale, Form L or Form L—M. No such data were available for the control group. The non-brain injured subjects were matched with the brain injured subjects for age, sex and grade placement. Both the brain injured group and the control group were taken from the same socioeconomic area and attended the same schools for the most part. It is hoped that differences in IQ or sex ratio between the two groups have been minimized by increasing the N in the control groups.

The Bender Test was administered to each brain injured subject as part of the total psychological examination which he underwent. The control subjects were tested individually in school by the author as subjects for a larger research project. All Bender protocols were scored according to the Developmental Bender Scoring System for Children. The Bender scores for the brain injured and the control subjects were analyzed and compared in the following three ways:

1) *The total Bender score for each subject was studied.* Chi-squares were computed comparing the number of subjects in the two groups whose Bender scores were above or below the normative Bender scores for their respective age level.

2) *Each individual Bender scoring item was examined next.* Chi-squares were computed comparing the number of subjects in the two groups whose Bender record showed a given scoring item as being present or absent. Since the degree of difficulty in drawing the Bender figures varies from one design to the next, the age at which most children are able to copy a given Bender design varies too. It stands to reason that a deviation on the Bender will not become diagnostically important for brain injury as long as it normally occurs among young children with as yet immature visual-motor perception. Therefore, special emphasis was placed on analyzing the diagnostic importance of each Bender scoring item in relation to the child's age.

3) *The relationship between IQ and Bender scores for children with neurological impairment was investigated.* A chi-square was computed comparing the number of subjects with at least average IQ and with below average IQ and with above or below average Bender scores compared to the normative Bender scores for their respective age levels.

1) Total Bender Score and Brain Injury

Table 17 shows the results when the total Bender scores of brain injured and non-brain injured children were compared. All chi-square values are significant

Table 17. Bender Performance of Brain Injured Subjects and Controls

	Brain Injured		Controls			
Age	Good Bender	Poor Bender	Good Bender	Poor Bender	Chi-square	P
5 & 6	0	10	23	7	15.04	<.001
7	5	21	58	16	26.00	<.001
8	2	28	64	16	45.88	<.001
9	2	21	46	17	25.71	<.001
10	0	14	23	11	15.56	<.001

at the .001 level. It was found that none of the brain injured subjects at the five and six year old level, nor at the ten year old level had above average Bender Test scores. Only very few that is nine, of the seven, eight, and nine year old subjects had good Bender records. Thus it appears that children with neurological impairment have only rarely, above average Bender scores. Good Bender scores may be found among brain injured youngsters who have difficulty primarily in auditory perception rather than in visual-motor perception, who are able to compensate (p. 83) for malfunctioning in visual-motor perception, or who have outstanding artistic ability. Because of these special cases it is not safe to assume that a good Bender performance rules out the presence of brain injury. The reverse conclusion that a poor Bender score indicates necessarily neurological impairment is even less defensible.

The great majority of all brain injured subjects revealed poor visual-motor perception, but about one out of four of the control subjects did likewise. It is quite probable that some of the 67 control subjects with poor Bender scores were also brain injured. Undoubtedly many more children suffer from neurological impairment than come to the attention of the psychologists. However, it is unlikely that *all* 67 control subjects with poor Bender scores were brain injured. It is probable that the poor Bender performances of these children reflect a variety of factors all of which can effect the performance on the Bender Test. It was shown earlier (p. 38) that some children mature more slowly than others in visual-motor perception. They may obtain a poor Bender score at an early age but improve their score considerably in subsequent years. Other children may well have a genetically determined weakness in visual-motor perception. Again others may have performed poorly on the Bender because they lacked motivation or were temporarily upset or emotionally preoccupied during the test administration. In some cases there may have been visual problems which had not been recognized or the child may have been ill or tired. Bender (1938) has pointed out that fatigue and illness will effect a person's performance on the Bender Test. Thus a poor Bender score may result from many different factors, but the most important of these is immature or malfunctioning visual-motor perception.

It appears safe therefore, to state that a poor Bender record may be thought of as indicating the possibility of brain injury especially if the Bender score is more than minus one standard deviation from the mean normative Bender score for a given age group. But a definite diagnosis of brain injury should never be made solely on the basis of a single Bender Test score or, for that

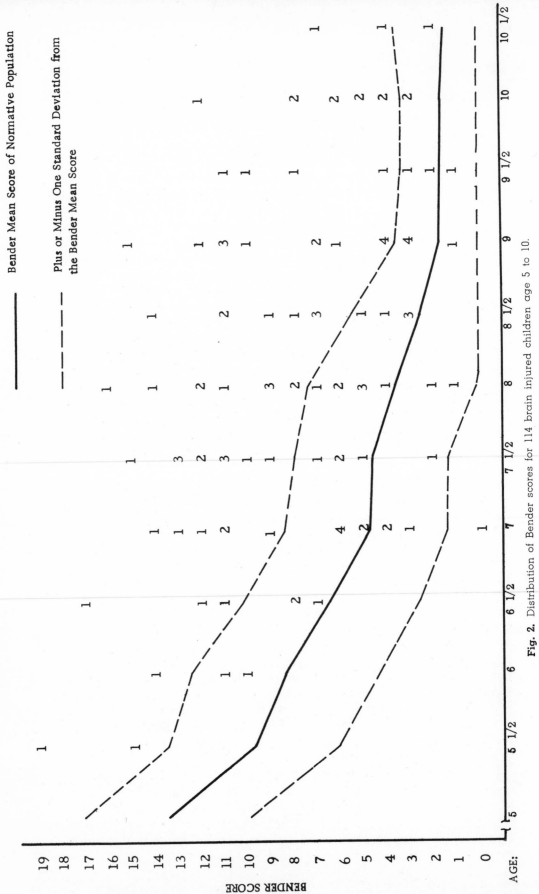

Fig. 2. Distribution of Bender scores for 114 brain injured children age 5 to 10.

matter, on the basis of *any single* psychological test score. Nor can the presence of neurological impairment be definitely ruled out because of a good Bender Test performance.

Figure 2 shows the distribution of Bender scores for 114 children with neurological impairment in relation to the mean scores and standard deviation of the normative population for the Developmental Bender Scoring System for Children (p. 76). The 114 brain injured children include the 103 subjects of the study reported above. None of the children were classified as mentally retarded; their IQ scores ranged from 75 to 138. It can be seen that there is a considerable spread of Bender scores for children with neurological impairment at any given age level though the great majority of all subjects show evidence of marked immaturity or malfunctioning in visual-motor perception. It was found that 69 children, or about three-fifths of all brain injured subjects scored more than minus one standard deviation from the normative Bender score for their respective age groups. Thirty-six or about one-third of all subjects scored between the Bender mean score and minus one standard deviation. Nine subjects, or about one in twelve scored above the normative Bender score and only one of these obtained a perfect score of 0 or more than plus one standard deviation.

2) *Individual Bender Scoring Items and Brain Injury*

As mentioned above Barnes, Baroff, Bensberg, and others (p. 72) had found that specific distortions and deviations on the Bender Gestalt Test seemed to be able to differentiate between brain injured and non-brain injured individuals. Because of this, each of the 30 separate scoring items on the Developmental Bender Scoring System for Children was tested individually to see how well it could distinguish brain injured from non-brain injured children. *Table 18* shows the chi-squares and P values when comparing the number of subjects in the brain injured and the control groups whose Bender record showed a given Bender deviation as being present or absent. Scoring item #12b for Figure 3 and scoring items #18b and #19 for Figure 6 are omitted from *Table 18*. These three distortions occurred so seldom that the theoretical frequencies did not reach the critical frequencies necessary to use chi-square statistics.

The data on *Table 18* show that no deviation on the Bender protocols was present exclusively among either the brain injured or the non-brain injured group of children. All Bender distortions are essentially manifestations of immature or poor visual-motor perception and occur normally on the Bender records of children at some point in their development. However, once a child has reached the age and level of maturation at which a given Bender deviation no longer normally occurs, the presence of this deviation takes on diagnostic significance. *Table 18* shows that different Bender scoring items become diagnostically significant at different age levels depending on the difficulty of that particular design or part of it. As was to be expected, the number of Bender scoring items which are able to differentiate between children with and without neurological impairment increases as the age of the children

Table 18.   Relationship Between Individual Bender Scoring Items and
Brain Injury in Young Children

Bender Scoring Items	5 & 6 year olds Chi-square	P	7 year olds Chi-square	P	8 year olds Chi-square	P	9 & 10 year olds Chi-square	P
Figure A								
1a) Distortion	13.81	<.001	24.74	<.001	9.99	<.01	20.54	<.001
1b) Disproportion	—	—	2.97	<.10	12.80	<.001	14.88	<.001
2) Rotation	—	—	—	—	—	—	4.57	<.05
3) Integration	—	—	3.67	<.10	5.66	<.02	2.96	<.10
Figure 1								
4) Circles for dots	—	—	7.96	<.01	—	—	4.96	<.05
5) Rotation	—	—	—	—	—	—	7.36	<.01
6) Perseveration	—	—	—	—	9.99	<.01	—	—
Figure 2								
7) Rotation	—	—	—	—	—	—	7.39	<.01
8) Integration	9.25	<.01	2.55	>.10	2.34	>.10	—	—
9) Perseveration	—	—	—	—	7.59	<.01	2.51	>.10
Figure 3								
10) Circles for dots	—	—	4.47	<.05	—	—	—	—
11) Rotation	—	—	—	—	10.31	<.01	17.56	<.001
12a) Integration	9.25	<.01	—	—	4.59	<.05	—	—
Figure 4								
13) Rotation	5.05	<.05	13.79	<.001	24.35	<.001	9.59	<.01
14) Integration	4.85	<.05	—	—	8.29	<.01	12.67	<.001
Figure 5								
15) Circles for dots	—	—	—	—	—	—	5.94	<.02
16) Rotation	6.06	<.02	—	—	—	—	8.57	<.01
17a) Shape lost	—	—	4.13	<.05	—	—	2.28	>.10
17b) Lines for dots	12.88	<.001	5.29	<.05	2.34	>.10	4.76	<.05
Figure 6								
18a) Angles for curves	3.39	<.10	17.31	<.001	19.54	<.001	23.26	<.001
20) Perseveration	—	—	—	—	8.42	<.01	19.37	<.001
Figure 7								
21a) Disproportion	—	—	—	—	10.99	<.001	17.53	<.001
21b) Distortion	7.67	<.01	4.12	<.05	23.89	<.001	63.57	<.001
22) Rotation	—	—	15.02	<.001	14.54	<.001	11.36	<.001
23) Integration	—	—	14.75	<.001	17.95	<.001	17.44	<.001
Figure 8								
24) Distortion	—	—	16.95	.001	19.83	<.001	30.86	<.001
25) Rotation	3.33	<.10	—	—	4.82	<.05	—	—

increases. Relatively few Bender scoring items are of value for diagnosing brain injury at the five and six year old level.

Each scoring item of the Developmental Bender Scoring System will be discussed here briefly in relation to its usefulness in diagnosing brain injury in young school children of normal intelligence.

Figure A

1a) *Distortion* was one of the few scoring items which differentiated significantly between the two groups of subjects at all age levels. At age five and six all children in the control group with two exceptions drew the circle and square correctly; hardly any of the brain injured subjects did so before age seven.

1b) *Disproportion* between the circle and square occurred equally often among five and six year old children in both groups. It gradually diminished in frequency in both groups but at a much faster rate among the control subjects.

2) *Rotation* was found consistently more often in the brain injured group but the difference was not statistically significant until age 9.

3) *Integration* of parts was consistently harder for brain injured children at all age levels. It became statistically significant at age 7.

Figure 1

4) *Substitution of circles and loops for dots* occurred significantly more often among brain injured children at all age levels.

5) *Rotation* occurred very rarely and was found almost exclusively among the brain injured subjects.

6) *Perseveration* was common among all children through age 7, by age 8 it occurs mostly among the brain injured group.

Figure 2

7) *Rotation* was found in both groups through age 8, thereafter it no longer occurred in the control group.

8) *Integration:* The omission or addition of rows of circles was common in very young children. It no longer occurred in the control group by age 6. Among the brain injured subjects it persisted through age 8. This scoring item has considerable diagnostic value for children six years old and older.

9) *Perseveration* was common among all children through age 7. By age 8 it was only found among the brain injured group and became highly significant diagnostically.

Figure 3

10) *Substitution of circles for dots* occurred to some extent in both groups though more often among the brain injured subjects.

11) *Rotation* was not uncommon among all children through age 7. By age 8 it tended to drop out in the control group but persisted among the brain injured group.

12a) *Integration of shape:* Most normal children were able to reproduce the basic Gestalt of Figure 3 after age 5. Brain injured children had difficulty with this item until age 9. It became diagnostically significant by age 6.

12b) *Substitution of line for dots* occurred very rarely. When it did occur it was highly significant as it was found almost exclusively among brain injured children of school age.

Figure 4

13) *Rotation* was of great diagnostic significance at all age levels. By age 7 it rarely occurred in the control group.

14) *Integration of the curve and the square* was very hard for most brain injured children at all age levels. Most children in the control group had no difficulty with this item.

Figure 5

15) *Substitution of circles for dots* did not seem to differentiate between the brain injured and the control groups before age 9.

16) *Rotation* was found to some extent among both groups; however, it occurred significantly more often among the brain injured subjects at all age levels.

17a) *Distortion of the basic configuration of design* was found rarely in either group at any age level. This item did not discriminate well between the brain injured and the control subjects.

17b) *Substitution of lines for dots* was found only among the brain injured subjects. This type of drawing is very primitive. It was of high diagnostic value for school children at all age levels. (The deviation is common among nursery school children.)

Figure 6

18a) *Substitution of angles for curves* was found consistently more often among the brain injured group, but at no age level was the control group entirely without this distortion. No brain injured child was able to draw the sinusoidal curves correctly before age 7.

18b) *Substitution of straight lines for curves* is a very primitive response. It occurred occasionally in the brain injured group, but not often enough for statistical computation. When it did occur it had high diagnostic value. (This deviation is normally found among children in nursery school.)

19) *Integration:* Failure to cross the two lines is a very primitive type of drawing; it is rare among school age children. When it did occur, it was diagnostically significant for brain injury.

20) *Perseveration* was common among all children through age 7. After age 8 it became diagnostically highly significant. It was observed among the brain injured group at all age levels.

Figure 7

21a) *Disproportion of the two hexagons* was not uncommon among all children through the age of 7. After age 8 it was found significantly more often among the brain injured subjects.

21b) *Missing or extra angles on hexagons* were quite common among brain injured children of all age levels. None of the neurologically impaired subjects were able to draw hexagons correctly before age 8. However, a large number of the control subjects also had difficulty with this task. Despite the high statistical significance of this scoring item at all age levels, this particular point has only limited diagnostic value. Its greatest usefulness is in suggesting the *absence* of brain injury in children who draw the angles correctly when they are less than eight years old.

22) *Rotation* was common among all children through age 6. By age 7 this type of drawing tended to drop out in the control group and became diagnostically significant for brain injury.

23) *Integration of hexagons* was hard for all children through age 6. Thereafter the failure to integrate the two hexagons occurred primarily in the brain injured group.

Figure 8

24) *Distortion:* Extra or missing angles on the hexagon or diamond were common among all children through age 6. Thereafter it took on diagnostic significance and occurred much more frequently among the brain injured subjects.

25) *Rotation* occurred rarely among school age youngsters. When it did appear it was almost exclusively on the records of brain injured children. This item appears to have considerable diagnostic value at all age levels.

The findings discussed in detail above are summarized on *Table 19** to facilitate their use in the analysis of Bender protocols. On this table the Bender scoring points are grouped according to the type of deviation they represent. For example, all Rotations are grouped together so that it can be seen at a glance that Rotations on Figures A, 1, 4, 5, and 8 have diagnostic implications for brain injury for school children of all age levels, whereas Rotations on Figures 2, 3, and 7 are not diagnostically significant until after age 8, 7, and 6 respectively. In similar fashion it can be seen that substitutions of circles for dots becomes diagnostically significant at different ages for different designs.

Most scoring items of the Developmental Bender Scoring System are classified on *Table 19* as diagnostically "significant" or "highly significant." "Significant" means in this case, that the particular scoring item is statistically significant in its ability to differentiate between brain injured and non-brain injured children and that *it occurs more often but not exclusively among children with neurological impairment.* "Highly significant" implies that the scoring item *occurs almost exclusively among brain injured children.* Once again, it should be emphasized that the presence of diagnostically significant indicators for brain injury is not sufficient by itself to make a definite diagnosis of neurological impairment. Such indicators offer strong hypotheses that brain injury may be present, but all Bender deviations can and do occur with more or less frequency on the records of non-brain injured children at some level of maturation.

The validity of a diagnosis of brain injury is greatly enhanced when a Bender record is examined for both the total Bender score and for individual scoring items which are associated with neurological impairment. The presence of indicators of brain injury on a Bender record may serve as a valuable clue in differentiating among children with poor Bender scores. A poor total Bender score *and* the presence of several indicators of brain injury may suggest that the child is neurologically impaired, while an equally poor Bender score with a minimum of organic indicators may suggest that the child is slow maturing but does not have any malfunctioning in visual-motor perception. The Bender records of Jimmy *(Plate 2,* p. 40) and Mike *(Plate 4,* p. 42) illustrate this point.

---

* See Appendix, page 189.

Jimmy, age six years two months, obtained a total Bender score of 10 which is below average for his age group. He scored on the following scoring items: #1a, 1b, 10, 14, 15, 18a, 20, 21a, 21b, and 24. Of these scoring items only #1a (distortion on Figure A) and #14 (failure to integrate parts of Figure 4) are considered to have diagnostic implications for brain injury on the six year old level. But these two items also occur to some extent on the records of non-brain injured children. Thus it seems safe to hypothesize that Jimmy is primarily a slow developing child. The fact that his Bender score was near perfect when he was retested a year later *(Plate 3,* p. 41) supports this hypothesis.

Mike, age six years two months, also had a Bender score of 10 *(Plate 4).* His total score was made up of the following scoring items: #2, 8, 12a, 13, 14, 18a, 20, 21a, 21b, and 24. Of these ten scoring items five are considered significant indicators for brain injury. They are #2 (rotation of Figure A), #8 (omission of row in Figure 2), #12a (loss of shape on Figure 3), #13 (rotation of Figure 4) and #14 (failure to integrate Figure 4). Two of these items, #8 and #13, are *highly* significant and occur almost exclusively among brain injured children. Thus it seems safe to hypothesize on the basis of *both* the total Bender score *and* the individual scoring items that Mike is a brain injured child and that his poor Bender performance is due to impairment in visual-motor perception. This hypothesis was supported by Mike's failure to show any progress on his Bender when he was retested a year later *(Plate 5,* p. 43). In fact, there seemed to be a regression on the maturity level of some designs. Since then Mike has been medically diagnosed as suffering from a progressive brain disease.

3) *Relationship of IQ and Bender Scores Among Brain Injured Children*

It had been shown earlier *(Table 10,* p. 46) that intelligence test scores and Bender scores are highly correlated for young children who have been referred to a child guidance clinic or to a school psychologist. An investigation was conducted to discover whether the same close relationship exists between IQ and Bender scores of brain injured children and whether the poor Bender performance of most children with neurological impairment is primarily due to low intelligence.

The IQ scores for the 103 brain injured subjects in this study were derived from the Wechsler Intelligence Scale for Children (WISC) or from the Stanford-Binet Intelligence Scale, Form L or Form L-M. It was found that the magnitude of the IQ scores, i.e., the high and the low IQ scores, were quite evenly divided among the five age levels tested. Thus there were the same proportion of subjects with high average, average and low average intelligence test scores among the five and six year olds, the seven year olds, the eight, nine and the ten year olds. It was therefore possible to treat all brain injured subjects as one group. Each child's Bender performance was compared with the normative Bender score for his respective age group. *Table 20* shows the distribution of the subjects in relation to their IQ scores and their Bender Test performance. All subjects were divided into two groups. One group included children with above average IQ scores, i.e., IQ scores of 100 or above, and the other included subjects with below average IQ scores, i.e., IQ scores of 99

Table 20. IQ and Bender Performance of Brain Injured Children

IQ Score	N	Above Average Bender	Below Average Bender
120 and above	1	0	1
110 to 119	12	2	10
100 to 109	19	4	15
90 to 99	22	2	20
80 to 89	33	0	33
75 to 79	16	1	15
75 to 126	103	9	94

or less. A chi-square was computed comparing the number of children with above and below average IQ scores and above and below average Bender scores for their respective age groups.

The chi-square value obtained was only 3.79 making the difference between the two groups statistically significant at the 10 per cent level of confidence. This indicates that the relationship between IQ and Bender scores for brain injured children is not very close. A high IQ score does not necessarily mean that the child will also do well on the Bender Test. *Table 20* reveals that 94 of the 103 subjects with neurological impairment had below average Bender scores. *It seems safe therefore, to conclude that brain injured children as a group tend to do poorly on the Bender Test regardless of their IQ scores.* Only nine subjects had above average Bender records. Eight of these had IQ scores of at least 90, while six of the nine subjects had an IQ score of 100 or above. It seems that brain injured children who perform well on the Bender Test are most likely to have at least, average intelligence. However, there are occasional exceptions to this rule. For instance, one little girl in this study produced one of the best Bender protocols of the entire group of subjects despite borderline intelligence. She had inherited outstanding artistic ability from her artist parents. This type of child is rare. Usually a good Bender record indicates the probability of at least average IQ scores for brain injured children.

It seems significant that only one of the subjects in this study was classified as being of superior intelligence, i.e., had an IQ score of above 120. Two explanations suggest themselves. One is that children with neurological impairment rarely obtain superior IQ scores, and the other is that brain injured children of superior intelligence are usually able to compensate for their perceptual impairment and do not come as readily to the attention of psychologist working in clinics or schools. It is probable that both explanations hold true to a certain extent.

COMPENSATING FOR POOR VISUAL-MOTOR PERCEPTION

The presence of a brain lesion implies that neural tissue has been destroyed which cannot be restored. However, the human brain has a miraculous capacity to compensate for malfunctions due to injuries it has suffered. If one area of the brain has been injured a reorganization of the brain processes takes place gradually, which allows other parts of the brain to take over functions of the damaged area unless specific centers for vision, hearing, speech, etc., are impaired. Many brain injured children learn to compensate for their perceptual impairment adequately if conditions are favorable, i.e., if 1) the extent of the brain injury is not too extreme, 2) if they have sufficient intellectual ability to learn different ways of solving problems, and 3) if they are not handicapped by serious emotional problems which may develop as a consequence of the brain injury, as a result of unfavorable home situations, or both.

Compensating for problems in visual-motor perception means that a child learns to overcome or to adapt to his difficulty in such a way that it no longer seriously interferes with his functioning. Visual-motor perception involves *both visual perception* and *motoric expression,* i.e., the reproduction of that which has been perceived. This is not to be confused with motor coordination (p. 95). If a child's problem is primarily one of visual perception then he will have to learn to adapt to his handicap and will have to get along in spite of it. That this can be done was demonstrated by Robbie. *Plate 8* (p. 85) shows Robbie's Bender record. Robbie was a 9 year 2 months old boy of high average intelligence whose neurological impairment resulted in serious problems in visual perception. He was completely unaware that his drawings of the Bender designs were incorrect. When his drawings were placed right next to the stimulus cards Robbie was unable to recognize that he had distorted the square in Figure A, had drawn too many dots on Figure 1, had substituted circles for dots on Figures 1, 3, and 5, and had failed to integrate the parts of Figures 4 and 7 correctly. In fact he was quite pleased with his production and with his achievement in general. And he had reason for being satisfied. Robbie had been slow in getting started in school and repeated kindergarten because of immaturity. But over the years he had been able to catch up with his age group and was working at the fifth grade level in all subjects except arithmetic where he was at the fourth grade level. Robbie's poor coordination made his writing difficult to read and may account for his poor angles on the Bender Figures 7 and 8, but it did not explain the more serious distortions mentioned above. Robbie's Bender record leaves little doubt that he is a brain injured child which was confirmed by medical diagnosis. But the Bender record tells nothing about his actual functioning. By virtue of his good intelligence, high motivation for learning, and a great deal of support and understanding from his parents Robbie had learned to compensate for his perceptual problem. He had *adapted* to it and was functioning well academically despite high distractability and restlessness.

If a brain injured child has no problems in visual perception but has great difficulty in the motoric expression of the perceived designs, he will be aware of his poor performance on the Bender Test. If he has sufficient intelligence and motivation for learning he will try to overcome his difficulty. How well he succeeds will depend on the severity of his impairment as well as on his ability and his efforts. *Plate 9* shows the Bender record of Nancy, a 7 year 2 months old girl of high average intelligence. Nancy was an attractive little girl, well liked by adults and peers but she had difficulty with reading and her achievement was poor. Her developmental history and medical examinations indicated the presence of neurological impairment. On the Bender Test

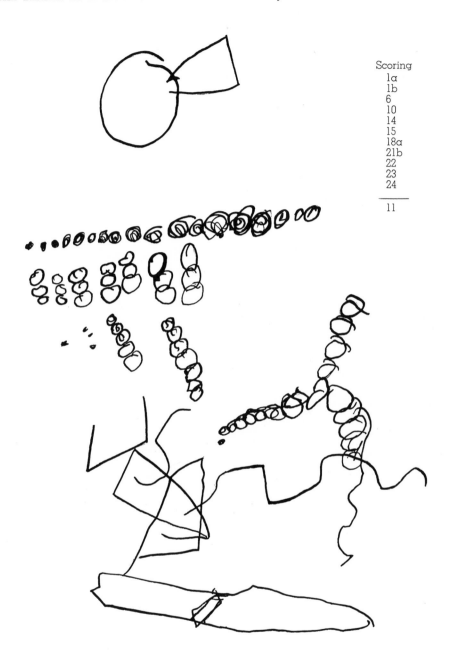

Scoring
1a
1b
6
10
14
15
18a
21b
22
23
24
___
11

Plate 8. Robbie, C. A. 9-2.

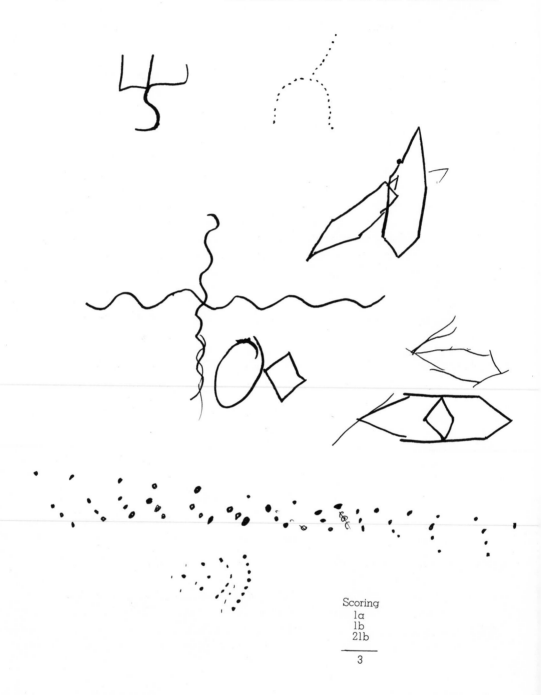

Scoring
1a
1b
21b
___
3

Plate 9. Nancy, C. A. 7-2.

Nancy obtained a score of 3 which is above average for her age group and is in itself not suggestive of brain injury or of problems in visual-motor perception. However, the way in which Nancy went about drawing the Bender designs told a different story. In this case the method of copying the figures told more than the final test score.

Nancy worked extremely slowly and required 17½ minutes to complete the test; this is almost three times as long as the time required by most children (p. 36). She was very much aware of the mistakes she made indicating that her visual perception was good. She expressed much dissatisfaction with her work and erased freely. She redrew spontaneously parts of Figures 2, 3, 6, 7, and 8. It was quite apparent that copying the Bender designs was extremely difficult for Nancy and she had considerable problems in controlling her motoric expression despite good visual perception. Her ultimately good performance on the Bender Test was the result of intensive effort on her part to overcome her handicap in motoric expression. It was also clear that the amount of time and effort required by Nancy to complete a motoric task seriously interfered with her school progress. On the other hand her good motivation and intelligence may enable her ultimately to compensate sufficiently and effectively enough so that she may be able to improve her functioning in school in the years to come.

Nancy's example demonstrates how important it is to analyze not only the finished Bender protocol but also to observe the child while he is taking the test. Behavior during the test administration often reveals the presence of underlying problems in visual-motor perception which are not necessarily apparent on the completed Bender record. The following is a list of different types of behavior observed in brain injured children who were trying to compensate for difficulties in visual-motor perception:

(a) *Excessive amount of time* required to complete Bender Test (*Table 7*, p. 36).

(b) *Tracing of design with finger* before drawing it.

(c) *"Anchoring"* design with finger, i.e., placing finger on each portion of design on the stimulus card as it is drawn.

(d) *Glancing once briefly at picture of design* and then removing card from sight and working entirely from memory, as though the presence of the stimulus card were confusing.

(e) *Rotation of stimulus card and of drawing paper* and then copying design in rotated position but turning paper back to correct position after the drawing has been completed.

(f) *Checking and re-checking of dots and circles* several times and still being uncertain about the correct number involved.

(g) *Impulsive, hasty drawings which are spontaneously erased and then corrected with much effort.*

(h) *Expressed dissatisfaction with poorly executed drawings* and repeated efforts to correct these which may or may not be successful.

All of these behaviors are found among brain injured children, but not all brain injured children show any or all of these actions. Behavior types (b), (c), (d) and (e) have been observed exclusively among children with neuro-logical impairment and reflect attempts at compensating for perceptual diffi-culty. Behavior types (a), (f), (g) and (h) are similar to those also found in perfectionistic or compulsive non-brain injured children and reflect an *emotional attitude* which is not found exclusively in brain injured children.

However, there are differences between the behavior of brain injured and non-brain injured perfectionistic children. For example, a perfectionistic child without neurological impairment will count dots and know how many there are, he will correct a drawing which is carefully drawn to begin with and which is most likely well drawn, he will express dissatisfaction with his produc-tion even though it may be quite satisfactory by the examiner's standards. The compulsive child without brain injury may use a long time to complete the test because he cannot meet his own high standards and is dissatisfied with himself, he does not have the same difficulty in drawing that the compulsive brain injured child has. Perfectionism and compulsivity occur in children with and without brain injury. Many neurologically impaired children will adopt an attitude of perfectionism and compulsivity as a defense against their inherent impulsiveness. A certain degree of compulsiveness and perfectionism is neces-sary in order for a brain injured child to be able to compensate for problems in visual-motor perception.

Once again it should be emphasized that the behavior indicators discussed here cannot and should not be used by themselves in the diagnosis of brain injury. But clinical experience has shown that behavior indicators can serve as valuable supporting evidence for brain injury in combination with the total Bender score and individual scoring items on the Bender records of young children.

The discussion has centered so far on ways of compensating for difficulties in visual-motor perception through more or less deliberate effort on the part of the brain injured child. But by far, the most important single factor in aiding neurologically impaired children in the struggle to function adequately despite poor visual-motor perception is *time*. Maturation in perception occurs in brain injured children just as it does in non-brain injured children, only it is usually a much slower process. And even where the perception is so greatly impaired that it shows little improvement over the years, the ability to compensate for it tends to develop in the course of time. The rate of maturation in visual-motor perception or compensation for malfunctioning of the same will depend of course, on the extent of the brain lesion, the child's age, his intellectual endowment, and his social and emotional state. Strauss (1947, p. 41) warns of underestimating the growing child's capacity to overcome in time, the effects of neurological impairment.

The extent to which even a seriously brain injured child of low average intelligence can overcome problems in visual-motor perception is illustrated by means of four Bender records of Karl. They were taken over a twelve months' period and reveal a marked improvement brought on by the passage of time primarily, although the class placement and the teacher were also of great help in this case. When Karl was first seen at the end of the first grade (*Plate 10*)

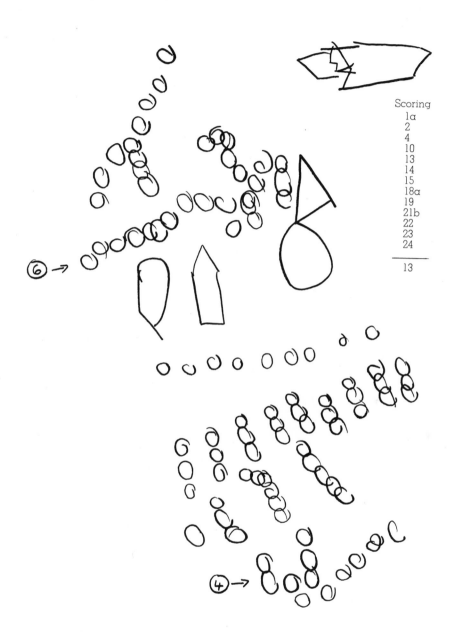

Scoring
1a
2
4
10
13
14
15
18a
19
21b
22
23
24
_____
13

Plate 10. Karl, C. A. 7-4.

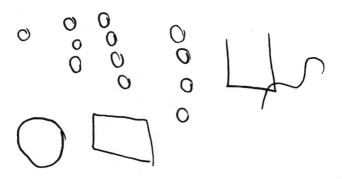

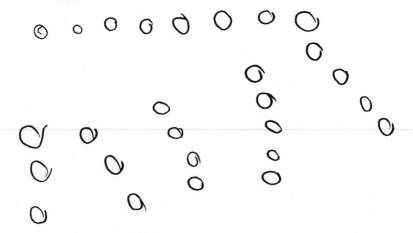

Plate 11. Karl, C. A. 7-9.

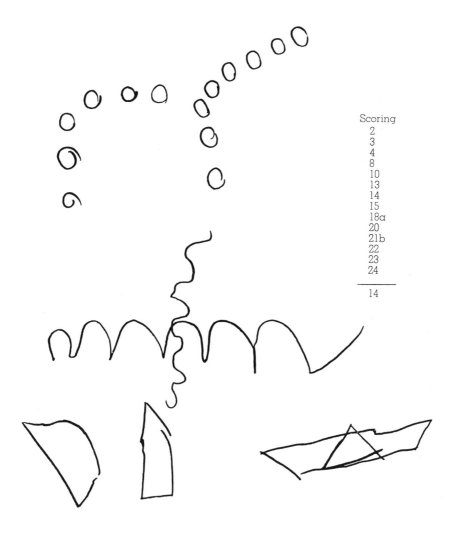

Scoring
2
3
4
8
10
13
14
15
18a
20
21b
22
23
24
___
14

Plate 11. (cont'd)

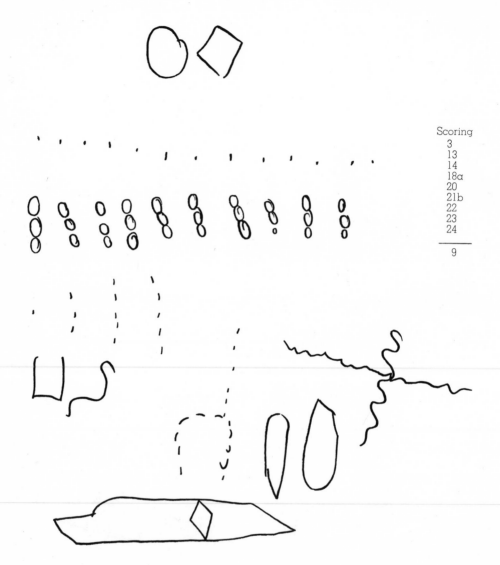

Scoring
3
13
14
18a
20
21b
22
23
24
___
9

Plate 12. Karl, C. A. 8-2.

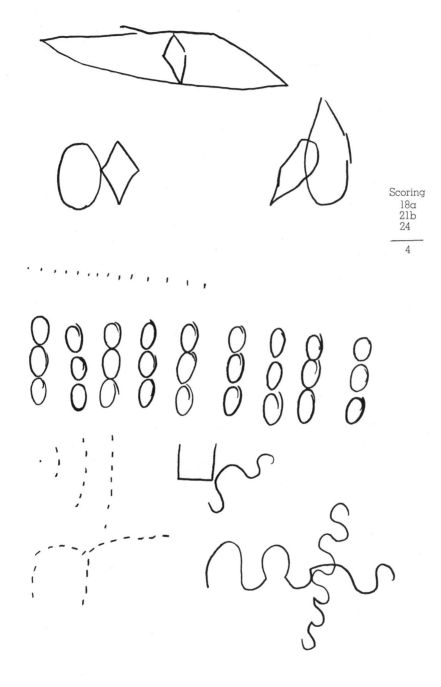

Scoring
18a
21b
24
———
4

Plate 13. Karl, C. A. 8-5.

he was a very immature and confused little boy. His Bender score and the maturity level of his drawings were similar to those of a five year old child. Karl was at the time seven years and four months old. He had spent a whole school year sitting in the classroom without comprehending what was going on; he had learned next to nothing and had no friends. Signs of withdrawal were evident and Karl was developing serious emotional problems. His teacher was a very informal, stimulating person who accomplished wonders with the large number of bright children in her class, but Karl was too immature to profit from this unstructured first grade experience. He would have done much better during this year if he had been permitted to repeat kindergarten. *Plate 10* shows Karl's rather unusual tendency to perseverate in drawing immature round loops even on Figures 4 and 6 where straight and curved lines are required. This seems to reflect both immaturity and serious emotional maladjustment. Karl shows a large number of Bender deviations which are associated with neurological impairment and with poor academic progress. He was in no way ready for second grade, in fact not even for the first grade. So it was decided to let Karl repeat the first grade.

At the end of the summer Karl returned to the first grade but was given a different teacher who provided a more structured program for Karl. When he was retested (*Plate 11*) he revealed no improvement in his Bender score and still showed only the maturation level of an immature five year old child, in visual-motor perception. However, he was more relaxed and less confused. He showed fewer signs of emotional disturbance and was much more outgoing. This was also reflected in his expansiveness on the Bender protocol. He drew oversized figures and spread them over two pages. Karl was still not ready to begin even with pre-primer work and his teacher was urged not to push him but to let him progress on the kindergarten level at his own speed. It can be seen on *Plate 11* that Karl still had difficulty integrating the parts on Figures A and 7, he used loops for dots on Figures 1, 3, and 5, he had difficulty with angles and curves, and perseverated on Figure 6 and on Figure 2 where he drew four circles instead of three in the majority of columns. He rotated Figures A, 4, and 7.

By March, Karl's new first grade teacher became concerned because he showed a complete lack of academic progress up to this point. Karl was again retested; at this time he was eight years and two months old. *Plate 12* shows a marked improvement in Karl's Bender performance. His Bender record now resembles that of an immature six year old child and he shows signs of being ready to begin pre-primer work. His controls and adjustment had greatly improved; Karl used only one sheet of paper, his Bender drawings are more nearly the correct size and are placed in logical sequence for the first time. He made dots where required and was able to draw the square on Figure A and the diamond on Figure 8 correctly. There was still a tendency to perseverate on Figure 6 and the integration of Figures A, 4, and 7 had not yet been accomplished. But in view of Karl's rate of maturation in visual-motor perception during the preceding five months there was reason to be optimistic about his academic progress from here on in.

When Karl was tested a fourth time in June, at age 8 years 5 months, his Bender record (*Plate 13*) had improved so much that it actually was average for his age group. He obtained a Bender score of only 4. Karl had also shown marked improvement in his ability to relate to other children. There was no doubt that Karl had finally "caught on"; he had learned to compensate for serious neurological impairment and at last was able to begin with reading and simple arithmetic. His teacher reported enthusiastically that Karl had suddenly begun to work and that he was reading on the same level as the slower children in his class. Before this he had done little or no academic work at all. *Plate 13* shows that Karl was now able to integrate the parts of Figures A, 4, and 7, perseveration had almost entirely disappeared, and dots and circles were well differentiated. He still had difficulty with angles and curves but this was not too unusual for his age group. It is interesting how Karl's academic progress coincides with his maturation in visual-motor perception.

Karl's case shows how over a period of time, a child of dull average ability was able to achieve what bright children like Robbie (p. 84) and Nancy (p. 84) could accomplish in a shorter period of time by virtue of their intelligence and effort.

BENDER TEST-RETEST FOR BRAIN INJURED CHILDREN

Repeated testing with the Bender Test offers valuable clues to a child's rate of maturation in visual-motor perception (p. 37). The Bender Test was administered more than once by the author to 28 children with neurological impairment. The time interval between tests ranged from three months to three years. An analysis of the test-retest scores revealed no significant pattern characteristic for brain injured children. The Bender scores for all 28 subjects were below average for their respective age levels both at the time of the first test administration and at the second test administration. Twenty-one of the children showed varying degrees of progress between the first and second execution of the Bender Test. The improvement in test scores ran all the way from one to twelve points regardless of the time interval between testing. Four children showed no progress on their Bender records and three did worse on their second Bender than on the first. They regressed one or two points each.

Repeated Bender test scores have their greatest value for brain injured children in pointing up possible regression and the presence of a progressive brain disease. Whenever a child shows a marked negative change in his Bender Test score or in the quality of his drawings, then a further investigation is definitely indicated.

RECEPTIVE VERSUS EXPRESSIVE DISTURBANCES

If the total process involved in visual-motor perception were divided into four steps they would include: (a) seeing a stimulus or *vision*, (b) understanding what has been seen or *perception*, (c) translating the perception into action or the motoric *expression*, and (d) the actual motor action or *coordination*. Steps (b) and (c) are the complex higher integrative functions which are under discussion here.

The question is frequently raised whether the Bender Test can help to differentiate between brain injured children who suffer primarily from receptive disturbance, i.e., *problems in visual perception*, and those who suffer from expressive disturbances, i.e., *difficulty in reproducing that which has been perceived*. Expressive disturbances do not refer to motor coordination as such. The answer to this question is "yes" if only one or the other disturbance is present. However, the majority of young children with neurological impairment show disturbances in both the receptive and the expressive areas.

Visual-motor perception, as the name implies, is a complicated integrative function which involves both visual perception *and* the motoric expression of the perception. Both these functions are subject to maturation in young children. In most youngsters *both* functions are as yet immature and the attempt to distinguish between them is difficult. It has been observed in groups of unselected school children that the rate of maturation in the receptive and the expressive function of visual-motor perception differs from one child to the next child. Thus one youngster may have matured early in perception; he may perceive the total configuration of the Bender designs perfectly, yet his expressive function may still be immature and he may lack the ability to reproduce accurately what he has perceived. Another child may have the ability to reproduce in perfect detail, designs which he as yet perceives incorrectly, e.g., he may draw the parts of Figure 4 correctly but may fail to integrate them or may be unaware that he is drawing them upside down. Such differences are common in young children. One can only begin to talk about a disturbance in the receptive or the expressive function of visual-motor perception when the discrepancy between the two is extreme at a time when most children have reached a certain degree of maturity in both functions.

The differentiation between receptive and expressive disturbances is more meaningful when working with older children or adults. In young children the presence of neurological impairment usually results in increased immaturity in the *total* function of visual-motor perception. Differences in the two component parts of this integrative function are usually not pronounced and are difficult to recognize on the Bender records of young children. But there are cases where a clear distinction is possible. Robbie, the 9 year old boy whose Bender record is shown on *Plate 8* (p. 85) is a case in point.

Robbie was a brain injured child of high average intelligence whose primary difficulty was in visual perception. The disturbance in visual perception was discovered when Robbie was asked whether his drawings resembled the designs on the stimulus cards. Each card was placed separately next to Robbie's reproduction of the same but Robbie could not "see" the differences between his drawings and the stimulus designs even when they were pointed out to him. Thereupon Robbie was asked to redraw several of the Bender Figures and he was retested with the entire Bender Test three months later. In both instances he reproduced almost identical drawings with the same errors. Improvement was minimal. Yet Robbie did very well in school in all academic subjects. It has been repeatedly observed that a bright child with neurological impairment can *adapt* to faulty perception and can function quite adequately in school as long as he does not have difficulty in the motoric expressive function.

Another child with disturbances primarily in the perceptual area was Sally, a brain injured, 10 year 4 months old girl of borderline intelligence. Her Bender record is shown on *Plate 14*. Sally substituted circles for dots consistently on Figures 1, 3, and 5, she had difficulty with angles on Figures 7 and 8, she showed a disproportion in size between the parts of Figure A, and inverted Figure 5. Sally worked very carefully and was completely at ease. She seemed pleased with her production and was unable to recognize her errors even when they were pointed out to her. When asked to redraw some of the designs she reproduced identical drawings over again. Sally showed definite evidence of disturbance in visual perception. Her drawings showed little trouble with motoric expression. But in contrast to Robbie, Sally has not been able to adapt too successfully to her perceptual problem because of limited capacity in conceptualization and poor memory. Sally has serious difficulty in all academic subjects.

Earlier in this chapter, the case of Nancy was cited to illustrate a bright little girl's ability to compensate for malfunctioning in motoric expression. Nancy was the 7 year 2 months old brain injured child whose Bender is shown on *Plate 9* (p. 86). Nancy had very good visual perception. The presence of expressive disturbance was inferred from the following: 1) The fact that a bright child like Nancy had so much difficulty with the copying of the Bender designs. 2) The fact that Nancy was keenly aware of her own mistakes and could describe in detail how the drawings should look. 3) The absence of any distortions of the basic Gestalten of the nine Bender designs drawn by Nancy. 4) The fact that Nancy showed poor school progress despite good intelligence, high motivation for learning, good visual perception, and much effort on her part.

A second very interesting example of a young child with primarily expressive disturbances was Byron. His Bender record is shown on *Plate 15*. Byron was a 6 year 10 months old boy of good intellectual potential and keen visual perception. But Byron was a brain injured child with serious expressive disturbances in both the language and the visual area. He did not learn to talk clearly until he was five years old and still stammered at times. He was very restless and had an extremely low frustration tolerance. Byron was very hyperactive while taking the Bender Test. He could not sit still for more than 30 seconds and became more and more frustrated because he could not draw the designs the way he knew they should look.

He was able to tell the examiner how the designs were supposed to look, clearly showing that he could perceive them correctly, but could not reproduce them. His was not a problem of coordination since Byron could draw angles correctly on Figures A, 4 and 7. But he was unable to draw the position of the designs or the parts thereof. He rotated Figures A, 3, 4, and 7 even though he could verbalize that they should *not* be rotated. He was also unable to integrate the parts of Figures A, 3, 4, and 7. Byron was still very young. It

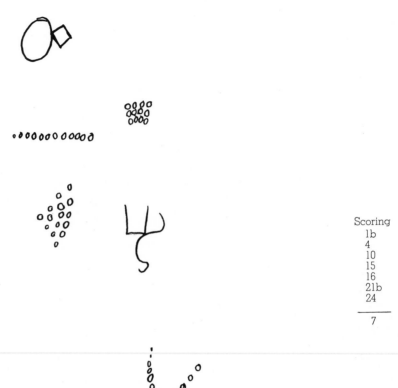

Scoring
1b
4
10
15
16
21b
24
───
7

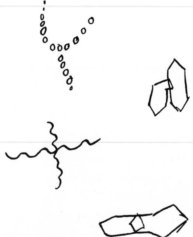

Plate 14. Sally, C. A. 10-4

Scoring
2
3
8
10
11
12a
12b
13
14
17b
18a
20
21a
21b
22
23
24
25

18

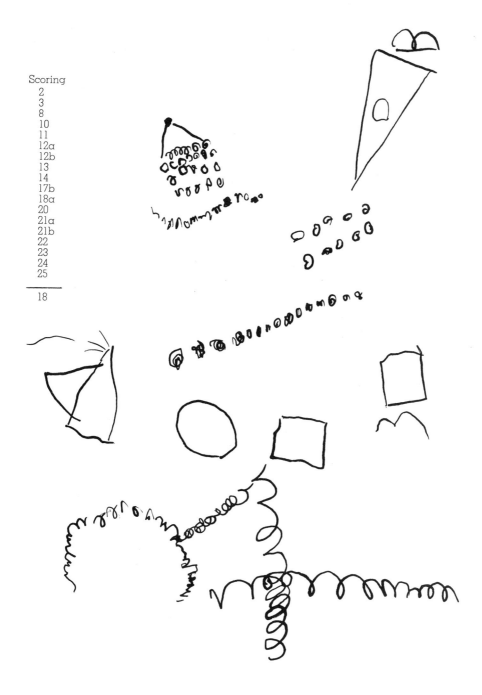

Plate 15. Byron, C. A. 6-10.

was predicted that he would learn in time to compensate for his expressive difficulties because of his good intelligence and keen motivation for learning.

It was mentioned earlier that most young brain injured children show immaturity in all aspects of visual-motor perception. *Plate 16* shows Tommy's Bender. Tommy was a 9 year 8 months old boy of average intelligence with serious receptive *and* expressive disturbances. He was aware of *some* of his mistakes but not of others. He realized that his angles and curves were incorrect on Figures A, 6, 7 and 8, but he was unable to correct them. He was unaware that he perseverated on Figures 1, 2, and 6, and that he distorted Figure 4. Since Tommy's handicap was severe and his endowment not outstanding, he had not been able to compensate for or to adapt to his difficulty in visual-motor perception. His academic progress has been extremely poor and the prognosis for his future achievement is guarded.

TIME AND SPACE USED BY BRAIN INJURED CHILDREN ON THE BENDER TEST

There are two aspects of the Bender Gestalt Test which are not related to visual-motor perception but which are nevertheless valuable aids in the diagnosis of brain injury in young children. These two aspects are: 1) the *time* and 2) the *space*, i.e., the number of pages required by a child to complete the Bender Test. Both these factors are related to the child's temperament, to his inner controls, and to his attitudes. These and other emotional indicators are explored more fully later on (p. 123). At this time the discussion will be limited to their diagnostic implications for neurological impairment.

1) *Time:* The majority of brain injured children use the same amount of time to complete the Bender Test as do most school children. It was pointed out previously (p. 37) that the time factor becomes important only if a child requires an unusually long period or an extremely short period to finish the Bender Test (*Table 7*, p. 36). *Impulsive* children tend to work very hastily and usually do poorly on the Bender Test. Most brain injured children are characterized by impulsiveness, i.e., by hasty actions on the spur of the moment without much forethought or planning. They also tend to have poor inner controls. Even though the majority of neurologically impaired children are impulsive, not all impulsive children are necessarily brain injured. Whenever a child dashes off all nine Bender designs in less than four minutes the possibility of impulsiveness associated with neurological impairment should be considered. The Bender protocol should be scrutinized for other indicators of brain injury.

Compulsiveness is one of the most effective defenses against impulsivity. Compulsiveness is often considered a neurotic disorder, but for brain injured children it is a very realistic and efficient way of controlling their impulsiveness. The compulsive child attempts to regulate his behavior by carefully structuring his actions and by following a rigid routine. This usually requires a great deal of time and deliberate effort. Whenever a child is observed working on the Bender Test extremely slowly and with a great deal of effort, the presence of underlying problems of impulse control associated with brain injury should be explored.

Scoring
1a
1b
6
9
13
14
18a
20
21b
24
___
10

Plate 16. Tommy, C. A. 9-8.

Don, the 10 year old boy whose Bender record is shown on *Plate 6* (p. 67) was a case in point. Don was a highly distractible and restless child who learned to cope with school assignments by carefully structuring them and by working very, very slowly and carefully. On the Bender he numbered all the designs from one to nine and lined them up along the outer edge of the paper. He erased frequently and required twice as much time as most children his age to finish the test. The same was true for Nancy, the 7 year old girl who tried to compensate for her disturbance in motor expression. She needed three times longer than most children to complete the Bender record shown on *Plate 9* (p. 86). Her method of working, clearly showed that her deliberate slowness and perfectionism were a defense against impulsiveness. She first dashed off all designs only to then carefully correct each one of them. Don and Nancy's examples illustrate how the use of time can provide insight both into underlying organic impairment and into the child's method of dealing with the same.

2) *Space:* Expansiveness or the use of two or more sheets of paper for the drawing of all nine Bender designs *(Plate 11,* p. 90-1) is found not infrequently among preschool children and among very impulsive and acting-out school children with poor inner controls. The emotional implications of expansiveness on the Bender will be discussed more fully later on (p. 129). Since impulsiveness and poor inner controls are characteristic of brain injured children, it is not surprising that expansiveness on the Bender Test is also characteristic for this group of youngsters.

The Bender records of the 103 brain injured subjects and the 281 control subjects of the previously cited study (p. 73) were examined for expansiveness. It was found that 17 brain injured children or 16.5 per cent of the organic group used two or more sheets of paper on the Bender Test while only two control subjects or 0.7 per cent of this group did likewise. A chi-square was computed comparing the number of subjects in both groups who used two or more sheets of paper. The result was 26.84 which is significant at the .001 level. The 17 brain injured subjects who used two or more sheets of paper for the Bender Test were distributed throughout the whole age range. That is, one child was 5 years old, two children were 6 years old, five subjects were 7 years old, three were 8 years old, five more were 9 years old, and one was 10 years old. It follows therefore that expansiveness occurs on the Bender records of brain injured children regardless of age. Among non-brain injured children it is limited almost exclusively to preschool children. When a school age child uses two or more sheets of paper to complete the Bender Test the possible presence of brain injury should be carefully investigated.

BEHAVIOR AND ACHIEVEMENT OF BRAIN INJURED CHILDREN

The preceding discussions and studies have dealt with the diagnosis of neurological impairment in young children. That is, an attempt was made to demonstrate how different aspects of the Bender Test can be used to determine whether or not a child is brain injured. Little has been said about the relationship between performance on the Bender Test and the actual functioning of brain injured children. Research findings showed (*Table 17*, p. 75) that Bender scores are closely related to neurological impairment. It was also found that the Bender scores derived from the Developmental Scoring System for Children correlate highly with school achievement (*Table 13*, p. 58), learning problems (*Table 15*, p. 63), and with emotional problems (*Table 24*, p. 125). It therefore follows that brain injured children as a group may be expected to have a high incidence of learning difficulties and emotional problems. This does not mean, however, that each brain injured child who does poorly on the Bender Test will also have learning problems and emotional difficulties. And even when a child has emotional problems the Bender score cannot predict what form and expression these problems will take. There is no one-to-one relationship between the Bender score and a child's behavior or degree of disturbance.

The variance in behavior among brain injured children is even greater than among non-brain injured children. There is no such thing as *the* brain injured child. But the author concurs with Strauss (1947, p. 23) that any damage to the higher centers of the brain will affect the personality-as-a-whole and its organization, in addition to the specific disabilities resulting from the specific locations of the brain lesion.

As a group, children with neurological impairment are more vulnerable than other children. They tend to mature more slowly not only in visual-motor perception but also in their attitudes and behavior. They also cannot adapt as easily to new situations and are usually less able to cope with the stresses and strains of daily life. But the specific reaction of brain injured children to stress will depend on many factors including the location and extent of the brain lesion, the child's mental ability, and above all the interpersonal relationships he has experienced. The Developmental Bender score can give no information about this last factor. However, a child's underlying attitudes are reflected in emotional indicators on the Bender protocol (p. 123). Underlying attitudes may be expressed overtly in many different ways. The author believes that *it is not possible to predict accurately a brain injured child's overt behavior from his performance on the Bender Test.*

This point is illustrated by a brief description of the varied reactions to pressure by some of the brain injured children whose Bender records are reproduced in this volume. All of these children had low frustration tolerance and could not endure much strain. When the demands made on Don (*Plate 6*, p. 67) were too much for him he just withdrew and sat and stared; he reacted with complete passivity and lack of action. The opposite reaction was observed in Byron (*Plate 15*, p. 99). When frustrated, this little boy threw a temper tantrum, hit other children and destroyed his own work as well as the work of others. Jeff (*Plate 7*, p. 68) was an unfortunate youngster who was burdened with multiple handicaps. In addition to brain injury he had limited intelligence and an unfavorable home situation. The pressures on Jeff have been extreme and he reacted to these in the past with at least one schizoid episode with complete withdrawal, bizarre behavior, hallucinations and muttering to himself. More usually he reacted to pressure by pulling out his hair and by withdrawing temporarily from others. Occasionally, when teased he would lose his temper and strike back at other children. Nancy (*Plate 9*, p. 86) on the other hand was her father's favorite and one of four siblings in a close knit family. She showed good emotional and social adjustment. Her only problem was school achievement. When she was unable to complete her work in school she would start to cry and suck her thumb. When helped by her teacher or a classmate she would smile readily and once more be her usual sunny self.

Another friendly, cheerful child was Tommy (*Plate 16*, p. 101) but when frustrated by constant failure in school and by lack of ability to compete with siblings at home he became defiant and stubborn. At times he was also enuretic and encopretic. In addition Tommy had a tendency to develop somatic complaints. Uneven behavior is characteristic of many brain injured children. Sally (*Plate 14*, p. 98) was usually a shy, quiet, cooperative child but she had her off days when even minimal stress upset her very much. At such times Sally withdrew and became negativistic and uncooperative. She also tended to get headaches fairly often.

Then there was Fred, a 10 year 11 months old boy whose Bender record is shown on *Plate 17*. Fred was a good student but he had extremely low frustration tolerance and a hairtrigger temper. Despite superior intelligence, weekly psychotherapy session, medication which he took three times daily, and placement in a residential treatment center, Fred found it extremely difficult to control himself. The least unexpected demand or casual statement made to him could upset him. Everyday living was very stressful for this child. When upset he reacted with somatic complaints, i.e., vomiting, stomach cramps, headaches, or with silliness, overtalkativeness and with overt aggression.

The brain injured children described above vary as much in their school achievement as they do in their behavior. Robbie (*Plate 8*, p. 85) was a good student, so was Fred (*Plate 17*). At the other extreme are Byron (*Plate 15*, p. 99) and Tommy (*Plate 16*, p. 101) whose achievement was negligible. Jeff (*Plate 7*, p. 68) could read but could not add, while Don (*Plate 6*, p. 67) could do arithmetic but could not read.

DIAGNOSING BRAIN INJURY: SUMMARY

In the preceding sections, each aspect of the Bender Gestalt Test was explored separately to determine its usefulness for the diagnosis of brain injury. When the findings of these individual explorations were presented, a note of caution was usually added. It was repeatedly pointed out that brain injury in young children should not and could not be diagnosed on the basis of a *single* test score, a *single* deviation on the Bender Test, or any *one* type of behavior. But if one considers *all* these findings on the Bender in combination, then the validity of this test as a diagnostic instrument is greatly enhanced. It is suggested, therefore, that a complete evaluation of a child's performance on the Bender Test include:

1. *Recording of the time* required by the child to complete the test (p. 100).
2. Careful *observation of the child's behavior* while taking the test (p. 87).

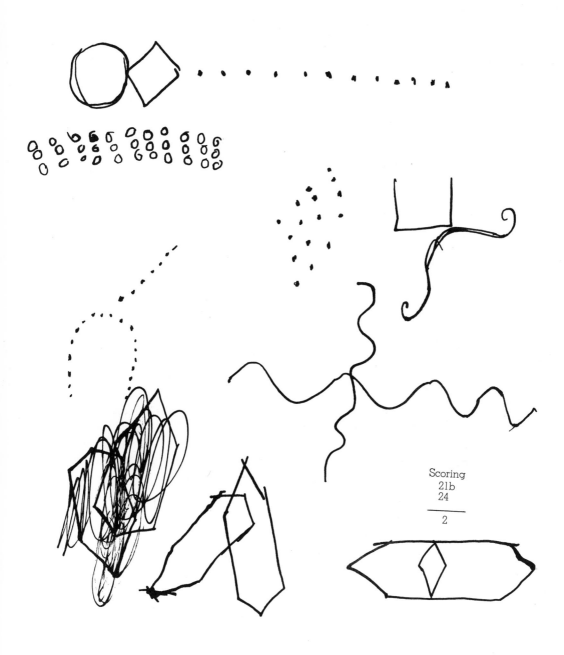

Scoring
21b
24
—
2

Plate 17. Fred, C. A. 10-11.

3. *Inquiry into whether the child is aware of the errors* on his drawings and, if necessary, a *redrawing* of some Bender designs (p. 96).

4. Scoring of Bender protocol with the Developmental Scoring System for Children and *evaluation of total Bender score* (p. 16 and Table 6, p. 188).

5. A *detailed analysis of individual deviations* on the Bender record to determine their diagnostic significance (*Table 19*, p. 189).

6. *Evaluation of the amount of space* required to finish the Bender Test (p. 102).

A tentative diagnosis of brain injury should only be made if *several* of these areas show positive findings. Any one diagnostic sign in isolation should be regarded with great caution. All diagnoses of brain injury made with the Bender Gestalt Test should always be regarded as hypotheses which should then be validated against supporting evidence from developmental, medical, and other psychological data.

In summary it may be stated that the Bender Test has considerable value for diagnosing neurological impairment in children, age five to ten. The diagnosis should always be made on the basis of a complete evaluation of the Bender Test performance including the total test score, individual deviations on the protocol, observation of the child's behavior while taking the test, and the amount of time and space required by the child to complete the same. A diagnosis with the Bender Test should be limited to whether brain injury is present or not. Most youngsters diagnosed as brain injured will also be found to be vulnerable, i.e., they may be expected to show a high incidence of emotional problems and learning difficulties. But not every brain injured child inevitably has problems in one or both of these areas. It is not possible to predict from a Bender record the specific behavior or the level of school achievement a brain injured child will be able to reach in time. Since most brain injured children tend to do poorly on the Bender regardless of IQ score caution should also be used in estimating the intelligence of a neurologically impaired child from his Bender performance.

PART V. The Bender Test and
Mental Retardation in Young Children

A survey of the literature reveals that the Bender Test has been used in four different ways in the study of mental retardation: 1) *As a test of differential diagnosis* between patients suffering from organic and familial retardation. 2) *As a test of emotional adjustment* of retarded patients. 3) *As a test of intelligence* for retarded individuals. 4) And *as a test of school achievement* for retarded pupils. The published research findings in each of these areas will be discussed briefly.

1) *The Bender as a test of differential diagnosis:* Investigators do not fully agree as to the Bender Test's effectiveness in differentiating between groups of retarded patients on the basis of etiology, nor is there a consensus as to the need or desirability to do so. Bender (1938, p. 137) assumes that the Gestalt Test reflects different kinds of disturbances underlying mental retardation, i.e., whether a patient suffers from organic or familial retardation. Baroff (1957), Bensberg (1952) and Feldman (1953) report findings that tend to support Bender's claim. They obtained significant differences between the Bender Test performance of endogenous and exogenous institutionalized patients. Bensberg noted that rotation of design, perseveration, and the substitution of lines for dots occurred more often among the exogenous group. This difference did not become statistically significant until the subjects had reached a mental age of five. Feldman found that perseveration, poor integration of parts, and the omission of parts of a design differentiated his groups of patients. Yet within the two groups he found a comparable range and variability of deviations on the Bender records. Baroff describes similar results. It seems important to note that the subjects in these studies ranged in age from young children to elderly patients; all groups of subjects were mixed with regard to age and sex.

In contrast to these findings other investigators, using retarded school children as subjects, did not discover any statistically significant differences between endogenous and exogenous groups. Beck (1959) did not observe any specific deviation on the Bender which differentiated his groups of subjects, although he did find that organic children tended to have a higher total incidence of deviations. Halpin (1955) reported no statistically significant difference in the number of rotations produced by organic and familial children. Similar results were obtained by Garrison (1958) whose subjects were institutionalized Training School boys. While he found some differences between groups of "familial," "unexplained," and "organic" children, none of these differences were statistically significant, and they did not follow the same pattern as Bensberg, Baroff, and Feldman's results. In Garrison's well designed study, the subjects were tested four times in the course of two years. The test results with the control group of normal children differed markedly from the three retarded groups. The latter remained quite constant and close in their relationship to each other.

These findings seem to suggest that the Bender Test cannot discriminate between exogenous and endogenous retarded school children and can differentiate with uncertainty between groups of institutionalized retarded adult patients. Pascal and Suttell (1951, p. 57) found it not possible to distinguish the Bender records of adult retarded patients from those of individuals suffering from organic brain disease or injury. Thus there appears to be a lack of agreement as to the Bender Test's effectiveness in the differential diagnosis of retarded subjects.

The author has always had some difficulty in accepting the classifications of "endogenous" or "familial" retardation. The diagnosis of "exogenous" or "organic" retardation is usually based on clear cut medical or developmental evidence. The "familial" diagnosis often appears to be based on a lack of information. This skepticism was enhanced when the author conducted two weekly group therapy sessions over a period of one year with twelve institutionalized teenagers, six boys and six girls, who had serious emotional problems. All children had been previously diagnosed as suffering from "familial" retardation. Most of them came from very deprived, unstable home backgrounds. Only a very limited amount of information was available concerning the early development and medical history of these youngsters. By the end of the year it was discovered that three of the girls no longer tested in the defective range of intelligence. They could not be considered as being truly retarded. All three had suffered severe early neglect and deprivation which made them appear retarded. Another child was found to be autistic and suffered from childhood schizophrenia rather than from retardation. And at least three of the boys showed strong evidence of brain injury in both their behavior and on psychological tests. Additional information gathered during the year confirmed these impressions. The remaining five youngsters revealed behavior and test results that made it impossible to rule out with certainty, minimal organic involvement. Lack of information, on the other hand, prevented a confirmation of such a diagnosis.

The writer believes that poor endowment alone is not sufficient to bring about serious mental retardation in a child if he has a well functioning central nervous system, warm, supporting parents, and good physical care. In most so-called familial children we find not only poor endowment but also poor physical care and inadequate nutrition during the prenatal period and during infancy, frequent illnesses, accidents, and often, emotional deprivation and neglect—all of which contribute to the child's level of functioning. These children are also more likely to have suffered minimal brain injury in early life than more privileged children (Pasamanik, 1954). It is hypothesized that most "familial" children suffer from multiple handicaps including poor endowment, social and emotional deprivation, and minimal neurologic impairment.

The author is inclined to agree with Gallagher (1957) that little is accomplished by trying to differentiate between "vague and oversimplified neurological classifications." The writer does not believe that the Bender Test can achieve its greatest usefulness in the study of mental retardation as a test for differential diagnosis between "familial" and "organic" retardation.

2) The Bender as a test of emotional adjustment: Some investigators have used the Bender as a test for assessing the emotional and social adjustment of retarded children. Eber (1958) found the Bender Test useful in differentiating pupils who were considered well adjusted from those who were considered poorly adjusted in school. His subjects were "non-brain damaged" educable retarded public school children.

F. Goldberg (1957) on the other hand was unable to find any significant differences on the Bender performance of his subjects. He used two groups of subjects, age 11 to 16 years, who were matched for IQ. One group consisted of schizophrenic patients, while the other was made up of children with "familial" retardation who had serious emotional problems. Both groups differed significantly from a normal control group. Goldberg believes that the performance on the Bender Test is mainly a function of the IQ. Both Eber and Goldberg used Pascal and Suttell's scoring system in their studies.

Problems of emotional and social adjustment are not peculiar to retarded children but may occur among all youngsters regardless of age and intelligence. Manifestations of emotional disturbances are common to all children with problems. It may be expected therefore that the same emotional indicators would be found on the Bender records of retarded children with emotional problems and on the Bender records of youngsters with emotional difficulties who are not classified as retarded. It appears therefore unnecessary to make a special study of the Bender Test as a measure of emotional adjustment of retarded children. Emotional indicators on the Bender Test are discussed in detail later on (p. 123). The findings presented there are believed to apply also to retarded children.

3) The Bender as a test of intelligence: There appears to be agreement among investigators that the Bender performance of retarded children is primarily related to their mental age. Bensberg (1952) and Baroff (1957) reported significant correlations between Bender scores and the mental age of their subjects. Feldman's (1953) results are similar, but he found a higher correlation for his endogenous group than for his exogenous group. Baroff suggests the need for Bender Test norms based on mental age for use with retarded children. He offers a tentative outline for such norms. It would appear that the Bender Test holds considerable promise as a screening device to assess the mental ability of retarded children.

4) The Bender as a test of school achievement: One of the most interesting studies of the Bender Test with retarded children was carried out by Keller (1955). He developed a unique Bender scoring system for retarded school children. While most Bender scoring systems score for errors, thereby obtaining negative scores, Keller scores for accomplishments and achievement on the Bender. Thus he obtains positive scores. He uses a 114 item scoring system based on maturational levels. This scoring system was found to be related to the school achievement of retarded subjects. Neither Bensberg nor Garrison found any significant differences in the scholastic achievement of their endogenous and exogenous groups. It appears therefore that the Bender Test could be used effectively to assess a retarded child's level of academic achievement and that the test could serve as a predictor of future achievement.

RESEARCH STUDIES

An evaluation of the research literature led to the conclusion that the Bender Test could be of greatest value in the study of retarded children if used as a screening test for mental ability and as a test of a child's achievement level. In this capacity it could be readministered to retarded children from time to time to measure the rate of their mental growth and to predict their readiness for academic training as well as their achievement potential. A study was conducted by the author to determine the relationship between Bender scores derived from the Developmental Bender Scoring System for Children and the mental age of retarded pupils.

Mental Age and Bender Scores

The findings in a study by the author mentioned earlier (p. 46) had been in agreement with those of Baroff, Bensberg and Feldman. The correlation between the Bender performance of retarded subjects and their mental age was found to be considerably higher than between their Bender and IQ scores. For 63 retarded school children the correlation between IQ and Bender scores was −.44, while the correlation between mental age and Bender scores for the same group of subjects was −.85. Both correlations are statistically significant at the .001 level.

The subjects for the following study were 91 retarded public school children who were attending either special classes for slow learners or who were under consideration for placement into such classes. The age of the subjects ranged from 5 years to 16 years. Their IQ score range was from 40 to 74, with an IQ mean score of 63. The IQ scores were derived from the WISC or the Stanford-Binet Intelligence Scale depending on the age and mental ability of the children. The author administered the Bender Test to all subjects in school. The Bender records were scored according to the Developmental Bender Scoring System for Children.

The 91 subjects were divided into two groups. *Group I* included 54 children, age 5 years 6 months to 10 years 10 months, with a mental age range of 3 years 7 months to 7 years 5 months. The children in Group I conformed in chronological age to the age generally under discussion in this volume. But the mental age of these children was below that of the normative population. *Group II* included 37 youngsters whose chronological age extended from 11 years 1 month to 16 years 2 months. That is, Group II was considerably above the age level of the normative population (*Table 4*, p. 33) but their mental age was approximately within the designated age limit. Group II had a mental age range from 4 years 0 months to 10 years 10 months. Pearson product moment correlations were computed between the Bender scores and the mental ages for each of the two groups separately and for both groups together. The results are shown in *Table 21*.

The three correlations obtained were −.84, −.50, and −.70 respectively. A t test (Croxton, 1959, p. 312) showed that all three are statistically significant at the .001 level and support the findings of Baroff, Bensberg and Feldman.

Table 21.   Relationship Between Bender Scores and M.A. of Retarded Children

Group	N	Mean C.A.	Mean M.A.	Mean Bender Score	Range of Bender Scores	Correlation[1]
I	54	8–5	5–4	13.3	25 to 4	−.84*
II	37	13–5	7–9	6.9	21 to 0	−.50*
Total	91	10–7	6–2	10.7	25 to 0	−.70*

[1] Correlations are negative since Bender is scored for errors.
* Significant at the .001 level.

Since the Bender Test scores of retarded public school children are so closely related to their mental ages it appears that the Bender Test can be used with some confidence as a screening test of mental maturity for retarded youngsters. The findings further show that the subjects in Group I had a mental age mean of 5 years 4 months and a Bender mean score of 13.6 which corresponds to the Bender normative score for five year old children *(Table 6,* p. 188). In Group II the mental age mean was 7 years 9 months and the Bender mean score was 6.9 which is not unlike that of a somewhat below average 7 year 9 months old child. It appears that the Bender Test scores of retarded children tend to be located in the lower half of the normative distribution of Bender scores for nonretarded school children of the equivalent mental age. That is, a retarded child of nine with a mental age of 5 years 11 months will tend to produce a Bender protocol not unlike that of a somewhat immature five and a half year old child. In children of normal intelligence, the mental age and the chronological age are, of course, the same or at least very close.

The Bender records of Mary and Alice *(Plate 18* and *Plate 19)* illustrate this point. Mary, age 8 years 2 months, was a retarded child with a mental age of 4 years 5 months. She was attending a special class for slow learners and was functioning on the nursery school level. Mary's Bender is shown on *Plate 18.* Her Bender Test score is 19 which is approximately what one would expect from a four year old child. *Plate 19* shows Alice's Bender. Alice also has a Bender score of 19. This little girl was attending nursery school; she had just celebrated her fourth birthday a few days earlier.

The Bender records of Mary and Alice reveal very similar indicators of immaturity in visual-motor perception. Both children are unable to draw angles and curves correctly. They show a disproportion of size in the parts of Figure A and 7 and they cannot integrate the parts into wholes successfully. Figure 3 is as yet nothing but a single vertical scribble or line of dots. Figure 2 consists of a curved row of crude loops bearing no resemblance to the configuration of this design. Figure 4 is rotated and the open box becomes a closed, poorly drawn square. The drawing of Figure 8 is the most nearly accurate on both Bender records. The chief difference between the two Bender protocols is the age of the children who drew them. In Alice's case *(Plate 19)* the poor performance on the Bender is a function of age and perceptual immaturity, in Mary's case *(Plate 18)* the Bender record reflects serious mental retardation.

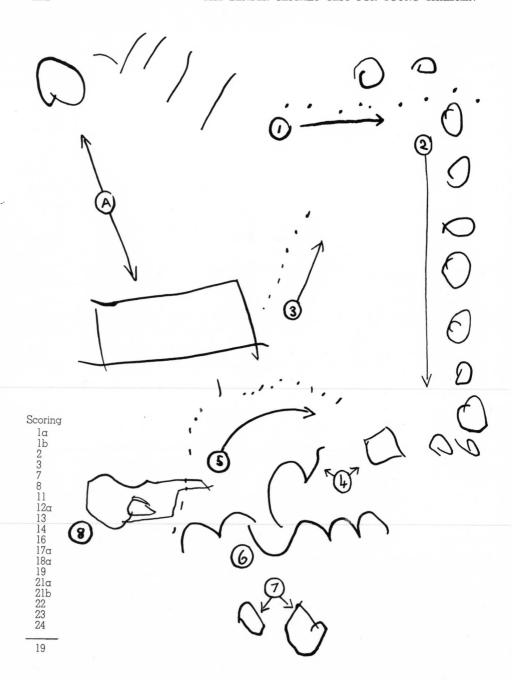

Scoring
1a
1b
2
3
7
8
11
12a
13
14
16
17a
18a
19
21a
21b
22
23
24
___
19

Plate 18. Mary, C. A. 8-2, M. A. 4-5.

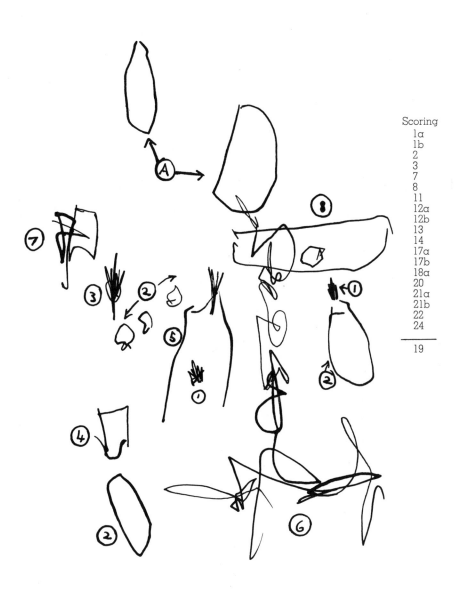

Scoring
1a
1b
2
3
7
8
11
12a
12b
13
14
17a
17b
18a
20
21a
21b
22
24
___
19

Plate 19. Alice, C. A. 4-0.

Test-retest on the Bender for retarded children

The author administered the Bender Test twice to 15 of the retarded subjects. The time interval between the first and the second test administration was from 4 to 14 months. The first set of Bender Test scores was extremely poor. The Bender scores for all 15 subjects fell outside the normal range of Bender scores for their respective age levels. That is, they were all more than one standard deviation from the normative scores. The second set of Bender scores was also very poor for all 15 retarded children. No consistent pattern was revealed by the test-retest scores of the retarded children.

Eight of the subjects showed some improvement on their second Bender record though their Bender scores remained quite poor for their age level. One youngster produced two almost identical Bender protocols despite a time interval of ten months between his first and second test. The remaining six youngsters did worse on the second Bender Test than on the first one. The degree of improvement or worsening on the Bender scores differed greatly from one child to the next and bore no relationship to the time elapsed between the first and the second administration of the Bender Test. The factors affecting a retarded child's Bender performance were the same as those affecting a normal child's Bender Test score, i.e., age, maturity or functioning in visual-motor perception, intellectual endowment, emotional adjustment, motivation, and ability to concentrate on the task.

It was found that a lack of improvement on the Bender Test between the first and second administration was associated with a lack of progress in school achievement. Similar results had been found earlier in the study of school children who were not mentally retarded (p. 44).

School Achievement Level and Bender Scores for Retarded Children

Mentally retarded children are usually placed in special classes on the basis of age and IQ scores. It is almost unavoidable that this results in a wide range of mental ages in a given classroom of slow learners. Yet for retarded children academic achievement is more a function of their mental age than of their chronological age or their IQ scores. The mental age determines a child's readiness to profit from formal instructions in academic subjects. The mental age of a child is among other things, a reflection of his maturation in visual-motor perception. It was shown above that the Bender Test, which measures maturation of visual-motor perception in young children, is closely related to the mental age of retarded children. It may be expected therefore that the Bender Test is also related to the achievement level of retarded children. There is no reason why the findings from earlier studies regarding the Bender Test and school readiness and achievement of normal school beginners (p. 52) cannot also be extended on a modified level, to retarded children. If this is the case then the Bender Test would be of great value in determining the time for, and level of a training program best suited for a retarded child.

To test this hypothesis, the achievement level and the Bender scores of the retarded subjects were compared. For ten of the subjects no information was available concerning their functioning in school. Thus the number of subjects for the following investigation was reduced to 81. The 81 subjects were divided into four groups according to their achievement level. The grouping was based on actual school work and on teachers' ratings. *Group I* consisted of 20 children who were functioning on the nursery school level. *Group II* contained 19 subjects who were on the kindergarten level. *Group III* included 19 youngsters who were able to do first or second grade work. And finally *Group IV* was made up of 23 pupils who were engaged in third grade work or in beginning fourth grade studies. For each of these groups the Bender mean scores and the standard deviations were computed. *Table 22* shows the results. The number of subjects in the four groups is small yet the findings are most interesting and highly suggestive. It can be seen that the retarded children who function on the nursery school level have a Bender mean score of 18.4 which is

Table 22. Bender Scores and Achievement Level of Retarded Children

Group	Achievement Level	N	Bender Mean Score	Bender S.D.	Plus–Minus one S.D.
I	Nursery School	20	18.4	2.5	20.9 to 15.9
II	Kindergarten	19	12.4	2.8	15.2 to 9.6
III	1st & 2nd Grades	19	9.3	3.1	12.4 to 6.2
IV	3rd Grade and higher	23	4.3	2.5	6.8 to 1.8

not unlike that of four year old children. Those functioning on the kindergarten level have a Bender mean score of 12.4 which is comparable to normal five year old children (*Table 6*, p. 188). Those retarded subjects who are functioning on the level of first and second graders have a Bender mean score of 9.3 which is similar to immature six year old school children. And finally, retarded children with an achievement level of third grade or better have a Bender mean score of 4.3 which is approximately what one would find in normal seven and eight year old children.

These results indicate clearly that the Bender scores of retarded children are closely related to both their mental age and their level of functioning in school. Thus the findings offer support for the hypothesis that the Bender Test can help to determine the level of training best suited for a retarded child. A few cases may help to illustrate the practical application of these findings. A teacher of 12 educable retarded children (IQ 50 to 75) asked the author to observe her children and to give her suggestions on the planning of suitable programs for each child. The author not only observed the children but also administered the Bender Test to them. It so happened that the class included four eight year old children: Joey, Mary, Albert and Ronnie. These four children differed greatly in their behavior and ability.

Joey was a tall, quiet boy who was eager to learn. He presented no behavior problems. The teacher had placed Joey with a small group of youngsters who were doing readiness work. Joey seemed to enjoy this work a great deal. He worked diligently on the Bender and obtained a test score of 13. His Bender record is shown on *Plate 20*. Joey's Bender performance is similar to that of a normal five year old child or that of a somewhat immature six year old (*Table 6*, p. 188). His level of maturity in visual-motor perception resembles that of

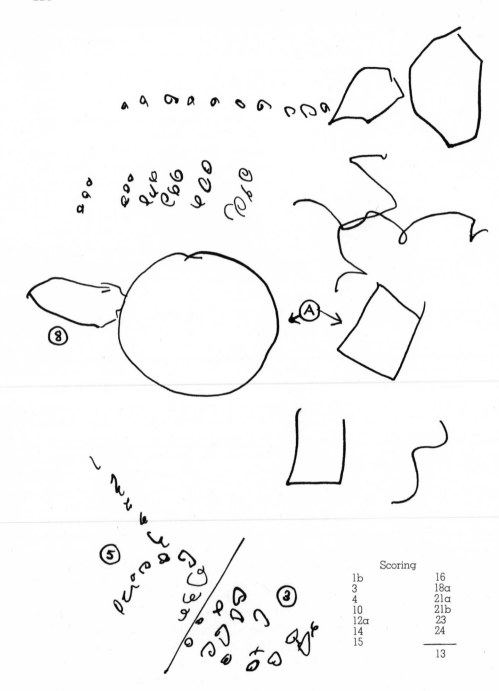

	Scoring	
1b		16
3		18a
4		21a
10		21b
12a		23
14		24
15		
		13

Plate 20. Joe, C. A. 8-11; M. A. 6-0.

normal kindergarten children or of retarded children who function on the kindergarten level. Since readiness work is usually begun in kindergarten it appears that Joey was well placed in his present school program. The teacher was encouraged to continue with her planning for him. Joey obtained a mental age of 6-0 on the Stanford-Binet Intelligence Scale.

Then there was Mary whose Bender record was shown on *Plate 18*. Mary was a cheerful little girl with excellent manners and good training from home. She was a happy and outgoing child who appeared to be alert. She was eager to learn in school and wanted to please her teacher and parents. The teacher was planning to put Mary in the advanced group of pupils with Joey. Yet despite all her efforts Mary seemed to be unable to understand and to remember even simple tasks. The teacher was puzzled. Mary enjoyed taking the Bender Test; she smiled as she worked and seemed pleased with her accomplishment. Her Bender score is 19 which is similar to that of normal four year old nursery school children or the Bender mean score of retarded children functioning at the nursery school level. It is therefore clear that Mary was as yet too immature to be able to profit from formal instructions in academic subjects. Her well poised and appealing behavior was misleading and made her appear more capable than she really was. The teacher was urged not to attempt any readiness work with this little girl until she gained more maturity in visual-motor perception. This was further supported by Mary's performance on the Stanford-Binet Intelligence Scale. She obtained on this test a mental age of 4 years 5 months.

In the case of Albert the reverse situation was found. Albert was an aphasic youngster who had just begun to talk and had much difficulty communicating with others. His behavior was very immature, he was restless and excitable. He was placed with the less advanced children in his class where his hyperactivity proved disturbing much of the time. Albert showed much interest in the Bender Test. His ability to concentrate and to complete the test was much better than had been anticipated. His Bender record is shown on *Plate 21*. Albert obtained a Bender score of 10 which is similar to that of a normal five and a half year old child or a somewhat immature six year old. The score also resembles that of beginning first graders and of retarded children functioning on the first grade level. The Bender Test gave every indication that Albert had more potential mental ability than had been realized due to his serious speech impairment. It was recommended that Albert be placed with the more advanced group of pupils in his class. Albert was delighted with the challenge of readiness work and studied very hard. For the first time he settled down in school and concentrated for longer periods of time. He became less restless and his behavior improved, even his efforts at verbal communication increased markedly. Albert was tested with the WISC Performance Scale and obtained on this test a mental age of 5 years 10 months. Thus the WISC and the Bender Test showed identical results.

The fourth child in this group was Ronnie, a friendly, rather vague youngster with very limited mental capacity. Ronnie had spent two years in a special class for retarded children where he had made no academic progress to speak of. He was happy playing with toys but had trouble following even the

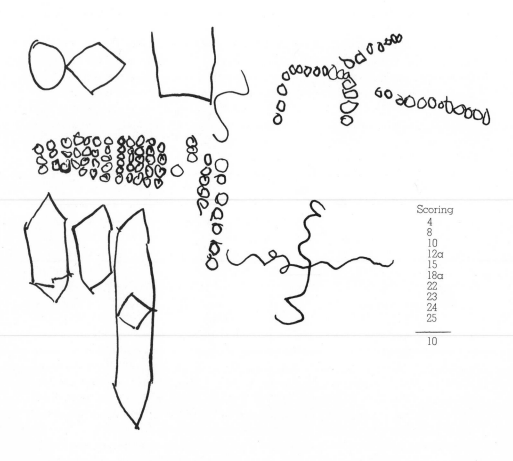

Scoring
4
8
10
12a
15
18a
22
23
24
25
___
10

Plate 21. Albert, C. A. 8-2, M. A. 5-10.

simplest directions. His extreme immaturity was reflected in his poor Bender performance. His Bender record is shown on *Plate 22*. Ronnie's Bender score was 22 which is about what would be expected of an immature four year old child and of retarded children who function on the level of immature nursery school children. Ronnie's teacher had wisely refrained from any attempt at formal work for this youngster. Even though the Bender Test offered no new insights, the teacher was pleased to have her judgment confirmed by means of an objective test. Too often teachers feel personally responsible if a child fails to show appreciable progress in school. In this case it was felt that Ronnie would become in time, a candidate for the trainable classes, particularly since he showed no improvement on the Bender Test when he was retested six months later. On the Stanford-Binet Scale Ronnie obtained a mental age of 4 years 8 months.

Every now and then a teacher of retarded children realizes that a pupil has been misplaced in her class. Usually an immediate testing or retesting of the child is not feasible due to other commitments on the part of the psychologist. However, a quick administration of the Bender Test is a matter of minutes and can serve to clarify the teacher's impression. In the case of Timmy, for instance, the teacher felt that he fell below the standards expected of trainable children. She was unable to accomplish anything with this child and felt that he demanded too much of her time. She was unable to meet his needs and to do justice to her other pupils. The teacher questioned seriously whether Timmy belonged in a class for trainable children. The author saw Timmy briefly and attempted to administer the Bender Test. He was cooperative and pleasant but was unable to draw even round loops; he merely scribbled like a two year old. Timmy's Bender record is shown on *Plate 23*. This Bender protocol is so immature that it cannot be scored. In fact there is no recognizable resemblance between Timmy's pencil marks and the Bender designs. This type of performance is usually found among normal two year old children. On the Stanford-Binet Scale, Tim obtained a mental age of 2 years 3 months which concurs with the Bender findings. The teacher's impression appeared valid.

Another example was Lois, a thirteen year old girl attending a class for educable retarded children. In regular class Lois had failed repeatedly all academic subjects and had been very defiant and aggressive. Several teachers had refused to have Lois in their class. When tested with the Stanford-Binet Scale Lois had been none too cooperative but the examining psychologist had felt confident that her IQ score was valid and that Lois was a retarded child. So Lois had been placed in a class for slow learners. In the therapeutic atmosphere of the small special class and with the help of an understanding teacher Lois showed considerable improvement in her attitude and her achievement. In fact her progress was so outstanding that her teacher questioned whether Lois was truly a retarded child. A quick check with the Bender Test revealed that Lois was functioning on this test well within the normal range for a child her age. When tested later on with the WISC these impressions were confirmed. Lois obtained a WISC Full Scale IQ of 90. Lois was transferred to a regular class in a different school where she was able to hold her own for the remainder of the school year.

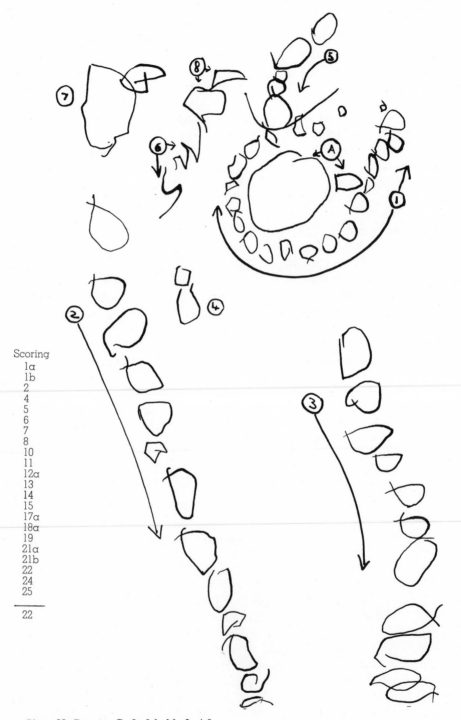

Scoring
1a
1b
2
4
5
6
7
8
10
11
12a
13
14
15
17a
18a
19
21a
21b
22
24
25

22

Plate 22. Ronnie, C. A. 8-1, M. A. 4-8.

Plate 23. Timmy, C. A. 10-9, M. A. 2-3.

In some cases, teachers of regular classes suspect a child of being retarded when this is not the case. Charles, a seven year old boy was repeating the first grade. He was referred to the school psychologist because of lack of academic progress in two years of school attendance. One of his brothers was in a class for slow learners and the teacher believed that Charles also belonged in such a class. It was noted that he seemed to day-dream a great deal and frequently fell asleep in class. When the author first met Charles she found a scared, neglected little boy with sullen expression. He was noncommunicative and cooperated only reluctantly. Yet his Bender performance was average for his age level and showed no indication of mental retardation. His IQ score on the WISC was 96 thus concurring with the Bender results. It became evident that Charles was a severely deprived youngster with serious emotional problems. He was one of eleven siblings and lived in a crowded home where he received neither enough sleep nor food. He was therefore constantly tired and hungry. He lacked self-confidence and had little motivation for learning despite average mental ability. Charles was not a candidate for a class for slow learners but needed more love and encouragement, more rest at night and an adequate diet, and he was in need of psychotherapy. Charles was referred to the welfare department for case work services. His problems were interpreted to his teacher and every effort was made to help this youngster develop his adequate intellectual potential which had been reflected on the Bender Test.

THE BENDER TEST AND RETARDED CHILDREN: SUMMARY

In summary it can be stated that the Bender Test is an important aid in the study of mental retardation in young children. *Its greatest value is seen in its use as a test of mental maturity and as an indicator of the academic achievement level of retarded children.* The Bender Test scores are closely related to both the mental age and the scholastic achievement of retarded children, just as the Bender scores were found to be related to the mental ability and the achievement of normal school children. Thus no special scoring system or method of test analysis is required for use of the Bender Test with slow learners. The Developmental Bender Scoring System for Children (p. 15) can be used for children age five through ten years regardless of IQ and for retarded children with a mental age of five through ten years regardless of their chronological age.

There is some doubt as to whether the Bender Test can and should be used as a test of differential diagnosis between familial and organic retardation in young children. But the indicators of neurological impairment on the Bender records of normal children can also be applied to the records of retarded children if so desired (p. 71).

The same applies to the evaluation of the emotional adjustment of retarded children with the Bender Test. The emotional indicators on the Bender (p. 123) are applicable to all children age five to ten years regardless of their intelligence. There are no special "signs" or deviations on the Bender Test which differentiate retarded children with emotional problems from normal children with emotional problems.

PART VI. The Bender Test and
Emotional Disturbances in Young Children

Survey of the Literature

Research data indicate that the Bender Test is useful in the identification and evaluation of children with emotional problems. In a well designed study Byrd (1956) examined the Bender Test records of 200 maladjusted and 200 well adjusted children. His subjects were divided into four different age levels ranging from 8 to 16 years. Byrd compared the Bender protocols on 15 test factors. Six of these were found to differentiate significantly between the maladjusted children and the controls. The six deviations include: orderly sequence of designs, change in curvature and in the angulation of figures, difficulty in closure, rotation of designs and change in the size of the designs. Byrd found no significant differences between maladjusted and well adjusted subjects in the following Bender deviations: use of margins, compression of all Bender designs into a small space, fragmentation of designs, perseveration on figures, collision of designs, retrogression in quality of drawings, and placement of figure in the extreme upper corner of the paper.

Eber (1958), using Pascal and Suttell's (1951) scoring system in his study, found significant differences in the total Bender scores of well adjusted and maladjusted retarded school children who were not brain injured.

A somewhat different approach was employed by Simpson (1958). He compared the Bender performance of 50 boys attending first grade. Twenty-five were emotionally disturbed while the other 25 were well adjusted. The two groups did not differ in the ability to copy simple squares and circles, nor in the perception of visual likenesses and differences. But they showed significant differences on their Bender records. Simpson hypothesizes that children with emotional problems do not differ from well adjusted children in coordination and perception, but they reveal disturbances in the integration of the two, i.e., they show malfunctioning in visual-motor perception as a result of their emotional disturbance.

A comprehensive and interesting study with the Bender Test and young emotionally disturbed children was carried out by Clawson (1959). Clawson used 80 young patients from the Wicheta Guidance Clinic as subjects and 80 school children as controls. Her subjects ranged in age from 7 to 12 years. The Bender records of the two groups were compared for quantitative differences in arrangement of the Bender designs on paper, modification in the size of the figures, use of space, modification of the Gestalt of the designs, and work method. Following Hutt's suggestions (1950) Clawson also attempted to relate Bender deviations to behavior symptoms. And finally she related the Bender performance of her subjects to Rorschach determinants. Clawson's findings are very similar to those of Byrd.

All four studies mentioned above give strong evidence that the Bender Test can differentiate between children who are well adjusted and those who are maladjusted. The four studies have one thing in common, they compare two groups of subjects on a variety of Bender deviations some of which are related to age and to maturity in visual-motor perception while others reflect attitudes and personality characteristics. Byrd recognizes the effect of maturation on the Bender Test but no attempt is made by him to differentiate between the meanings of the various Bender deviations found on the records of emotionally disturbed children. It does not necessarily follow that all Bender distortions on the protocols of youngsters with emotional problems reflect these problems nor that the same causal relationship exists between all Bender distortions and emotional disturbances.

The author is inclined to concur with Bender (1938, p. 157) who claims that neurotic disturbances do not result in disturbances in perception or in visual-motor function. On the contrary, it is this writer's observation that emotional problems develop secondary to perceptual problems. Children with problems in visual-motor perception experience much frustration and frequent failure in school and at home. As a result many of these children develop negative attitudes and emotional maladjustment. *It is hypothesized that children with immature or malfunctioning visual-motor perception not only tend to reveal learning problems* (see p. 61) *but also have a much higher incidence of emotional problems than do children with well functioning visual-motor perception.* But not every child with poor visual-motor perception necessarily develops learning difficulties and not every child with perceptual problems inevitably develops emotional problems. A child's emotional adjustment depends partly on his integrative capacity but even more on his social and emotional experiences with the significant people in his life. An emotionally secure child can learn to tolerate the frustrations arising from impaired visual-motor perception.

Deviations and distortions of the Gestalt of the Bender designs are associated primarily with immaturity *in visual-motor perception.* A child's method of working on the test, e.g., the size of the drawings, the organization of the figures, their placement on the paper, and the quality of the pencil line, are all emotional indicators which are primarily related to personality factors and attitudes. *It is hypothesized that children with problems of adjustment will show a much higher incidence of emotional indicators on the Bender Test than children who are well adjusted.*

The testing of these two hypotheses requires different methods of analyzing Bender records. When testing for problems in visual-motor perception the Bender is evaluated as a perceptual test and the records are scored according to the Development Bender Scoring System for Children (see p. 15). When testing for emotional factors the Bender is interpreted as a projective test. An investigation was conducted by the author analyzing the Bender records of the subjects both ways: 1) for maturation in visual-motor perception, and 2) for emotional indicators.

RESEARCH STUDIES

The subjects for the following study were 272 children, age five to ten years. The subjects consisted of two groups: 136 were children who had been referred to a child guidance clinic or to the school psychologist because of emotional problems, while the other 136 subjects were school children who had no known history of emotional maladjustment. The two groups were matched for age and sex. *Table 23* shows the distribution of all subjects. No retarded children were included in this study. All the subjects with emotional problems

Table 23.   Distribution of Subjects by Age and Sex

Age	Subjects with Emotional Problems			Control Group		
	Boys	Girls	Total	Boys	Girls	Total
5	8	8	16	8	8	16
6	12	3	15	12	3	15
7	19	5	24	19	5	24
8	19	9	28	19	9	28
9	26	8	34	26	8	34
10	13	6	19	13	6	19
	97	39	136	97	39	136

took the Bender Test as part of a comprehensive test battery at the time of their psychological examination. The children in the control group were tested individually in school by the author.

1) The Bender as a Developmental Test for Children with Emotional Problems

All Bender records were scored according to the Developmental Scoring System. Chi-squares were computed for the younger and older subjects comparing the number of children with and without emotional problems whose Bender score was above or below the normative score for their respective age level *(Table 6,* p. 188). The results are shown on *Table 24.* The chi-squares

Table 24.   Bender Test Performance and Emotional Problems in Children

Subjects	Good Bender	Poor Bender	Chi-square	P
Age 5 to 7				
Emotional Problems	17	38	10.54	<.001
Controls	35	20		
Age 8 to 10				
Emotional Problems	26	55	26.99	<.001
Controls	60	21		

for both the younger and the older group of subjects were significant at the .001 level. Thus it is shown that children with emotional problems also tend to have significantly more often immature visual-motor perception, i.e., poor Developmental Bender scores. It was found that about two-thirds of all the children with poor visual-motor perception had emotional problems. It is again emphasized that immature visual-motor perception is considered to be the primary symptom in these children, while the emotional problems are thought of as secondary symptoms which developed as a consequence of the first. It is therefore suggested that the Bender scores obtained with the Developmental Scoring System should *not* be used for the identification of emotional disturbance in children but rather in the investigation of underlying factors contributing to the child's emotional maladjustment.

2) *The Bender as a Projective Test for Children with Emotional Problems*

The Bender records of all subjects were next evaluated on the basis of eleven emotional indicators which were believed to reflect emotional attitudes and personality structure. These eleven scoring categories were derived from the author's clinical experience and from the findings of other investigators (Byrd, 1956; Clawson, 1959; Hutt and Briskin, 1960; Kitay, 1950; Murray and Roberts, 1956; Pascal and Suttell, 1951; Tucker and Spielberg, 1958). The emotional indicators are not considered to be a function of visual-motor perception. A child may be free from problems in visual-motor perception and yet may show a high incidence of emotional indicators on his Bender record, while another child with marked difficulties in visual-motor perception may be free from emotional indicators on his Bender Test protocol.

The eleven emotional indicators on the Bender Test are listed below. (Detailed definitions and scoring examples of the emotional indicators are shown in the scoring manual on p. 132).

    I.   *Confused Order*
   II.   *Wavy Line* (Figures 1 and 2)
  III.   *Dashes for Circles* (Figure 2)
   IV.   *Progressive Increase in Size* (Figures 1, 2, and 3)
    V.   *Large Size of Drawings*
   VI.   *Small Size of Drawings*
  VII.   *Fine Line*
 VIII.   *Overwork, reinforced lines*
   IX.   *Second Attempt*
    X.   *Expansion*
   XI.   *Constriction*

Chi-squares were computed comparing the number of subjects with and without emotional problems who showed a given emotional indicator as being "present" or "absent" on their Bender record. The results for the younger and the older subjects are shown on *Tables 25* and *26*. It was found that six of the eleven emotional indicators showed statistically significant differences between the subjects who were emotionally disturbed and the control group. Four additional indicators showed differences between the two groups but these were not statistically significant. The emotional indicators appear to be not entirely independent of the age factor in young children. Some indicators were found to be related to emotional problems in five to seven year olds only, while others were significant only for eight to ten year olds. Only "Expansion" was diagnostically significant for all age levels tested. One indicator, "Constriction," showed a difference between the groups of subjects which was in the wrong direction but this difference was not statistically significant. The following is a brief discussion of the findings on each of the eleven emotional indicators on the Bender Test:

Table 25. Relationship Between Individual Emotional Indicators on the Bender Test and Emotional Problems in Children Age Five to Seven

	Subjects with Emotional Problems		Control Group			
Emotional Indicators	Present	Absent	Present	Absent	Chi-square	P
I. Confused Order	46	9	40	15	not significant	
II. Wavy Line	27	28	13	42	6.64	<.01
III. Dash for Circle	6	49	2	53	not significant	
IV. Increasing Size	9	46	8	47	not significant	
V. Large Size	12	43	7	48	not significant	
VI. Small Size	6	49	7	48	not significant	
VII. Fine Line	7	48	2	53	not significant	
VIII. Overwork	23	32	9	46	7.44	<.01
IX. Second Attempt	7	48	5	50	not significant	
X. Expansion	17	38	1	54	14.94	<.001
XI. Constriction	3	52	8	47	not significant	

Table 26. Relationship Between Individual Emotional Indicators on the Bender Test and Emotional Problems in Children Age Eight to Ten

	Subjects with Emotional Problems		Control Group			
Emotional Indicator	Present	Absent	Present	Absent	Chi-square	P
I. Confused Order	46	35	16	65	21.97	<.001
II. Wavy Line	10	71	10	71	not significant	
III. Dash for Circle	4	77	4	77	not significant	
IV. Increasing Size	4	77	1	80	not significant	
V. Large Size	6	75	3	78	not significant	
VI. Small Size	20	61	8	73	5.23	<.02
VII. Fine Line	2	79	3	78	not significant	
VIII. Overwork	34	47	28	53	not significant	
IX. Second Attempt	19	62	6	75	6.81	<.01
X. Expansion	10	71	0	81	8.63	<.01
XI. Constriction	20	61	19	62	not significant	

I. *Confused Order:* This indicator appears to be related to a lack of planning ability, to an inability to organize material and to mental confusion. Planning ability develops gradually in young children. Confused Order of Bender designs is common among all five to seven year old children. Not until age eight does this indicator on the Bender Test take on diagnostic importance. Only one in five children in the control group showed Confused Order on his Bender record while more than half of the older children with emotional problems scattered the Bender figures in arbitrary fashion over the sheet of paper (see *Plate 36*, p. 182).

II. *Wavy Line* (Figures 1 and 2): This indicator seems to be associated with lack of stability. It was found significantly more often on the records of five to seven year old children with problems, than on the Bender records of the control group. This indicator appears to be related also to age, since it did not differentiate between the older subjects. Young children with emotional problems appear to be quite unstable not only emotionally but also in their coordination and fine muscle control. (See *Plate 4*, p. 42.)

III. *Dashes Substituted for Circles* (Figure 2): This indicator has been associated with severe emotional disturbance in adults; it appears to be related to impulsivity and lack of interest or attention in young children. It was found relatively rarely and did not differentiate significantly between either the younger or the older subjects. Its total occurrence was however more frequent among the subjects with emotional problems than among the control group *(Plate 16,* p. 101).

IV. *Progressively Increasing Size* (Figures 1, 2, and 3): This indicator is supposedly related to low frustration tolerance and to explosiveness. It was found equally often among the younger subjects with and without emotional problems suggesting that it is not unusual for young children to be somewhat explosive. Among the older subjects, it occurred rarely but then more often on the records of children with problems *(Plate 27,* p. 154).

V. *Large Size of Drawings:* An increase in the size of drawings has been associated with acting out behavior in children. It was found more often on the records of younger and older children with emotional problems than on the Bender protocols of the control subjects. However, the differences were not statistically significant *(Plate 11,* p. 90-1).

VI. *Small Size of Drawings:* A decrease in the size of drawings is related to anxiety, constriction, timidity, and withdrawal behavior in children. This indicator occurred relatively rarely on the records of all younger subjects both with and without problems. There was a statistically significant difference between the number of older children with and without emotional problems who showed this indicator. Since small drawings require a fairly high degree of inner control and fine muscle coordination this type of drawing does not become diagnostically important until age eight at which time children have sufficient control to produce small drawings (See *Plate 14,* p. 98).

VII. *Fine Pencil Line:* A very fine line is usually associated with timidity and withdrawal in young children. It was found more often among the younger subjects with emotional problems than among the control group. The difference was not statistically significant. This indicator seems to reveal similar attitudes and behavior as the Small Drawings of Bender designs. Withdrawal and shyness in very young children may be reflected in the quality of the line while older children show their withdrawal and shyness in the size of the drawing. Fine lines were very rare among all older subjects. This indicator appears to be related to a child's age as well as to his emotional adjustment *(Plate 28,* p. 156).

VIII. *Overwork and reinforced lines:* This indicator has been related to overt aggressiveness and impulsiveness. It was found significantly more often on the Bender records of the five to seven year old children with emotional problems than on the records of the control group. It occurred also more often among the older subjects with problems but here the difference was not statistically significant *(Plate 17,* p. 105).

IX. *Second Attempt to draw design:* This indicator may be related to impulsivity or to anxiety. That is, it was found among children eight years old and older with emotional problems who were aware that their drawings were incorrect but who lacked the patience and inner control to correct their drawings by erasing the errors and redrawing the design. Instead these children gave up and started all over again (*Plate 17*, p. 105). These same youngsters will start many different activities and give up easily. They lack stick-to-itiveness and rarely complete what they begin. Another group of children who show second attempts at drawing Bender figures are those who associate the particular Bender design with a threatening idea or impulse, i.e., they may regard Figure 8 as a phallic symbol and may reveal their anxiety over impulse control or fear of castration by an inability to complete this figure despite repeated attempts (see *Plate 24*, p. 146). This emotional indicator occurred relatively rarely among the five to seven year old subjects who are less critical of their drawings and are less aware of their errors. It differentiated significantly between the older subjects with and without emotional problems.

X. *Expansion or the use of two or more sheets of paper:* This indicator is associated with acting out behavior and impulsiveness in children. It is the only emotional indicator which differentiated significantly between subjects with and without emotional problems at all age levels. This indicator was also found to occur significantly more often among children with neurological impairment than among non-brain injured children (see p. 102). This seems to suggest that children with neurological impairment who show Expansiveness on the Bender tend to have emotional problems and reveal acting out behavior. Expansiveness is not unusual among normal preschool children, but for school age youngsters it is considered to be a pathological sign (*Plate 11*, p. 90-1).

XI. *Constriction: The use of less than half a sheet of paper* is supposedly related to withdrawal, shyness, and depression. While this indicator appears to have pathological implications for adults it has been found to show no significant relationship to emotional problems in children. This indicator was the only one which occurred more often in the control group than in the group of children with problems. This finding is consistent with that of Byrd (1956). It seems to suggest that constriction is a sign of a moderate degree of anxiety which may serve as a motivating factor for learning and good behavior. There is little evidence that constriction signifies depression in young children. This emotional indicator appears to have little value in the diagnosis of children with emotional problems and was therefore eliminated from the list of emotional indicators (*Plate 6*, p. 67).

In the subsequent investigation, the indicator of "Constriction" is no longer included among the emotional indicators on the Bender Test. In the foregoing study the emotional indicators were analyzed singly. All ten emotional indicators were found to differentiate in the right direction between the subjects with and without emotional problems but only six of the ten indicators showed statistically significant differences. In the following study the Bender records are examined for *the total number of emotional indicators for each subject*. In this study each indicator was only counted once even when a given emotional indicator was present more than once, i.e., when several figures were drawn in Large or Small Size or when Wavy Line was present on Figure 1 and Figure 2 of a given Bender record. *Table 27* shows the incidence of emotional indicators on the Bender protocols of children with and without emotional disturbance.

Table 27. Number of Emotional Indicators on the Bender Records
of Children with Emotional Problems and Controls

Subjects	N	Number of Emotional Indicators						
		0	1	2	3	4	5	6
Age 5 to 7								
Emotional Problems	55	2	10	10	13	11	7	2
Controls	55	6	22	12	11	4	0	0
Age 8 to 10								
Emotional Problems	81	15	24	16	9	13	3	1
Controls	81	26	35	17	2	1	0	0

The results show that the subjects with emotional problems have anywhere from 0 to 6 indicators on their Bender records while the control group did not reveal more than a maximum of four emotional indicators on their Bender records. The mean number of emotional indicators for the five to seven year old subjects with problems was 2.9, whereas the mean for the control subjects was 1.7. For the older group of children the mean number of emotional indicators was 1.9 and .9 respectively. Chi-squares were computed comparing the number of subjects in the two groups with "above average" and "below average" occurrence of emotional indicators on their Bender records. "Above average" was defined as three or more emotional indicators on a single Bender record and "below average" indicated two or less emotional indicators on a given Bender protocol. The findings are shown on *Table 28.*

Table 28. Relationship Between Number of Emotional Indicators on the
Bender Records and Emotional Problems in Children

Subjects	0 to 2 Emotional Indicators	3 to 6 Emotional Indicators	Chi-square	P
Age 5 to 7				
Emotional Problems	22	33	10.68	<.01
Controls	40	15		
Age 8 to 10				
Emotional Problems	55	26	20.33	<.001
Controls	78	3		

The differences between the incidence of emotional indicators for the subjects with and without emotional problems were statistically significant at the .01 and .001 level. It was found that among the younger subjects about ⅔ of all children with two or less emotional indicators on their Bender records were well adjusted while ⅔ of all children with three or more emotional indicators were emotionally disturbed. For the older group of subjects about ⅗ of all children with two or less emotional indicators on their Bender records were found to be without emotional problems while all but three children with three or more emotional indicators were emotionally disturbed.

Thus it appears that both individual emotional indicators and the total number of emotional indicators on a given Bender record have diagnostic value in the study of children with emotional disturbances. Six of the indicators: *Confused Order of Designs, Wavy Line* (Figure 1 and 2), *Small Size of Drawing, Overwork, Second Attempt at Drawing,* and *Expansiveness* serve to reveal some of the child's personality characteristics and his attitudes. The total incidence of emotional indicators on a single Bender record appears to be related to the seriousness of the emotional disturbance. More than half of all children with three emotional indicators were emotionally disturbed, four out of five children with four emotional indicators on their Bender records had emotional problems, and all children with five or more emotional indicators were among those referred for psychological evaluation because of serious emotional maladjustment.

Scoring Manual for Emotional Indicators on the Bender Test for Children: Definitions and Scoring Examples

I. CONFUSED ORDER

Definition: Figures are scattered arbitrarily on paper without logical sequence or order. Credit is given for *any sort* of order or logical sequence. This may include arrangements from top of page down and up again, from left to right or from right to left. Subject is not penalized for placing Figure 8 at top of page if there is no room left at the bottom or side of the paper.

Implications: Confused Order of designs is associated with poor planning and inability to organize material. It is also related to mental confusion particularly in older or brighter children. Confused Order is common among all children 5 to 7 years old.

Scoring Examples:

acceptable, not scored

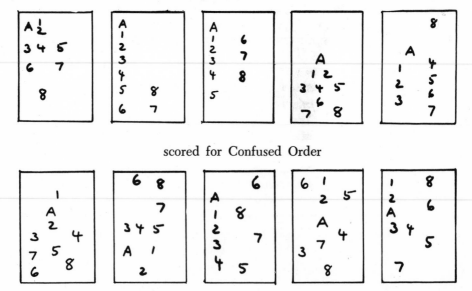

scored for Confused Order

II. WAVY LINE (FIGURES 1 AND 2)

Definition: Two or more abrupt changes in the direction of the line of dots or circles of Figure 1 and Figure 2 respectively. A continuous, gradual curve or rotation of line is *not* scored for this category. A change of direction must involve at least two consecutive dots or circles. A single dot or column of circles out of line is not scored. Wavy Line is only scored once regardless of whether one or both Figures show this deviation.

Implications: Wavy Line seems to be associated with instability in motor coordination and in personality. It may reflect emotional instability resulting from poor coordination and poor integrative capacity in a child, or poor motor control due to tenseness in a child with serious emotional disturbances. Wavy Line may come about from organic factors, from emotional attitudes, or both.

Scoring Examples:

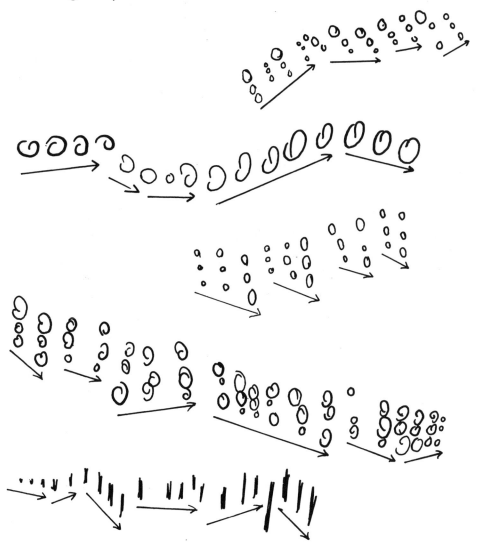

III.   DASHES SUBSTITUTED FOR CIRCLES (FIGURE 2)

Definition: At least half of all circles on Figure 2 are replaced with dashes ¹⁄₁₆″ long or longer. Substitution of *dots* for circles is *not* scored as this does not seem to differentiate between children with and without serious emotional problems.

Implications: Substitution of Dashes for Circles has been associated with impulsivity and with lack of interest or attention in young children. It is found among children who are preoccupied with their problems or who try to avoid doing what they are required to do.

Scoring Examples:

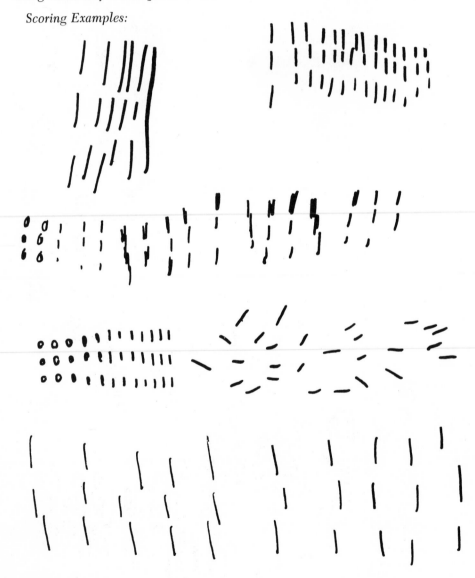

IV.   INCREASING SIZE (FIGURES 1, 2 AND 3)

Definition: Dots and circles increase progressively in size until the last ones are at least three times as large as the first ones. This item is scored only once regardless of whether it occurs on one or three figures.

Implications: Increasing Size on designs is associated with low frustration tolerance and explosiveness. Since very young children normally tend to have a lower frustration tolerance, the diagnostic implications on this Bender deviation increase as children grow older.

Scoring Examples:

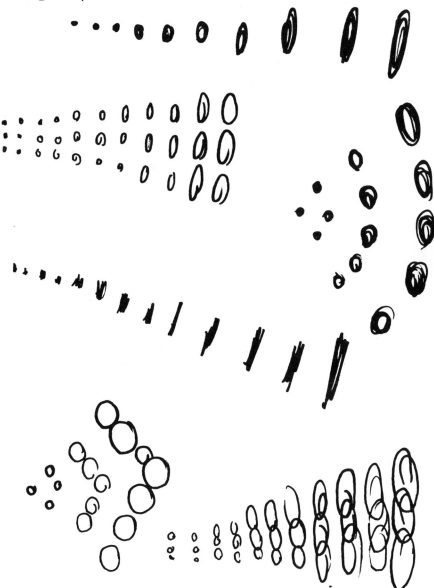

V. LARGE SIZE

Definition: One or more designs are drawn one third larger in both directions than design on stimulus card. When a design consists of two parts, e.g., Figure A and 7, then both parts have to be enlarged in size in order to qualify for this category. Large Size is only scored once regardless of whether one or all nine designs are enlarged.

Implications: Large Size has been associated with acting out behavior in children.

Scoring Examples:

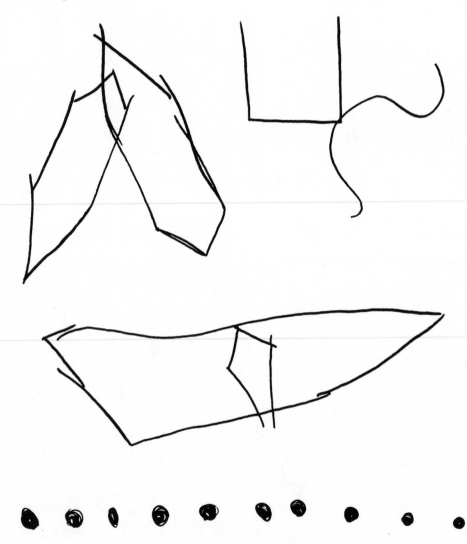

VI. SMALL SIZE

Definition: One or more designs are drawn half as large as the design on the stimulus card. The size of each figure is measured in both directions. When a design consists of two parts, e.g., Figure A and 4, then both parts have to be reduced in size in order to score in this category. Small size is only scored once regardless of whether one or all nine designs are reduced in size.

Implications: Small Size in drawings is associated with anxiety, withdrawal behavior, constriction, and timidity in children.

Scoring Examples:

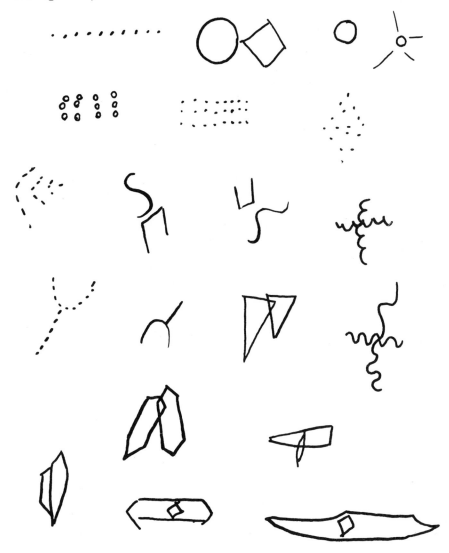

VII. FINE LINE

Definition: Pencil line is so thin that it requires effort to see the completed design.

Implications: Fine Line is associated with timidity, shyness, and withdrawal in young children.

Scoring Examples:

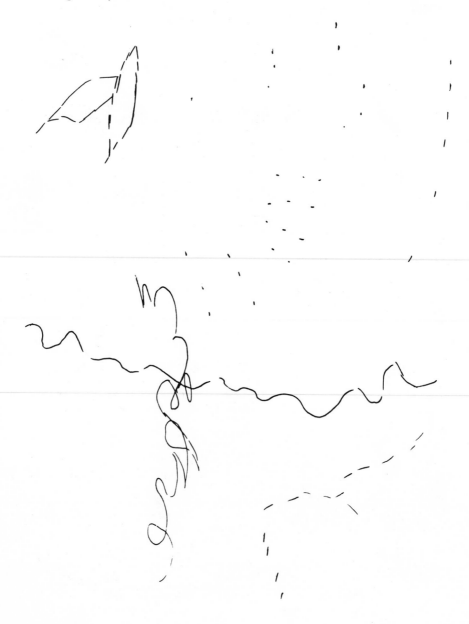

VIII. OVERWORK OR REINFORCED LINES

Definition: Total design or part of it is redrawn or reinforced with heavy, impulsive lines. The design may be first erased and then redrawn or it may be corrected without any erasures. This item is scored only once regardless of whether overwork occurs once or several times on a Bender record.

Implications: Overwork and reinforced line have been associated with impulsiveness and aggressiveness. It occurs frequently among acting out children.

Scoring Examples:

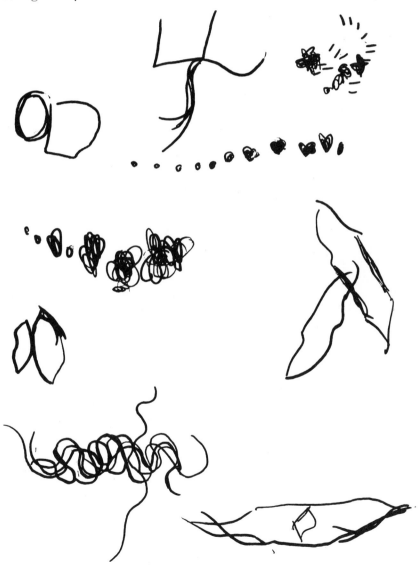

IX. SECOND ATTEMPT AT DRAWING FIGURES

Definition: Drawing of design or part of it is spontaneously abandoned before or after it has been completed and a new drawing of the design is made. This item is only scored when two distinct drawings are made of one design on two different locations on the paper. It is *not* scored when a drawing is erased and then redrawn on the *same spot* over the original drawing. When a drawing is erased and a second drawing is then made on a *different location* on the paper, it *is* scored.

Implications: Second Attempt at Drawing Figures has been associated with impulsiveness and anxiety. That is, it occurs among children who are aware that their drawing of a design is incorrect but who are too impulsive and lacking in inner control to correct the drawing by erasing and carefully redrawing the part that was incorrect. The impulsive child gives up easily and starts over again or starts something else rather than completing a difficult task. Another group of youngsters who make a Second Attempt at Drawing Figures are very anxious children who associate particular meanings with the shape of the design, i.e., Figure 6 may be associated with a snake and with masculinity. A child who has problems with masculine identification may react to Figure 6 with anxiety and may have difficulty completing the same. He may make several attempts at drawing the design before he can finish it.

Scoring Examples:

X. EXPANSION

Definition: Two or more sheets of paper are used to complete the drawing of all nine Bender designs. This item is scored regardless of whether each design is placed on a separate sheet of paper or if eight designs are on one page and the last design is on the reverse side of the paper.

Implications: Expansion is associated with impulsiveness and acting out behavior in children. This indicator seems to occur normally among preschool children. Among school age children it seems to occur almost exclusively on the Bender records of emotionally disturbed youngsters with neurological impairment (p. 102).

Scoring Examples:

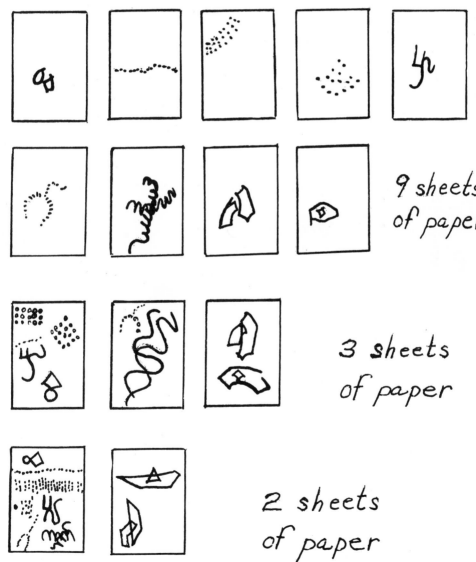

RELATIONSHIP BETWEEN DEVELOPMENTAL SCORES AND THE NUMBER OF EMOTIONAL INDICATORS ON THE BENDER TEST

Table 24 (p. 125) showed that children with poor visual-motor perception, as measured on the Bender Test, have a significantly higher incidence of emotional disturbance than children with good visual-motor perception. It was also demonstrated that emotionally disturbed children have significantly more emotional indicators on their Bender records than children without serious emotional problems (*Table 28*, p. 130). It was therefore hypothesized that children with poor visual-motor perception may be expected to show a higher incidence of emotional indicators on their Bender protocols than children with good visual-motor perception.

This hypothesis was tested by the author using the same subjects (*Table 23*, p. 125) as in the preceding study. All five to seven year old subjects were grouped together. A chi-square was computed comparing the children with above and below average Bender scores who had less than three or three or more emotional indicators on their Bender records. The same procedure was followed for all the eight to ten year old subjects. The results are shown on *Table 29*. The findings reveal that the relationship between Bender scores and the number of emotional indicators is statistically significant at the .001 and .01 level respectively. This supports the hypothesis that children with poor visual-motor perception also tend to have a high incidence of emotional indicators on their Bender records. Three out of four of all subjects with three or more emotional indicators were also found to have a poor Bender score. However, there were subjects with good Bender scores who showed a high incidence of

Table 29. Relationship Between Bender Scores and the Number of Emotional Indicators on the Bender Records

Number of Emotional Indicators	Good Bender	Poor Bender	Chi-square	P
		Subjects age 5 to 7		
0 to 2	40	22	15.40	<.001
3 to 6	12	36		
		Subjects age 8 to 10		
0 to 2	79	54	10.43	<.01
3 to 6	7	22		

emotional indicators while more than half of all children with poor Bender records revealed less than three emotional indicators. Thus it seems safe to assume that the Developmental score and the emotional indicators on the Bender Test measure different aspects of a child's functioning but that both are found more often together on the records of children with emotional problems than on those of children without emotional problems. A poor Bender score alone, does not necessarily imply emotional problems, but if a child shows several emotional indicators as well as a poor Bender score, then indications are that the child has serious emotional problems and that perceptual problems have probably contributed to his disturbance. If a child shows emotional indicators without any evidence of poor visual-motor perception, then it may be assumed that the child's problems are related primarily to his social and emotional experiences. The following case histories may help to illustrate how the Developmental scores and the emotional indicators on the Bender Test can be used together in the evaluation of emotionally disturbed children.

Jeff, the 8 years 4 months old boy whose Bender record is shown on *Plate 7* (p. 68) was mentioned earlier when children with problems in school achievement were discussed (p. 69). Jeff was a brain injured youngster with serious problems in both visual-motor perception and in emotional adjustment. His Developmental Bender score was quite poor; with a score of 16, Jeff's perceptual maturity was on the level of a preschool child. On the basis of the Bender score alone, it could be stated that Jeff was a boy with serious perceptual impairment who was probably very vulnerable. But the Bender score tells nothing about his emotional adjustment. Yet, it may be assumed that any eight year old with such serious disturbances in visual-motor perception is also likely to develop emotional problems.

When analyzing Jeff's Bender record as a projective test the presence of several emotional indicators is noted: Jeff shows I., *Confused Order* of the designs suggesting poor planning ability and/or mental confusion. There is evidence of II., *Wavy Line* on both Figures 1 and 2 probably indicating both poor coordination as well as emotional instability. On Figure 2 Jeff also reveals a tendency toward IV., *Increase in Size* which reflects low frustration tolerance and explosiveness. Jeff exhibits the paradox of drawing one design in VI., *Small Size* (Figure 8) and one design with a tendency toward V., *Large Size* (Figure 6). Thus it appears that Jeff vacillates between anxious withdrawal and aggressive acting out. VIII., *Overwork* on Figures 1, 3 and 5 gives additional indication that Jeff is a very impulsive and aggressive youngster.

The presence of four emotional indicators and the tendency toward two additional ones suggest that Jeff was a disturbed child who was in need of psychiatric help. He appeared to be a very impulsive, confused little boy who was torn between aggressive explosiveness and anxious withdrawal. It appears likely that both Jeff's perceptual problems and his difficulties in impulse control were related to his neurological impairment but that these were enhanced by his interpersonal relationships with significant adults at home and in school. It can be seen that both the Developmental Bender score and the emotional indicators contribute to the understanding and evaluation of Jeff. But it is not possible to predict from the Bender record which of the conflicting forces in Jeff determine his overt behavior. Observation showed that Jeff was actually a very anxious and withdrawn child most of the time, but when teased or frustrated he would lose his temper and showed aggressive behavior toward his peers.

Another child with both perceptual and emotional problems was Sally, the 10 years 4 months old girl with serious learning problems. Her Bender record is shown on *Plate 14* (p. 98). Her Bender score was poor, indicating that Sally had immature visual-motor perception and was probably a vulnerable child who might easily develop emotional problems, but it did not tell anything about the nature or presence of such problems. An analysis of her Bender record for emotional indicators reveals the following: Sally showed *Confused Order* in the arrangement of her Bender designs. This may reflect lack of planning ability due to limited intellectual ability and/or mental confusion. Of particular significance is the fact that Sally drew all nine Bender designs in *Small Size*. This suggests extreme anxiety and feelings of inadequacy. It reflects Sally's actual behavior. She was a very quiet, withdrawn child who presented no behavior problems in class. But she had some days when her withdrawal was extreme and when she showed indications of serious emotional disturbance. In view of Sally's perceptual problems, i.e., poor Bender Developmental score, and her emotional problems, i.e., confusion and anxious withdrawal, it was felt that Sally was in need of both academic and psychological help. In Sallys' case, it was shown how the two methods of analyzing Bender records supply information about different aspects of a child.

Plate 17 (p. 105) shows the Bender record of Fred. Fred was 10 years 11 months old. His Developmental Bender score is 2 which is just below average but well within the normal range for his age group. Fred presented no learning problems but showed serious emotional disturbances. The Bender record indicates that Fred probably had difficulty with visual-motor perception in the past since the drawing of angles and curves was still hard for him. But there was evidence that he had learned to compensate for problems in visual-motor perception by virtue of his age and good intelligence. The Developmental Bender score offers little insight into Fred's emotional problems.

The nature of Fred's problems was revealed more clearly when the Bender Test was analyzed as a projective test. Fred shows evidence of *Overwork* on Figures A, 4, 6, and 8 suggesting considerable aggressiveness and acting out behavior. This was even more vividly demonstrated on Figure 7. First Fred drew the design upside down but recognized his error at once. He became disgusted with himself and scribbled over the drawing with heavy impulsive lines. He made a *Second Attempt* at drawing Figure 7 rather than carefully erasing and correcting the first drawing. His second drawing still reflects his impulsiveness, the sides of the hexagons overlap and are not joined properly. Low frustration tolerance, explosiveness, and impulsive actions are typical for Fred. His problem with impulse control did not reveal itself on the Developmental Bender score but in the presence of emotional indicators on the Bender Test. The latter gave a good picture of how Fred deals with frustrations.

Laura's Bender record, as shown on *Plate 24* is quite unusual and most interesting. Laura was an 8 year old girl of high average intelligence. She was referred to the school psychologist because of daydreaming in class and failing to complete her assignments. She preferred playing with boys and frequently hit girls. During the administration of the Bender Test Laura was extremely anxious, she worked very slowly and with great effort, she sighed repeatedly and seemed dissatisfied with her performance. Laura obtained a Developmental score of 3 which is better than average for her age level. Thus it would appear that Laura's difficulty in school achievement was not related to immaturity in visual-motor perception. The Bender score gives no clue to the emotional factors influencing the child's behavior.

Laura's Bender record became highly significant when it was analyzed for emotional indicators. The presence of *Confused Order* of Bender designs on the record of a bright eight year old child suggests some mental confusion. Figure 2 reveals *Wavy Line* indicating emotional instability. Instead of circles, Laura drew dashes on Figure 2; the substitution of *Dashes for Circles* is usually associated with impulsivity and with preoccupation or lack of attention. The presence of both *Small Size* (Figure 3) and a tendency toward *Large Size* (Figure 6) on the same Bender record reflects a conflict between emotional withdrawal and aggressive acting out behavior. Most outstanding on Laura's Bender are three occurrences of *Second Attempt at Drawing a Design* (Figures 3, 7 and 8). This seems to reflect extreme anxiety.

It seems significant that Laura should have so much difficulty drawing designs which could be readily interpreted as phallic symbols. She apparently had no difficulty drawing angles as such; her original hexagon on Figure 7 is quite good. It may therefore be assumed that Laura's problem in drawing the Bender designs was related to her associations with the shapes she was asked to copy rather than with the difficulty of the designs. This was particularly true for Figure 8 which is usually one of the first ones young children draw correctly. It is also significant that Laura drew Figure 6 so large since this design is often associated with masculinity. Although this writer is usually reluctant to interpret deviations on the Bender records of young children in a symbolic way, the evidence in Laura's case pointed in this direction. There appeared to be every indication that this confused, unstable girl was suffering either from severe castration anxiety or penis envy and that she had great difficulty accepting her own female identity. Hutt (1962) suggests that the circle in Figure A represents the female element while the square represents the male element. The disproportion in the size between the circle and square on Laura's drawing may further reflect her conflict in sexual identification.

It is greatly emphasized that Laura's case is unusual and that symbolic interpretation of Bender records of young children is often far-fetched and frequently shows little validity. At best, symbolic interpretations are only hypotheses which have to be checked for supporting evidence. It would be unfortunate to assume that dynamic relationships and feelings actually exist in a child just because a given "sign" appeared on the Bender record. The author considers it much safer and more appropriate to use first, the simplest and most logical explanation for a Bender deviation and to resort to symbolic interpretations only when all other methods have been found insufficient. For young children a great deal can be explained in terms of age, immaturity in coordination and perception, and in as yet poor impulse control.

The hypothesis of castration anxiety and difficulty in sexual identification was fully supported by Laura's behavior and by her social history. It was learned that Laura was the oldest of four little girls. Her father was an officer in the Armed Services as was his father before him and his grandfather before that. It can be imagined how disappointed the father was by the birth of each succeeding daughter. His wish for a son and heir had been expressed many times. It was discovered that Laura was aware of this situation and had taken it upon herself to fulfill her father's wish. She decided to become a boy.

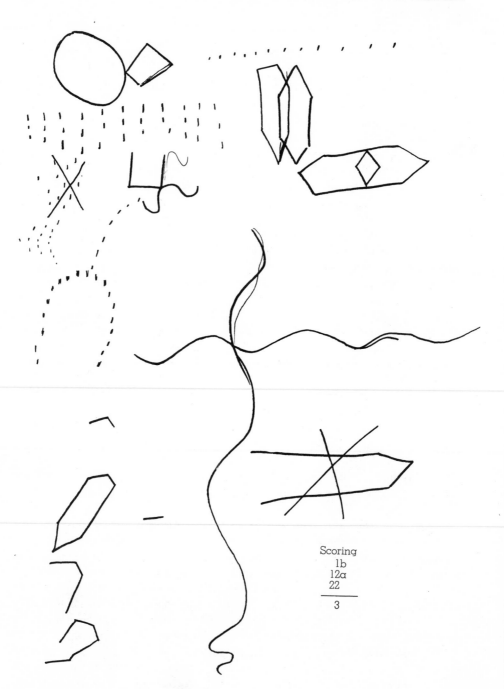

Scoring
1b
12a
22
———
3

Plate 24. Laura, C. A. 8-0.

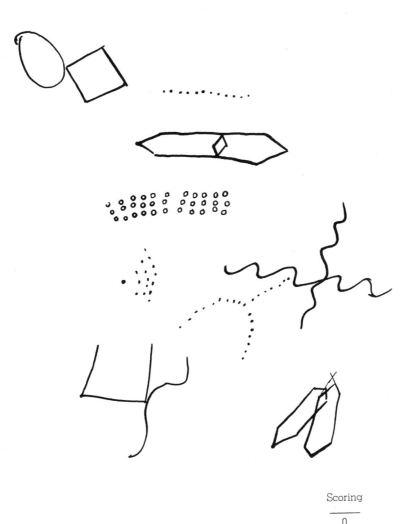

Scoring

0

Plate 25. Laura, C. A. 8-8.

Laura openly rejected her femininity by fighting with girls and seeking the company of boys. Her mother reported daily struggles to make Laura wear dresses to school; the child insisted on wearing slacks. Laura cut her own hair in an effort to look more boyish. But being a bright little girl she could not fully deceive herself and knew that she really was not a boy. She lived in fear lest she would be "found out." Laura felt very inferior about being a girl and tended to depreciate herself. She suffered from periods of depression and also had a history of nightmares.

It can be seen that Laura's Bender record reflected primarily her emotional conflicts, fears, and attitudes. In this case the Developmental scoring helped to rule out perceptual problems while the emotional indicators helped to formulate hypotheses which were then further investigated. The presence of six emotional indicators on Laura's Bender suggested that the child was seriously disturbed and was in need of help. Recommendations were made to obtain psychotherapy for Laura and guidance for her parents. This was accepted by the parents who went with their daughter to a child guidance clinic. Laura was able to profit greatly from this experience. Her behavior and attitudes changed markedly at home and in school. She learned to accept herself as a girl and seemed much happier and more outgoing. Her school achievement was above average. Eight months after Laura had first been seen she was again tested with the Bender Test. The results are shown on *Plate 25.* Laura's second Bender shows a lessening of anxiety and explosiveness and an improvement in the drawings of the designs. Laura's Bender score is 0 or perfect. The presence of Confused Order and Small Drawing on Figures 1 and 3 still suggests some tenseness but it is no longer extreme. Laura's Bender reflects her change in attitudes and her greatly improved emotional adjustment.

PART VII. Application of Research Findings on the Bender Test for Young Children

In the preceding chapters different aspects of the Bender Test were examined in relation to young children's maturation in visual-motor perception, school achievement, intellectual ability, and to the diagnosis and evaluation of neurological and emotional problems. Each of these areas was investigated separately and cases were cited to illustrate particular points under discussion.

In the following section, all the pertinent research findings described in this volume are integrated to demonstrate how they can be applied in the evaluation of Bender records of young children. The case histories presented in the subsequent pages are believed to be fairly typical of those encountered by clinical psychologists in guidance clinics and in private practice, and by school psychologists in elementary schools.

1. Case History: Eric

Eric was a sturdy little boy with a very sober expression. He was five years and five months old. His family moved into the community in March at which time Eric was enrolled in kindergarten. In the town where Eric had lived previously the schools did not have any kindergarten classes. Thus school attendance was a new experience for Eric. He seemed quite upset by kindergarten and cried a great deal, wandered about looking vague, and showed no interest in the other children or their activities. He participated in none of the games or songs directed by the teacher and seemed unable to follow even simple directions. Eric was very quiet. He seldom tried to speak and when he did attempt to communicate, a severe articulation defect made his speech unintelligible. Eric appeared very unhappy and lonely. At first his teacher tried to explain his behavior with the fact that Eric had missed seven months of kindergarten. But when he failed to show any improvement during the next four weeks Eric was referred to the psychologist for evaluation.

During the testing session, Eric was cooperative but not spontaneous. Verbal communication was difficult but it appeared that he understood what was requested of him. Eric's Bender Test record is shown on *Plate 26*. A step by step analysis of Eric's Bender protocol follows:

Scoring of the Bender record (p. 16): Figure A:1a. The square is grossly distorted since it consists of five disconnected lines. 1b. Disproportion in size between the circle and the square. 2. Rotation, i.e., the side of the attempted square closest to the circle is drawn in vertical position instead of in the diagonal. 3. The circle and the square are not connected.

Figure 2:7. Rotation, since the maximum expansion of Eric's drawing of this design is vertical instead of horizontal. 8. Since this drawing is scored as rotated it means that there are only two dots instead of three in each column.

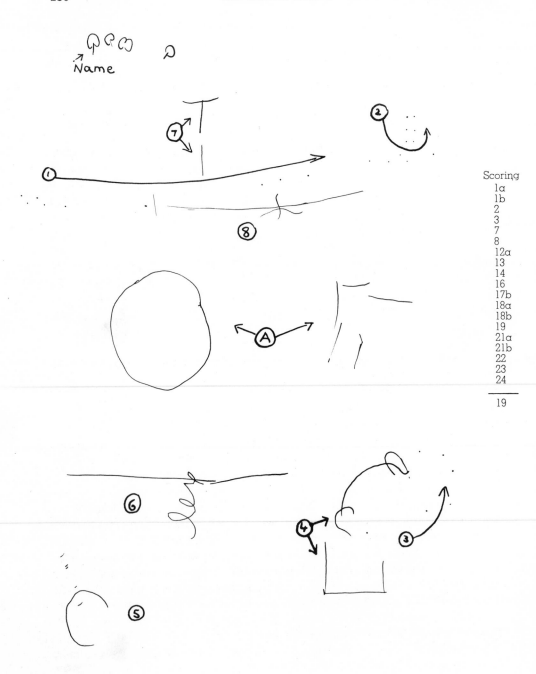

Scoring
1a
1b
2
3
7
8
12a
13
14
16
17b
18a
18b
19
21a
21b
22
23
24

19

Plate 26. Eric, C. A. 5-5.

Figure 3:12a. The shape of the design is lost; Eric drew just a conglomeration of dots.

Figure 4:13. Rotation, since the curve is placed above the square. 14. The parts of this design are not integrated.

Figure 5:16. The arc of this figure is rotated. 17b. The arc is drawn with a continuous line instead of dots.

Figure 6:18a. Drawing of four angles and loops instead of sinusoidal curves. 18b. Straight line instead of sinusoidal curves. 19. The vertical line loops across the horizontal line and curves back again; it does not truly cross it.

Figure 7:21a. Disproportion among "hexagons," i.e., one hexagon consists of one line, the other of two lines, hence it is twice as "big." 21b. Grossly misshapen hexagons, in fact they are unrecognizable. 22. Rotated position of hexagons or their equivalents. 23. Failure of parts to overlap.

Figure 8:24. Gross distortion of shape.

Total Bender Score: 19.

Interpretation of Bender Score (Table 6, p. 188): Eric's score of 19 is more than one standard deviation from the normative score for his age level. *His Bender score resembles that of a four year old child.* Compared with other kindergarten children, Eric's Bender score is more than one standard deviation from their Bender mean score. *Eric's performance on the Bender is not unlike that of a nursery school child.*

Time (Table 7, p. 36): Eric completed the Bender Test in three minutes ten seconds. He drew very rapidly and without hestitation. His time approaches the critical time limit for his age level. *The speed of his drawing suggests impulsivity and a short attention span.*

Intellectual evaluation (p. 45): Eric's chronological age was 5 years 5 months at the time he took the Bender Test. His perceptual maturity was on the 4 year 5 months level. This would suggest that *Eric's intellectual functioning was on the dull normal level and that his IQ score was approximately 80 to 85.*

School readiness (p. 52): Eric's extremely poor Bender score indicates that he was not yet ready for reading and writing and *it seemed unlikely that he would be ready to enter the first grade successfully in the fall.*

Diagnosing brain injury (p. 75): Since extremely poor Bender scores occur significantly more often among children with neurological impairment than among non-brain injured children, it is possible that Eric's immaturity and poor functioning may be the result of brain injury.

It was shown on *Table 19* (p. 189) that 13 individual Bender scoring items are significantly related to neurological impairment in five year old children. Eight of these 13 items occur much more often but not exclusively among brain injured children. Eric revealed six of these eight items on his Bender record. They were: 1a, 2, 3, 14, 16, and 19. Five scoring items are found almost *exclusively* on the Bender records of 5 year old children with neurological impairment. Eric's Bender showed three of these five items, they include: 13, 17b, and 18b. *Eric exhibits an usually high incidence of Bender deviations associated with brain injury in five year old children.*

Eric was still too young to be able to compensate for any neurological impairment that may have been present (p. 83).

Receptive versus expressive disturbance (p. 95): Eric appeared to have no difficulty understanding what was said to him. His severe articulation problem suggested difficulty in verbal expression. A similar problem was noted in the area of motor expression. Eric seemed to be able to perceive the Bender Gestalt fairly accurately. He did not draw vague immature loops as most four year olds or dull older children are inclined to do. His treatment of Figures A, 7 and 8 suggested that he was trying to draw angles and straight connecting lines between them. But Eric was as yet unable to integrate the parts of the designs. He could not put down on paper what he knew should be there. *Eric seemed to be suffering primarily from disturbances in motor and verbal expression.*

Time and Space (p. 100): Eric worked very rapidly suggesting impulsiveness, but he drew all nine designs on one sheet of paper *suggesting fairly good control of his impulsiveness.*

Behavior observations: During the test administration, Eric showed poor coordination and his attention span was short, but he was very cooperative and tried hard to do well. He appeared immature in all but his physical development.

Summary on diagnosing brain injury: On the basis of Eric's total Bender score, the number of indicators of brain injury on his protocol, and the speed of his drawing, it appears that Eric is a brain injured child who is suffering primarily from disturbances in motor and verbal expression.

Mental retardation (p. 107): It was indicated above that Eric was probably of dull normal intelligence with a mental age of about 4 years 5 months and an IQ level of about 80-85. The way Eric went about drawing the Bender designs suggests that he is not a mentally slow child but an impaired youngster. It is likely that his intellectual level of functioning will increase as he gains more maturity in visual-motor perception. It is believed that Eric has normal intellectual potential.

Emotional indicators on the Bender (p. 125): On the basis of Eric's poor total Bender score it can be assumed that he is a vulnerable child who may readily develop emotional problems. The following emotional indicators were found to be present on his Bender record (p. 126): I., *Confused Order* related to poor planning ability, is common among all five year old children. VI., *Small Size* on Figures 2 and 7 suggesting anxiety, timidity, and withdrawal. VII., *Fine Pencil Line* on Figures 1, 2, 3 and 6, further emphasizes Eric's shyness and anxiety. VIII., *Overwork* on Figure 8 may be associated with underlying aggressiveness or with impulsivity, probably the latter in this case. The presence of four emotional indicators suggests that *Eric is an extremely anxious child with emotional problems who seems to be under a great deal of pressure.*

Summary of Bender Analysis: Eric's Bender record reveals him to be an anxious youngster with immature visual-motor perception, who is functioning on the level of a nursery school child. He seems to have average intellec-
᠊l potential although his present IQ level is in the low 80's. His immaturity

and problems in visual-motor perception are probably due to neurological impairment. He appears to be suffering from a disturbance in verbal and motor expression. Kindergarten attendance at this time is very upsetting for Eric and he reacts to it with anxiety, withdrawal and unhappiness. A lessening of pressure on this little boy is essential to avoid the development of more serious emotional disturbances. Eric is in no way ready to enter first grade in the fall.

The impressions gained from the Bender analysis were supported by additional test findings. On the Stanford-Binet Intelligence Scale, Form L-M, Eric obtained a mental age of 4 years 6 months and an IQ of 80. Eric's Human Figure Drawing showed a "Kopffüssler," i.e., a head with arms and legs extending from it. This type of drawing is typical of four year old children. However, the extremely poor integration of the head and the limbs support the hypothesis of brain injury, while the rather sophisticated treatment of the eyes suggests that Eric is not a dull child but rather a child of normal intellectual potential who is developing somewhat slowly.

The recommendation was made that Eric repeat kindergarten in the coming year to enable him to gain more maturity in visual-motor perception and to develop better emotional adjustment. It was pointed out that Eric required one more year in the relaxed atmosphere of kindergarten, free from academic pressures. Eric's parents rejected these recommendations completely. The irate father, a successful professional man, let it be known that no son of his was going to "flunk" kindergarten. He was adamant that there was nothing wrong with Eric and that he was a perfectly normal child. Patient explanations of how some children mature more slowly due to possible neurological malfunctioning fell on deaf ears. Eric's father refused to listen to anything the school principal, the teacher, or the psychologist had to say. In desperation the author showed Eric's father the boy's Bender record and compared it with those of his classmates. She also quoted research findings with children like Eric. The statistical facts and figures, and the visual evidence of Eric's immaturity made an impression on Eric's father who was a scientist by profession. After having denied earlier anything unusual about Eric's development, he now reluctantly volunteered the information that Eric's mother had suffered from toxemia just prior to the child's birth. But he added quickly that the doctor had assured him that Eric was perfectly normal. Yet Eric's father expressed considerable concern when he admitted that Eric had developed much slower than his brothers. He did not start walking until he was 22 months old and he did not begin to talk until he was three and a half years old. He feared that Eric might be retarded and was greatly relieved when it was suggested that Eric probably had average intellectual potential but that he could not and should not be pushed into school work before he was ready to begin. The father finally agreed to let Eric repeat kindergarten.

In the course of the next school year Eric showed considerable improvement in all areas. He seemed more relaxed and became cheerful and outgoing. He related better to other children. His speech, while still poor, became for the most part intelligible. Eric showed keen motivation for learning and put forth great effort in everything he did, including readiness work. He accomplished through determination what comes easily to most other children.

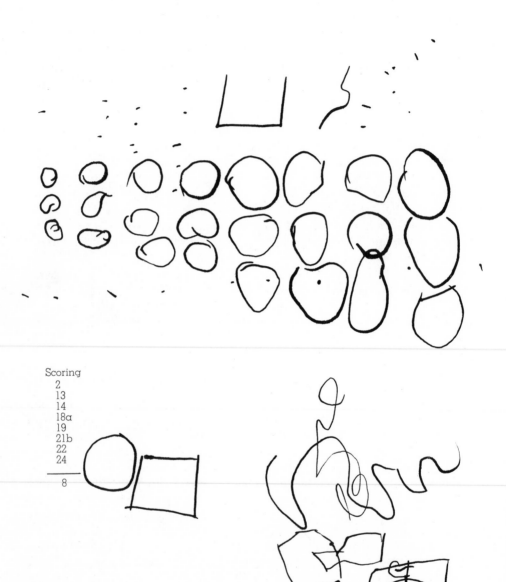

Scoring
2
13
14
18a
19
21b
22
24
——————
8

Plate 27. Eric, C. A. 6-6.

Eric was again tested with the Bender when he was 6 years and 5 months old. His second Bender record is shown on *Plate 27*. The difference between the first and second Bender Test is remarkable. The score on Eric's second Bender record is 8 which is average for a six and a half year old boy. His drawing is free from the anxiety and withdrawal indicators shown earlier, indicating that he profited greatly from the second year in kindergarten. He was now emotionally and perceptually mature enough to enter the first grade.

2. Case History: Gary

Late in October, Gary, age 5 years 7 months, was referred to the school psychologist by the kindergarten teacher bacause of persistent daydreaming, failure to participate in group activities, and inability to complete even simple assignments though he appeared to be of above average intelligence. Gary was an attractive, tall, well developed youngster who was very serious and appeared troubled. He seemed eager for attention and reassurance. Gary was very cooperative and worked carefully on the Bender Test. He was aware of his errors on Figure 7 and attempted to correct them. Gary's Bender record is shown on *Plate 28* (p. 156). A detailed analysis of his Bender protocol follows:

Scoring of Bender record (p. 16): Figure A:1a. Distortion since the square is excessively flattened. 1b. Disproportion between circle and square.

Figure 6:18a. More than three angles in curves. 20. Perseveration, i.e., more than five sinusoidal curves on the horizontal line.

Figure 7:21b. Distortion of both hexagons.

Total Bender score: 5.

Interpretation of Bender score (Table 6, p. 188): Gary's Bender score was more than one standard deviation above the normative score for his age group. This indicated that *his visual-motor perception was outstanding. Gary's level of perceptual maturation was similar to that of a seven and a half year old child and beginning second grade students.*

Time required to complete test (Table 7, p. 36): Gary finished the Bender in 8 minutes 39 seconds which is within the average time limits for young children.

Intellectual evaluation (p. 45): At the time of testing Gary was 5 years and 7 months old while his perceptual maturity was on the level of 7½ year old children. *This suggests that Gary is of superior intelligence and has an IQ of approximately 135.*

School readiness (p. 52): Gary's excellent Bender score showed that he had the mental capacity and the perceptual maturity to begin with academic work.

Diagnosing brain injury (p. 75): Gary's good Bender was not suggestive of neurological impairment. None of the five scoring points on Gary's Bender are significantly related to brain injury in five year old children (*Table 19*, p. 189). The time, space, and work method used by Gary to complete the Bender Test were all normal for his age level. *There is nothing on Gary's Bender record to suggest the presence of brain injury.*

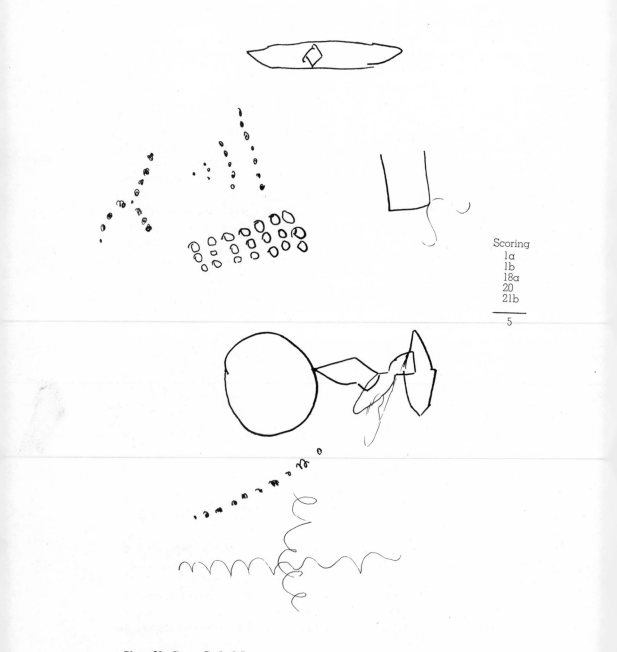

Scoring
1a
1b
18a
20
21b
──
5

Plate 28. Gary, C. A. 5-7.

Emotional indicators (p. 125): In view of Gary's good Bender score it did not appear that Gary was highly vulnerable nor that he would develop emotional problems easily. An analysis of his Bender record for individual emotional indicators (p. 126) showed the presence of two indicators: I., *Confused Order* which is not unusual among all five year olds. It reflects poor planning ability or mental confusion, particularly if it occurs on the Bender records of bright, perceptually mature children. VII., *Fine Line* on Figures 4 and 6 seemed to indicate anxiety and a tendency to withdraw in the face of stress. *It appeared therefore that Gary was anxious and showed signs of withdrawal and confusion at the time of testing.* A vulnerable child may react with anxiety to even minor stresses and strains, but a well integrated, bright child like Gary does not show these signs unless he has experienced something very disturbing and has reason to be upset.

Summary of Bender analysis: The Bender record revealed that Gary was a child of superior intelligence whose maturity in visual-motor perception was on the level of a seven and a half year old child. There were no indications of neurological impairment and he did not appear to be unduly vulnerable. However, Gary appeared to be a somewhat confused, anxious child with a tendency toward withdrawal in the face of stress. Since Gary showed only two emotional indicators on his record it was felt that his emotional upset must have developed fairly recently and that his behavior in school must be the reaction to some very specific experience which happened not too long ago. Gary had the capacity and the perceptual maturity to begin with formal academic work, however, it was probable that he could not use his ability fully as long as his emotional problem persisted.

Additional psychological test data confirmed the impressions from the Bender Test. Gary obtained an IQ of 138 on the Stanford-Binet Intelligence Scale, Form L-M. His Human Figure Drawing showed both signs of high intelligence and emotional problems. A home visit revealed that Gary's mother had suffered a period of depression during the summer and was still hospitalized. She came home on week ends only. Gary who was very close to his mother was greatly concerned about her. Gary's father was a brilliant but rather remote scholar who had little time or understanding for the child. Gary spent much time alone or in the company of adults.

3.   Case History: Concetta

Concetta, an attractive but ill kempt first grader, was 6 years and 7 months old. She was referred for psychological evaluation because of frequent aggressive conflict with other children and a complete lack of academic progress. Her teacher wanted to know whether Connie's difficulties were the result of language difficulties and culture conflict or whether Connie was a slow learner.

Connie was born in Italy and came to this country with her parents when she was two years old. Her parents spoke Italian at home and their knowledge of the English language was limited. But Connie spoke English with her older sisters and with other children. During the psychological testing session, Connie was able to express herself quite well in English. She was coopera-

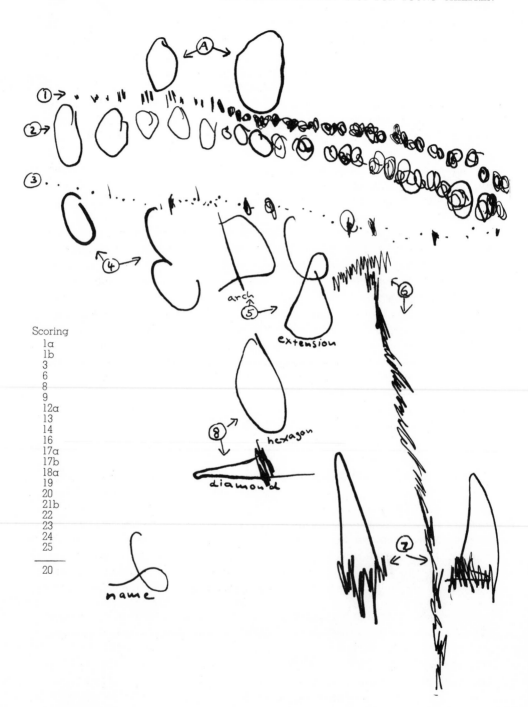

Scoring
1a
1b
3
6
8
9
12a
13
14
16
17a
17b
18a
19
20
21b
22
23
24
25
___
20

Plate 29. Concetta, C. A. 6-7.

tive but had a short attention span. She also appeared to be a very serious and troubled child who longed for attention and affection. Toward the end of the session, Connie snuggled up to the examiner and told long spontaneous stories of how others hit her and blame things on her. She described her parents as punitive and strict. "They all tell me to shut up . . . and mamma always tells me to write my name and hits me if I make it wrong." When asked what she would wish for if she could ask for anything she wanted, Connie replied: "I want a gun. I want to shoot everybody, all them neighbor kids. I mean it!"

When the Bender Test cards were presented Connie announced: "I can't do that." But with encouragement she completed the test and seemed quite pleased with her accomplishment. Her Bender record is shown *Plate 29* (p. 158). The following is a detailed analysis of Connie's Bender protocol:

Scoring of Bender record (p. 16): Figure A:1a. The square is grossly distorted and resembles an egg. 1b. The misshapen square is twice as large as the circle. 3. The square and the circle are not integrated.

Figure **1:6**. Gross perseveration, Connie drew 41 instead of 12 dots.

Figure 2:8. One row of circles instead of three rows of circles. 9. Perseveration since Connie drew 24 circles instead of 11 columns of circles in a row.

Figure 3:12a. Shape of design is lost; just a single line of dots.

Figure 4:13. Rotation of curve. 14. Curve and square are not integrated.

Figure 5:16. Extension on design curves down instead of going up. 17a. Gestalt completely destroyed. 17b. Arc and extension each consist of continuous lines instead of dots.

Figure 6:18a. Angles substituted for curves on both lines. 19. The two lines do not cross. 20. Perseveration on both lines.

Figure 7:21b. Gross distortion of both hexagons. 22. Left hand hexagon is rotated. 23. Two hexagons do not overlap.

Figure 8:24. Gross distortion of shape; hexagon resembles an egg while diamond resembles a triangle. 25. The misshapen hexagon is rotated.

Total Bender score: 20.

Interpretation of Bender score (Table 6, p. 188): Connie's Bender score is more than three standard deviations below the normative Bender score for her age group. This would indicate that *her maturity in visual-motor perception is extremely retarded. The Bender score is similar to that of a four year old child. Connie's functioning in visual-motor perception is on the level of a nursery school child.*

Time needed to complete Test (Table 7, p. 36): Connie finished the Bender Test in exactly six minutes which is about average for a six and a half year old child.

Intellectual evaluation (p. 45): At the time of testing Connie's chronological age was 6 years 7 months while her perceptual maturation level was 4 years. *Connie's IQ level is probably in the low 60's.*

School readiness (p. 52): A perceptual maturation level of at least five years is necessary before a child can begin to work successfully in school. *Connie's Bender record indicates that she is not yet ready for formal school work and cannot be expected to complete the first grade at this time.*

Diagnosing brain injury (p. 75): Connie's very poor total Bender score suggests possible brain injury. An analysis for individual Bender indicators of brain injury (p. 189) showed the following: Connie revealed seven of the nine scoring items which occur significantly more often but not exclusively on the Bender records of six year old children with neurological impairment; they are: 1a, 3, 12a, 14, 16, 18a, 19. Six additional scoring items occur almost *exclusively* on the Bender records of six year old brain injured children. Three of these items were present on Connie's Bender protocol. They were 12b, 17b, and 25.

Receptive versus expressive disturbances (p. 95): Connie appeared to be only partly aware of her errors on the Bender Test. At this point Connie revealed immaturity or disturbances in both the receptive and the expressive functions of visual-motor perception.

Time and space used for test (p. 100): Both the time and the space used by Connie on the Bender Test are normal for her age level and are not necessarily indicative of brain injury.

Behavior observation: Connie showed a very short attention span on the one hand and tended toward perseveration on the other hand. She either completed a drawing in great haste, e.g., Figure 4 and 5, or she continued repeating parts of a drawing over and over again, e.g., Figures 1, 2, and 6. Moderate, controlled action seemed to be difficult for this impulsive little girl.

Summary on diagnosing brain injury (p. 104): *Connie's poor Bender score, the high incidence of individual indicators of brain injury, and her behavior during the test administration indicate that Connie is probably a neurologically impaired child. She shows both receptive and expressive disturbances in visual-motor perception.*

Mental retardation (p. 107)): The great discrepancy between Connie's chronological age and her level of maturation in perception suggested some mental retardation. The quality of her drawings was extremely primitive. All her Bender designs consisted of crude loops and scribbles. The strong tendency toward perseveration was another very immature feature of her drawings. There was no indication that Connie even attempted to draw angles or curves. The uniformly low level of drawing suggests that Connie was a mentally retarded child who was developing slowly and who was probably not of potentially normal ability.

Emotional indicators (p. 126): Connie's very poor Bender score reflected strong vulnerability which would make her quite susceptible to emotional problems. The following individual emotional indicators were found on her Bender record: I., Confused Order indicates poor planning which is common among six year olds. II., Wavy Line on Figure 2 which suggests instability in personality. IV., Increasing Size in Figures 1 and 2—in Figure 2 the size of the loops actually decreases rather than increases. In both cases the drawings reflect poor inner control and explosiveness. VIII., Overwork on Figures 1, 3, 7, and 8 is associated with impulsiveness and aggressiveness. The presence of four emotional indicators shows that Connie has serious emotional problems. *She appears to be an impulsive, unstable, explosive little girl with considerable aggressiveness and underlying hostility.*

Summary of Bender record analysis: Connie's Bender indicates that she is probably a mildly retarded youngster who is functioning on the four year old level and who has an IQ somewhere in the low 60's. Her perceptual retardation is probably due to neurological impairment and is not believed to be the result of language difficulties or culture conflict. The latter factors would not be expected to effect maturation in visual-motor perception. Connie also appears to be an emotionally disturbed child who had difficulty controlling her aggressiveness. This hostility and her poor social and emotional adjustment seem to reflect an unsatisfactory home environment.

Since Connie's mother was a bit hazy about the development of Connie and her other four children, it was not possible to obtain an adequate social and medical history for the little girl. The diagnosis of brain injury could therefore not be confirmed. However, additional psychological testing supported the impression that Connie is a mildly retarded child. She obtained a Full Scale IQ of 66 on the WISC. Her Verbal IQ was 77 while her Performance IQ was 60. There was considerable inter-test scatter. Connie's highest WISC Subtest score was in common sense reasoning (Comprehension: 8) while her lowest score was in abstract reasoning (Similarities: 0) and in visual-motor perception (Object Assembly: 0). The Human Figure Drawing was extremely primitive and resembled that of a four year old child. It also revealed many aggressive features.

4. Case History: John

John, a 6 year 11 months old boy, was referred to the school psychologist early in spring to help determine the best grade placement for him. John was attending the first grade but seemed bored and unhappy despite special work assignments. He was functioning in all academic subjects on the second or third grade level. Since all his friends were attending the second or third grade John longed to be with them. John was a slender, rather small boy and his teacher was not certain if he was truly precocious in his mental and emotional development or if he had been pushed at home beyond his age level. As the only child of older parents, both of whom were professional people with very high standards, John had been exposed to considerable intellectual stimulation at home and had travelled a great deal.

When seen for testing John was relaxed and outgoing. He chatted with equal enthusiasm about his friends, baseball, reading, building things, camping out with boys and going to a concert with his parents. He appeared to be a poised and well rounded youngster. His vocabulary and his pronunciation of words were exceptional for such a young child. John worked very carefully on the Bender Test using the left hand. John's Bender record is shown on *Plate 30* (p. 161). A detailed analysis of the Bender protocol follows:

Scoring of Bender record (p. 16): John drew all nine Bender designs correctly with the exception of Figure 6: 19. is scored since the vertical line barely crosses the horizontal line. However this distortion is probably the result of the unfortunate placement of the design at the bottom edge of the

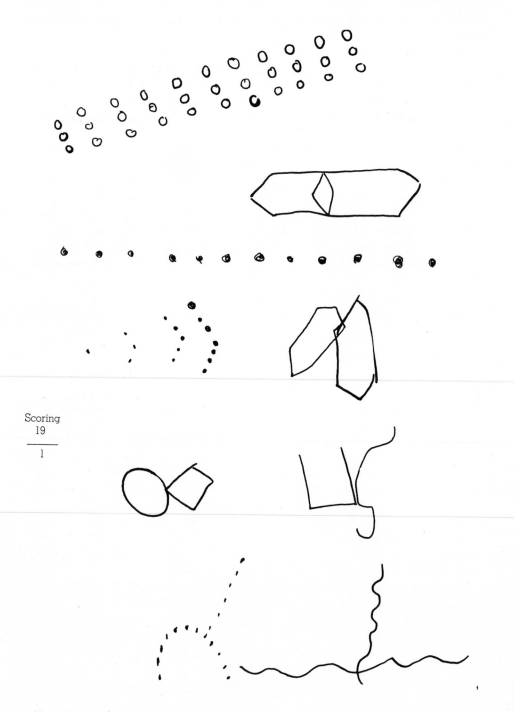

Scoring
19
——
1

Plate 30. John, C. A. 6-11.

paper and reflects primarily lack of planning rather than perceptual immaturity.

Total Bender score: 1.

Interpretation of Bender score (Table 6, p. 188): John's Bender score was outstanding, i.e., it was more than one standard deviation above the normative score for his age group. *His level of maturation in visual-motor perception was on the level of a 9 or 10 year old child. His Bender score was similar to that of a fourth grade pupil.*

Time used to finish test (Table 7, p. 36): John worked very slowly and carefully; he was aware of his errors and corrected them spontaneously. He erased several times and redrew parts of a design. All this required much time. He completed the test in 8 minutes and 46 seconds. This was somewhat longer than average for his age level, but it was within the acceptable limits for young children. *The time John required to complete the test seemed to reflect high motivation for achievement and a tendency toward perfectionism.*

Intellectual evaluation (p. 45): At the time of testing, John's chronological age was 6 years 11 months; his level of perceptual maturation was on the 9 to 10 year level. This would suggest that *John was of superior intelligence and had an IQ of approximately 130.*

School achievement (p. 52): John's exceptionally good Bender score indicated that he had the ability to be an outstanding student in the second grade at this time.

Diagnosing brain injury (p. 75): There was nothing on John's Bender record or in his behavior to suggest the presence of neurological impairment. *The quality of his drawings and his work method demonstrated that John was a child with well functioning and highly developed integrative capacity.*

Emotional indicators (p. 125): John's good Bender score indicated that he was a well integrated child who can tolerate considerable stress and strain. He would therefore not be expected to show many emotional indicators or emotional problems. Only one of the 10 emotional indicators (p. 126) was present on John's record. That was I., Confused Order. This indicator reflects poor planning ability and is common among *all* six and seven year old children. Since it was the only emotional indicator on John's record, it reflects primarily his age and not emotional disturbance. *The Bender protocol showed no signs of emotional disturbances.*

Summary of Bender analysis: The Bender record showed that John was a well integrated child of superior intelligence who showed no signs of emotional maladjustment. He could be expected to be an outstanding student in the second grade at this time since his perceptual level was similar to that of fourth graders and he revealed high motivation for achievement and good work habits.

The impressions from the Bender record found support in other psychological test results. On the WISC John obtained a Verbal IQ of 137, a Performance IQ of 132, and a Full Scale IQ of 138. His Human Figure Drawing was not outstanding but appropriate for his age level. It was concluded therefore, that John was a well functioning youngster of superior intelligence who has been able to profit from his stimulating home environment. It was not believed that John had been unduly pushed into high achievement by his parents or that he was under strain because of it. There was every indication that he was ready for the second grade despite his immature appearance. Socially, emotionally, and intellectually John much more resembled children in the second and third grade than first graders. It was therefore recommended that John be transferred to the second grade at this time. When the recommendation was put into effect John was overjoyed. He adjusted very well to his new class and was readily accepted by his new classmates.

5. Case History: Paul

The exasperated mother dragged Paul, age 7 years 6 months, to the Mental Health Clinic to seek help. She "had tried everything" but could not cope with her son. She complained that Paul wandered away from home, never did what he was asked to do, destroyed his toys, caused disturbances in school and refused to learn his lessons. He was repeating the first grade and still could not write his name. Paul's mother expressed considerable resentment toward the boy who seemed to be a threat to her. Since she was a severely handicapped polio victim who could walk only with great effort using crutches, she was no match for a lively seven and a half year old boy. She could not manage Paul herself but reported his wrongdoings every night to the father who then disciplined the child by spanking him "hard." But all this seemed to have no effect on Paul according to his mother.

Paul was attending classes for the hard of hearing. He was deaf in one ear and had a severe hearing loss in the other ear. He wore a hearing aid but managed to break it frequently. Despite his hearing aid and special class instructions he had made no progress in school. Paul's mother was convinced that he was a perfectly normal, healthy boy with a slight hearing loss who was just too "mean" to learn or to behave.

Paul was an attractive, well developed boy. He was cooperative and very responsive during the testing session. His attention span was rather short and he showed much restlessness. Verbal communication was difficult since Paul's vocabulary was very limited. But it was evident that Paul understood what was requested of him. He completed the Bender Test without difficulty working very rapidly. Paul's Bender record is shown on *Plate 31* (p. 165). The following is an analysis of Paul's protocol:

Scoring of Bender record (p. 16): Figure A:1a. The square is distorted. Figure 4:14. The square and curve are not joined.

Figure 5:16. The arc is rotated by 45°.

Figure 6:18a. Angles are substituted for most of the curves. 20. Perseveration since the horizontal line has more than five sinusoidal curves.

Figure 7:21b. The hexagons are distorted having an incorrect number of clearly defined angles. 22. The hexagons run parallel to each other instead of overlapping at an angle of 45°.

Figure 8:24. The hexagon shows extra angles at one end.

Total Bender score: 8.

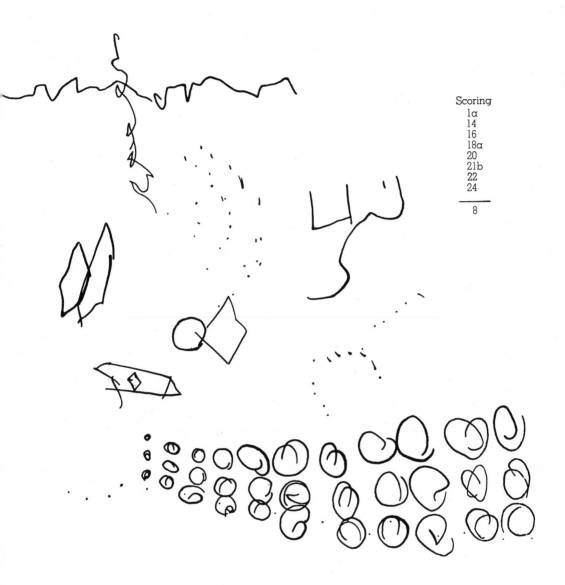

Scoring
1a
14
16
18a
20
21b
22
24
___
8

Plate 31. Paul, C. A. 7-6.

Interpretation of Bender score (Table 6, p. 188): Paul's Bender score is just one standard deviation below the normative score for his age group. This suggests that his maturity in visual-motor perception is at the lower end of the normal distribution of seven and a half year olds. *His visual-motor perception is on the level of a six year old child and resembles that of beginning first graders.*

Time required to complete Bender (Table 7, p. 36): Paul worked quite rapidly and completed the Bender Test in 4 minutes and 39 seconds. This is less time than most young children use but is still within the normal time range. *The short time reflects impulsiveness and restlessness.*

Intellectual evaluation (p. 45): At the time of testing Paul was 7 years and 6 months old, his level of perceptual maturity was 6 years. This indicates that *Paul was probably of low average intelligence with an IQ score in the low 80's.*

School readiness (p. 52): Paul's Bender score was at the maturation level of a six year old child; this indicates that *he was just now ready to begin first grade work.* Since Paul was repeating the first grade it appeared that he had started school long before he was ready to do so.

School achievement (p. 52): In view of Paul's lack of academic progress it was interesting to note that he showed many deviations on his Bender which are associated with reading problems. They include difficulty in drawing angles and curves on Figures A, 6, 7, and 8, and rotation of Figures 5 and 7. Paul also had trouble drawing the correct number of dots on Figure 3, he perseverated on Figure 6, and failed to integrate the parts of Figure 4. These particular deviations have been found to correlate with learning problems in arithmetic.

Diagnosing brain injury (p. 75): Paul's poor Bender score suggests possible brain injury. An analysis for Individual indicators of brain injury (*Table 19,* p. 189) shows that six of the eight deviations scored on Paul's record are significantly related to brain injury in seven year old children. They are: 1a, 14, 16, 18a, 22, and 24. The two remaining scoring points, 20 and 21b, occur frequently on the records of brain injured children as well as nonbrain injured seven year old children.

Receptive versus expressive disturbances (p. 95): Since there are no gross distortions on the configuration of the Bender designs, it is believed that Paul attempted to draw the designs correctly even when he did not succeed. It is therefore concluded that Paul's difficulty is primarily in the motor expressive area. But this could not be verified as verbal communication with Paul was difficult.

Time and space used to complete Bender (p. 100): Paul's use of space for the Bender drawings was normal for a young child. But, as was mentioned earlier, the speed with which he completed the test, 4 minutes and 39 seconds, was suggestive of impulsiveness and short attention span which are frequently associated with brain injury.

Behavior observations: Paul was cooperative but despite his efforts he found it difficult to sit still. He wiggled and moved about in his chair, pulled out desk drawers and reached for the Bender cards. It was also noted that he had particular difficulty shifting directions on the drawing of Figure 6.

Summary on diagnosing brain injury (p. 104): *Paul's poor Bender score, the high incidence of individual neurological indicators on his record, the short time required by him to complete the test, and his behavior during the test administration all indicate that Paul was probably a brain injured child.*

Emotional indicators (p. 126): Paul's poor total Bender score suggests that he was a vulnerable child who may easily develop emotional problems. The following individual emotional indicators were found on his Bender record: I., Confused Order which is common in seven year old children and reflects poor planning ability and confusion. II., Wavy Line on Figure 1 suggests emotional instability. IV., Increase in Size on Figure 2 indicates a low frustration tolerance and explosiveness. VI., Small Size on Figure 8 is related to anxiety and withdrawal. VII., Fine Line in Figure 1 was an additional sign of shyness and withdrawal.

The presence of five emotional indicators on Paul's Bender record can be considered as evidence that he has serious emotional problems. *He was shown to be an anxious, unstable, poorly organized child with low frustration tolerance.*

Summary of Bender analysis: Paul's Bender record revealed a child with serious disturbances in visual-motor perception probably due to neurological impairment. He had at least low average mental ability and was functioning on the level of a six year old child. He was just now ready to begin with school work. It was believed that his lack of academic progress was not only due to his hearing loss but also to his immaturity in visual-motor perception. In addition Paul showed signs of serious emotional problems. He seemed to be a sensitive, anxious boy with low frustration tolerance and poor inner controls who either explodes or withdraws when under pressure.

The impressions from the Bender Test were supported by additional psychological test results. Paul's Human Figure Drawing revealed a tiny, crudely drawn boy without any features at all. This drawing was highly indicative of both neurological impairment and serious emotional maladjustment. The Performance Scale of the WISC and the Progressive Matrices (Raven, 1945) were administered. Paul obtained a Performance IQ of 93 on the WISC and an IQ of 110 on the Matrices. The discrepancy between these IQ scores and the Bender performance level indicated that Paul was a child of normal intelligence who was suffering from neurological impairment which resulted in poor visual-motor perception. It was also probable that some of his speech and hearing difficulties were related to brain injury.

It was not possible to confirm the diagnosis of brain injury with developmental and medical data. Paul's mother insisted that his development had been perfectly normal. However, her very defensive attitude and her apparent rejection of Paul made her a somewhat unreliable informant.

It was concluded that Paul was a brain injured child of normal intellectual potential who was severely handicapped by a serious hearing loss, poor visual-motor perception, and emotional problems. It was recommended that Paul and his mother be seen at the Guidance Clinic for psychotherapy and guidance respectively. The school was advised not to pressure Paul for achievement at this time.

6. Case History: Kathleen

Kathleen's mother was puzzled. She came to the Child Guidance Clinic to seek advice. It appeared that Kathy, an 8 year 9 months old child, was having difficulties in the third grade. The teacher had complained about Kathy's behavior and had threatened to exclude her from class. The mother was at a loss to explain the situation. Kathy had always been a quiet, well behaved child at home and in school, although the mother acknowledged that Kathy had never been a good student and had always preferred playing by herself. But since the mother herself had been "just like that" as a girl, she accepted Kathy's poor grades and shyness without concern. Kathy had always liked school and had loved her first and second grade teachers. But recently Kathy had shown reluctance in going to school. She had suddenly developed headaches and stomach aches in the morning which quickly disappeared when she was permitted to remain at home and did not have to go to school. Kathy also seemed to be having bad dreams and had reverted to sucking her fingers.

In her report, the teacher described Kathy as a stubborn, uncooperative child who never completed her assignments. Her work habits were very poor and she was unable to work independently. Unless the teacher stood right over her, Kathy did nothing but rock in her seat and suck noisily on her fingers. This was disturbing to the rest of the class and to the teacher. When spoken to, Kathy would burst into tears. The teacher was certain that Kathy could do the work if she really tried since a group test in the second grade had shown that she was of normal intelligence. It was apparent that the teacher was losing her patience with Kathy.

Kathy was a frail, pale little girl who appeared immature for her age. During the testing session she was shy but friendly and cooperative. She was very restless and showed a very low frustration tolerance. As soon as a task appeared to be a little hard she gave up and put her fingers into her mouth. Kathy worked very rapidly and carelessly. She seemed to have a very short attention span. It required a great deal of encouragement on the part of the examiner to get Kathy to complete the psychological tests. Kathy's Bender Test is shown on *Plate 32* (p. 169). The following is a detailed analysis of Kathy's Bender protocol:

Scoring of Bender record (p. 16): Figure A:1b. Disproportion since the circle is twice as large as the square.

Figure 1:6. Perseveration since Kathy drew 16 dots instead of 12.

Figure 6:20. Perseveration since Kathy drew seven sinusoidal curves on the vertical line.

Figure 7:21b. Angles are missing on hexagons. 23. Hexagons do not overlap.

Figure 8:24. Angles missing on hexagon.

Total Bender score: 6.

Interpretation of Bender score (Table 6, p. 188): Kathy's Bender score was more than one standard deviation below the normative score for her age group. This indicated considerable immaturity in visual-motor perception. *Her level of functioning in visual-motor perception resembled that of a six and a half year old child or a first grader at the end of the school year.*

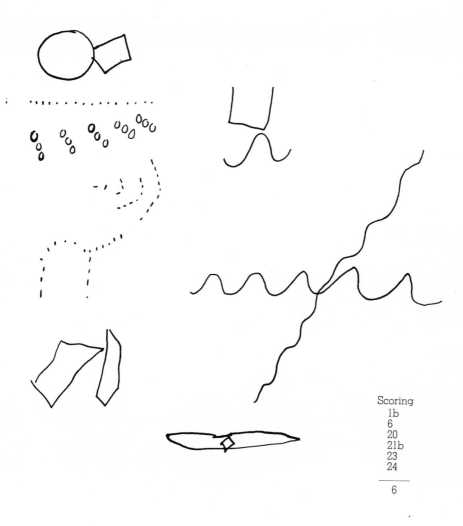

Scoring
1b
6
20
21b
23
24
___
6

Plate 32. Kathleen, C. A. 8-7.

Time required to complete Bender (Table 7, p. 36): Kathy finished the Test in 3 minutes 58 seconds. *Kathy's rapid rate of working showed impulsiveness and short attention span.* It also seemed to reflect a lack of involvement and a desire to avoid the task. Kathy's time was just within the normal range for her age group.

Intellectual evaluation (p. 45): Kathy's chronological age at the time of testing was 8 years 7 months; her level of perceptual maturity was 6 years 9 months. This would indicate that *Kathy was probably of low average intelligence* with an IQ score in the 80's.

School achievement (p. 52): In view of Kathy's poor Bender score *it could be expected that Kathy would be a poor third grade student.* Her difficulty in drawing angles on Figures 7 and 8 and her substitutions of dashes for dots on Figures 3 and 5 may be related to her reading problems. The tendency toward perseveration on Figures 1 and 6 and the difficulty to integrate parts of Figures A, 4 and 7 have been found to be related to problems in arithmetic. Kathy showed these deviations on her Bender record.

Diagnosing brain injury (p. 75): *Kathy's very poor Bender score resembles those frequently found among brain injured children.* An analysis of individual scoring items on her record *(Table 19,* p. 189) shows that two of Kathy's six scoring points, 6 and 20, are highly significant for brain injury, i.e., they occur *almost exclusively* on the Bender records of 8½ year old children who have neurological impairment. Three of Kathy's six scoring points, 1b, 23, and 24, are significantly related to brain injury, i.e., they occur significantly more often but not exclusively on the Bender records of 8½ year old children with brain injury. And the sixth scoring point, 21b, is found frequently on the Bender records of all 8½ year old children, but more often on those of brain injured children. Thus it appears that *Kathy shows an unusually high incidence of indicators for brain injury on her Bender record.*

Time and space used to complete Bender Test (p. 100): Kathy used one sheet of paper to complete the Bender Test which is normal for young children. *The short time of 3 minutes 58 seconds required by Kathy to finish drawing the designs is typical of many brain injured children.*

Behavior observations: Kathy was very restless and found it difficult to sit still, her attention span was short and she gave up easily. She worked rapidly and made no attempt to correct her errors.

Summary on diagnosing brain injury (p. 104): *Kathy's very poor Bender score, the high incidence of individual Bender indicators of neurological impairment, the short time required to complete the test, and her behavior indicate that Kathy was probably a brain injured child.*

Mental retardation (p. 107): While there is some discrepancy between Kathy's chronological age and her level of perceptual maturity it was not so great as to suggest mental retardation. The quality of her drawings was also more adequate than that of retarded 8½ year old children.

Emotional indicators (p. 125): Kathy's total Bender score indicates that she was probably a very vulnerable child who could easily develop emotional problems. An analysis of her Bender record shows the presence of two emotional indicators (p. 126). They are I., Confused Order which reflects confusion and poor planning ability and VI., Small Size on Figure 1 suggesting timidity and anxiety. Thus *it appears that Kathy was a somewhat confused, shy little girl who revealed a tendency toward withdrawal and anxiety.*

Summary of Bender analysis: The analysis of Kathy's Bender record indicates that she was a restless, somewhat anxious little girl with a short attention span and immature visual-motor perception probably as a result of neurological impairment. She appeared to be of at least low average intelligence and was doing as well in school as could be expected. Her perceptual maturation level was similar to that of 6½ year old children. Kathy tended to give up easily and withdrew when she felt a task was too difficult for her. She seemed to be a very vulnerable, sensitive little girl who showed signs of emotional upset.

Kathy's developmental history offered support for the hypotheses of neurological impairment. It seemed that Kathy's mother was very ill during her third month of pregnancy with Kathy and feared losing the child. But Kathy was a full term baby who appeared perfectly normal at birth. The mother noted, however, that Kathy was an unusually good baby who slept most of the time. She was very quiet and presented no problems. The mother reported that Kathy was always unusually sensitive to loud noises and tended to withdraw from people with loud voices. Kathy did not begin to talk or walk until she was more than 2½ years old. She was always a bit slow and immature for her age. Her first and second grade teachers accepted her on her level and did not push her beyond her ability. Since she presented no behavior problem they passed her on to the third grade despite poor achievement.

On the WISC Kathy obtained a Full Scale IQ score of 95. This suggests that Kathy had normal intellectual potential but was functioning academically on a lower level due to malfunctioning in visual-motor perception. Kathy's achievement scores on the Wide Range Achievement Test (Jastack, 1946) were on the beginning second grade level for reading, spelling, and arithmetic. Thus her level of academic functioning was in keeping with her perceptual maturity level. Her Human Figure Drawings also showed evidence of neurological impairment as well as feelings of inadequacy and anxiety.

It appears that Kathy was a very sensitive child with immature visual-motor development probably due to neurological impairment. She was able to get along in school as long as she was permitted to progress at her own speed and no unreasonable demands were made of her. In the third grade the school work was more difficult and the teacher was less accepting of Kathy. Kathy was unable to tolerate this increase in pressure and showed much anxiety and regression in her behavior, that is, she reverted to sucking her fingers, rocking in her seat, crying, and had developed somatic complaints as well as bad dreams. In view of her relative good adjustment during the first years in school, it was believed that Kathy was basically not a very disturbed child but rather that her present behavior was a temporary reaction in the face of excessive strain.

Recommendations were made for Kathy and her mother to come to the clinic for supportive therapy and guidance to help Kathy regain her self confidence. In a conference with the teacher, an attempt was made to explain

Kathy's difficulties and to assure the teacher that Kathy really could not be expected to do third grade work at this time despite normal intelligence. The teacher was urged to speak softly to Kathy as her rather loud voice frightened the child. It was agreed that Kathy should repeat the third grade in the coming year and that the remainder of the present school year should be devoted to making Kathy comfortable in school and helping her to relax so that she could work up to her capacity. She was to be permitted to work on the second grade level in the hope that she would be ready for third grade work in the coming year. It was also suggested that Kathy get individual tutoring in reading during the summer.

The recommendations were put into effect. Within a few weeks both the teacher and the mother reported such an improvement in Kathy's behavior that therapy was discontinued. Once again Kathy was a quiet but happy little girl free from nervous mannerisms and somatic complaints. She no longer resisted going to school. But as was to be expected, in view of her perceptual problems, her school progress was slow.

7. Case History: David

David, age 9 years 1 month, was brought to the mental hygiene clinic early in November by his foster mother. She was concerned about his shyness and his lack of progress in school. He was attending the third grade for the second time and seemed to be unable to do his homework. His teacher reported that he hardly ever talked in class and never finished his assignments. He did not interact with the other children who just ignored him since he did not bother them.

It appeared that David was an illegitimate child who had experienced severe rejection and neglect during the first three years of his life. He had been shifted from one inadequate home to the other until he was put in an orphanage at age three. During the next three years, he was twice placed unsuccessfully for adoption. Then at age seven he was finally sent to his present foster home. The foster parents were stable, mature people. Their own family was grown and married. They lived on a farm and took care of eight foster children. During the first year on the farm David hid in corners and would not talk to anyone. Only very gradually did he form an attachment to one of the other boys. At the present time David was a little more outgoing at home but still painfully shy in school. The foster mother tried to help David with his school work but all her efforts had failed so far. It troubled her that David was so unhappy despite all her efforts to make him feel wanted and loved.

David was a small, rather plain looking boy who was extremely timid. When seen for psychological evaluation he was barely able to whisper his name and volunteered no information. He answered all questions put to him with "yes" or "no." He was cooperative and drew the Bender Test very carefully. His record is shown on *Plate 33* (p. 173). The following is a detailed analysis of his Bender protocol:

Scoring of Bender Record (p. 16): Figure A:3. The circle and the square are not integrated, i.e., they are more than ⅛ inch apart.

Total Bender score: 1.

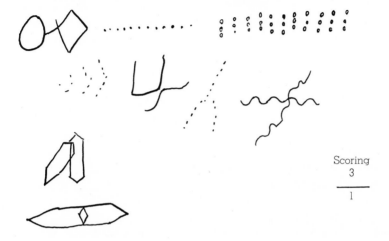

Scoring
3
―――
1

Plate 33. David, C. A. 9-1.

Interpretation of Bender score (Table 6, p. 188): David's Bender score is just above the normative score for his age group. *His maturity level in visual-motor perception is appropriate for nine year old children and is somewhat better than average for third graders.*

Time used to complete Bender Test (Table 7, p. 36): David worked very carefully and slowly. He finished the Test in 9 minutes 15 seconds. This means that he needed more time than most children his age to complete the Bender. *The long time needed seems to reflect primarily, David's extreme anxiety and timidity.* There was no indication of undue perfectionism, and David seemed to have little difficulty with drawing as such.

Intellectual evaluation (p. 45): David's chronological age and his level of maturation in visual-motor perception are about the same; this indicates that *David is of normal intelligence.* His IQ score is probably somewhere in the 90's or about 100.

School achievement (p. 52): David's good Bender score suggests an absence of learning problems due to perceptual malfunctioning. However, it was shown earlier *(Table 14, p. 59)* that the correlation between Bender scores and school achievement is not very high for fourth graders, i.e., nine year old children, since school achievement is determined by many factors besides perception at this level. Therefore, *if David has learning problems they must be related to factors other than visual-motor perception.*

Diagnosing brain injury (p. 75): David's good Bender score is not suggestive of brain injury since children with neurological impairment rarely have above average Bender scores. The single scoring point on David's record was 3, i.e., the failure to integrate parts of Figure A, which occur significantly more often but not exclusively on the Bender records of nine year old children with brain injury *(Table 19, p. 189).* In David's case, it is believed that the poor integration of Figure A was caused by a slip of his pencil due to anxiety and not as the result of perceptual impairment. It was found that the long time required to complete the test was probably due to emotional factors rather than to difficulties in perception and drawing. Thus it was concluded that *David's Bender record did not suggest presence of brain injury.*

Emotional indicators (p. 125): On the basis of his good Bender score David cannot be considered unduly vulnerable or likely to develop emotional problems. Vulnerable children react with emotional disturbance to even relatively minor stresses and strains. When well integrated children, i.e., those with good Bender scores, show emotional problems it is usually in response to severely traumatic experiences.

An analysis of David's Bender record for individual indicators of emotional disturbance (p. 126); reveals the presence of two such indicators. They are: II., Wavy Line on Figure 2 and VI., Small Size on more or less all nine Bender designs. His drawings of all figures were constricted into less than half the sheet of paper. *This together with the high incidence of Small Size seems to reflect severe anxiety, insecurity, and shyness, while the Wavy Line suggests emotional instability. It appears that David is a child with emotional problems.*

Summary of Bender analysis: David's Bender record indicates that he is a boy of normal intelligence whose maturation in visual-motor perception is appropriate for his age level. There are no indications of neurological impairment. David appears to have both the ability and the perceptual maturity to do average work in school. If he shows poor academic achievement despite this, then it must be due to emotional and social factors. The Bender record further reveals that David is a very insecure, unstable, anxious little boy who has a tendency to withdraw. Since David's Bender performance does not suggest that he is an unduly vulnerable child it is believed that his emotional disturbance reflects very traumatic experiences in early life.

Additional psychological test results confirmed the impression that David was of normal intelligence and had serious emotional problems. On the WISC David obtained a Verbal IQ of 85, a Performance IQ of 100, and a Full Scale IQ of 91. The low Verbal IQ score seems to reflect both cultural deprivation and a mild depression. His lowest Subtest scores were in Information, Vocabulary, and Digit Span. The Performance IQ score corresponds well with his Bender score and indicates average ability. David's Human Figure Drawing reflected average intelligence as well as emotional deprivation and anxiety. David's scores on the Wide Range Achievement Test (Jastak, 1945) in reading, spelling, and arithmetic were all on the first grade level.

It was concluded that David was essentially a child of normal intelligence whose poor school achievement and extreme shyness and anxiety were the result of his unfortunate early life. It was recommended that David come to the clinic twice a week for remedial reading and for psychotherapy. The foster mother was to come from time to time for guidance. David kept his appointments regularly. At first, progress was very slow but gradually he was able to express his fear of becoming attached to people because they always left him. He was also frightened lest he be "bad" and would be sent away from his present home which he liked very much. He wanted to please the foster mother and worked very hard during his reading lessons. The author observed David for the last time about ten months after the initial evaluation. At that time he had gained 16 months in reading and seemed much happier and a little less shy. Therapy was still being continued. The long-term prognosis for David was believed to fairly good, provided he could remain in his present home for many years to come.

8. Case History: Kenneth

Kenneth, age 9 years 3 months, was referred to a special class for children with emotional and neurological problems who were not mentally retarded. He had been unable to get along in a regular classroom because of his immature, silly, and disturbing behavior, his distractability and very short attention span, and his poor peer relationship. Despite superior intelligence Ken did only average work in reading and was more than a year below his age level in spelling and arithmetic.

Ken was seen by the psychologist to help determine a suitable program for him in the special class. Ken was an attractive, well developed boy who was

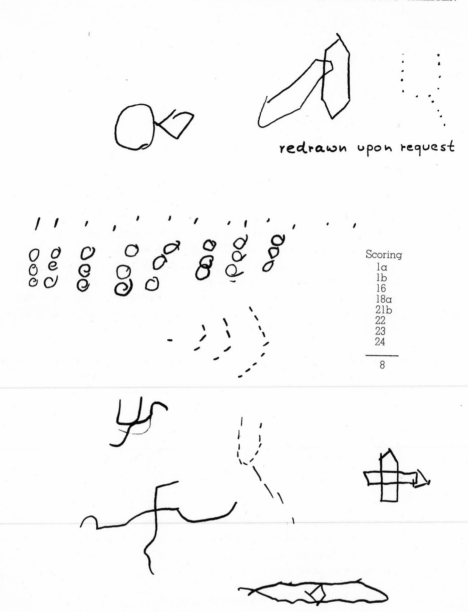

redrawn upon request

Scoring
1a
1b
16
18a
21b
22
23
24
———
8

Plate 34. Kenneth, C. A. 9-3.

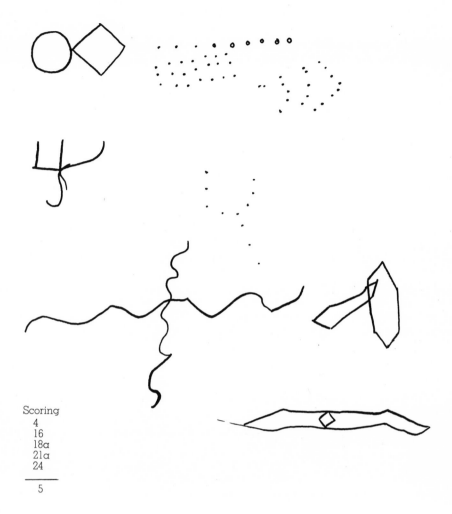

Scoring
4
16
18a
21a
24
_____
5

Plate 35. Kenneth, C. A. 9-3. (Retest)

friendly, chatty and spontaneous throughout the testing session. He seemed eager to impress the examiner with his material possessions and his father's eminence, but he showed much dislike for hard work. He drew the designs on the Bender test very rapidly and carelessly. Ken dashed through the test in less than three minutes. His Bender Test record is shown in *Plate 34.* Since it was felt that his performance could be better than it was, he was asked to redraw Figure 5 and Figure 7. The quality of the redrawn designs was much better than the first drawings, even though he again rotated Figure 5.

The examiner felt that Ken's Bender record *(Plate 34)* represented a typical sample of Ken's work in school. He dashed off his assignments with a minimum of involvement or effort and did poorly. But it was believed that this performance did not show what he was capable of. Since a special educational program has to be geared to a child's true ability it was deemed important to get a good measure of his maximum intellectual potential. It was therefore decided to readminister the Bender Test to Ken three days after the first testing. The psychologist talked to him for some time, elicited his full cooperation and she challenged him to do his best. Ken accepted the challenge and said, "I can do better." During the first testing session Ken had squirmed in his chair and had tried to get out of doing the task, but during the second test administration he settled down to work, concentrated with all his might, and drew very carefully. The examiner gave him a great deal of encouragement and praise. Ken required almost three times as long to complete the second Bender protocol as the first. His second Bender record is shown on *Plate 35.* It is felt that this second Bender protocol represents Ken's optimum functioning at this time. A detailed analysis of the second Bender record follows:

Scoring of Bender record (p. 16): Figure 1:4. Substitution of circles for dots. Figure 5:16. Rotation of design.
Figure 6:18a. Three angles in curves.
Figure 7:21a. Disproportion between hexagons.
Figure 8:24. Incorrect angles on hexagon.
Total Bender score: 5.

Interpretation of Bender score (Table 6, p. 188): Ken's Bender score is almost two standard deviations below the normative score for his age group. This indicates that he suffers from malfunctioning in visual-motor perception. *His level of maturity on visual-motor perception is like that of a seven and a half year old child or a beginning second grade student.*

Time needed to complete test (Table 7, p. 36): Ken finished the Bender in 6 minutes 19 seconds which is average for his age level. But *for Ken, this length of time spent in concentration represents hard work and an accomplishment.*

Intellectual evaluation (p. 45): Ken was 9 years 3 months old at the time of testing. His level of perceptual maturity was 7 years 6 months. Judging from the Bender performance Ken was of at least dull normal intelligence and has an IQ probably in the low 80's. In Ken's case the Bender score grossly underestimates his intellectual endowment. As was mentioned earlier

Ken was of superior intelligence, having a WISC Full Scale IQ of 128. His Verbal IQ was 131 while his Performance IQ was 118.

The marked discrepancy between the Verbal and Performance IQ's seems to reflect Ken's difficulty in visual-motor perception which was also revealed on his Bender score. The great difference between the WISC and the Bender score suggests that the malfunctioning in visual-motor perception is rather severe and is probably due to neurological impairment. It was shown on *Table 20* (p. 83) that there is no significant relationship between Bender and IQ scores among brain injured children who are not retarded.

School achievement (Table 14, p. 52): The correlation between Bender scores and fourth grade achievement is not statistically significant. It follows therefore that *no conclusions about Ken's school achievement can be drawn from his Bender score.* However, on the basis of the individual deviations on his Bender record (p. 61), it seemed probable that Ken had difficulty with reading, spelling, and arithmetic. He substituted circles for dots and dots for circles on Figures 1 and 2, distorted curves on Figure 6 and angles on Figure 8, and rotated Figure 5. These particular deviations have been found to be associated with reading and spelling problems. He also drew the incorrect number of dots on Figures 1 and 3, the wrong number of circles on Figure 2, and one too many sinusoidal curves on the vertical line on Figure 6. All these latter deviations are related to problems in arithmetic.

Diagnosing brain injury (p. 75): Ken's poor Bender score was highly suggestive of brain injury. An analysis for individual indicators showed that all items scored on Ken's Bender record *(Table 19*, p. 189) are significantly related to brain injury, i.e., they occur more often but not exclusively on the Bender records of brain injured nine year old children.

Receptive versus Expressive Disturbance (p. 95): Ken suffers apparently from both receptive and expressive disturbances in visual-motor perception. Receptive disturbance was evident on Figure 5 which he drew on three different occasions upside down without being aware of it. He did not perceive his error even when specifically asked about it. He did recognize his other errors and corrected them spontaneously. His poor angles and curves represent expressive malfunctioning.

Time and space used to finish test (p. 100): Ken completed the second Bender Test within the average time limit for his age group. But it is believed that the extremely short time he used to complete the Bender on the first test administration *(Plate 34*, p. 176) is more typical for him. It reflects his impulsiveness and short attention span. The amount of space he used for the Bender designs was normal.

Behavior (p. 87): Ken's behavior while working on the Bender Test *(Plate 35*, p. 177) was most revealing since he was determined to do well. Ken concentrated very hard and put forth great effort. He worked by glancing at each stimulus card briefly and then drew the design from memory. The cards seemed to distract him, so he removed them. Ken grew tense from concentrating so much. He had difficulty with Figure 7 and erased it several times before it met with his approval. The amount of energy he expended sitting still, working, and drawing, exhausted him. By the time Ken reached Figure 8 he could control himself no longer and dashed off the design; then he jumped up and ran off. He became extremely restless and excited and could not relax for the rest of the hour. Ken had a very short attention span; concentration was very hard for this youngster.

Summary on diagnosing brain injury (p. 104): *Ken's poor Bender score, the presence of individual Bender indicators for brain injury, the discrepancy between his IQ and Bender score, and his behavior during the testing session, all indicate that Ken is a brain injured child with disturbances in both the receptive and the expressive functions of visual-motor perception.*

Emotional indicators (p. 125): Ken's poor Bender score indicates that he is a vulnerable child who may easily develop emotional problems. The following individual emotional indicators (p. 126) were found on his Bender record (*Plate 35*): II., Wavy Line on Figures 1 and 2 suggesting emotional instability. VI., Small Size of Figure 2 indicates anxiety or constriction probably related to his great effort to control his impulsiveness. VIII., Overwork on Figure 4 reflects impulsiveness and aggressiveness. It seems therefore, that *Ken is an unstable, impulsive child who will make an attempt to control his impulsiveness when motivated to do so.*

Ken's first Bender record (*Plate 34*) reflects his instability and impulsiveness more strongly.

Summary of Bender analysis: The Bender Test indicates that Ken is a neurologically impaired youngster with a very short attention span and serious malfunctioning in visual-motor perception. He is emotionally unstable and acts hastily and carelessly unless motivated and encouraged to concentrate. But even then he can only work for very brief periods of time. Since Ken's deviations on the Bender Test are related to problems in reading and arithmetic, it is probable that his poor school progress is related to his difficulties in visual-motor perception.

The findings from other psychological tests supported the Bender results while a positive EEG confirmed the hypothesis of brain injury. A special program was planned for Ken with a frequent change of activities and lessons since he could only work at any one subject for a few minutes at a time. In view of his perceptual problems, his school work was adjusted to his actual functioning rather than to his IQ level. Special emphasis was given to helping Ken control his impulsiveness and to gradually increase his attention span. By enabling him to experience success it was hoped that he would have less of a need to disrupt his class and to tease other children.

9. *Case History: Rosalie*

Rosalie, age 10, was brought to the child guidance clinic in January by her mother. Since the irresponsible father had deserted the family more than a year ago, the mother was trying to raise her five children alone. It appeared that the other four children, a girl older than Rosalie and three younger boys, got along well in school and in the community; they presented no difficulties at home. But Rosalie was constantly in trouble. She beat up other children because they would not play with her, had frequent temper outbursts, cried easily and was disturbing in the classroom. She also showed nervous mannerisms, i.e., a facial tic and thumbsucking. Rosalie was attending the fourth grade but her achievement was only on the first grade level. The mother had tried to correct the child by scolding and beating her but Rosalie's behavior got worse rather than better. The mother was at a loss as to how to cope with the girl. The teacher too, was complaining about her. Rosalie had always been a difficult, headstrong child according to the mother. Now that she was getting older she became more aggressive and more difficult to manage.

When seen for psychological evaluation, Rosalie was found to be an attractive, sturdy little girl who was cooperative but quite restless and hyperactive. She seemed immature for her age and spoke with a childish lisp. Rosalie appeared to be quite comfortable in the testing session and spoke spontaneously about the "mean" children in school and at home. She seemed to crave recognition and was very responsive to praise and encouragement. She was very friendly but informed the examiner that she got mad easily and liked to fight. Rosalie tried to please the psychologist by working hard on all tests. Her Bender record is shown on *Plate 36*. The following is a detailed analysis of her test protocol:

Scoring of Bender record (p. 16): Figure A:1a. Distortion of square.

Figure 1:6. Perseveration since Rosalie drew 68 dots instead of 12.

Figure 2:9. Perseveration since Rosalie drew 22 columns of circles instead of 11.

Figure 3:11. Rotation of design by 90°.

Figure 4:14. Failure to join box and curve correctly (also gross perseveration, i.e., repetition of design, however, this is not scored).

Figure 6:18a. Angles substituted for curves. 20. Perservation since the design was repeated four times. This is scored even though each individual drawing of Figure 6 does not show perseveration.

Figure 7:21b. Incorrect number of angles on both hexagons. 23. Failure to overlap the two hexagons.

Figure 8:24. Incorrect number of angles on hexagon and diamond.

Total Bender score: 10.

Interpretation of Bender score (Table 6, p. 188): Rosalie's Bender score of 10 is more than five standard deviations below the normative score for ten year old children. This indicates that *Rosalie has serious malfunctioning in visual-motor perception. Her maturity in visual-motor perception is on the level of a five and a half year old child or immature beginning first graders.*

Time needed to complete test (Table 7, p. 36): Rosalie finished the Bender Test in 5 minutes 56 seconds which is average for her age group. However, since she drew many more designs and dots than were required it means that *she worked very rapidly and impulsively.*

Intellectual evaluation (p. 45): At the time of testing Rosalie was just 10 years old. Her perceptual maturity was on the level of a 5½ or a very immature 6 year old child. This suggests that Rosalie is probably a retarded child with an IQ somewhere in the high 50's or about 60, unless she has specific perceptual problems due to brain injury. The high incidence of perseveration on

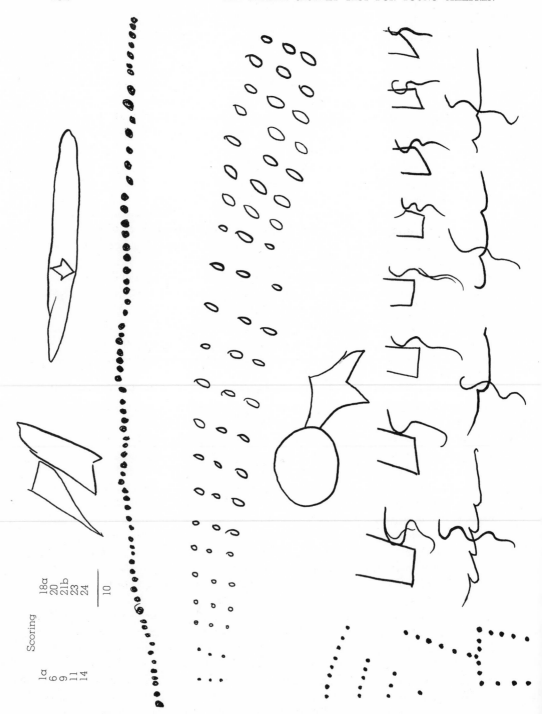

Plate 36. Rosalie, C. A. 10-0.

Rosalie's Bender record is very suggestive of neurological impairment. Because of this, Rosalie may actually have a higher intellectual potential than her low Bender score indicates.

School achievement (Table 14, p. 59): Research findings have shown that the correlation between Bender scores and fourth grade achievement is not high since achievement at this level depends on many factors besides visual-motor perception. But it appears unlikely that a child with as serious perceptual problems as those shown by Rosalie can do well in school. An analysis of specific deviations on Rosalie's Bender record (p. 61) shows difficulty in drawing angles and curves, and rotation of Figure 3, all of which are related in reading problems. The most striking feature of Rosalie's Bender protocol is the extreme perseveration on Figures 1, 2, 4, and 6, and the failure to integrate parts of Figures 4 and 7 correctly. These distortions are related to problems in arithmetic. *In view of Rosalie's severe disturbance in visual-motor perception she cannot be expected to function academically above the first grade level.*

Diagnosing brain injury (p. 75): Rosalie's extremely poor Bender score is highly suggestive of brain injury. An analysis for individual indicators on her Bender record *(Table 19,* p. 189) shows that three items, 6, 9 and 20, all related to perseveration, occur *almost exclusively* on the Bender records of ten year old children with neurological impairment. The other seven deviations on Rosalie's Bender record are found more often but not exclusively on the Bender protocols of ten year old brain injured children.

Time and space used to complete the Bender Test (p. 100): Rosalie worked very rapidly on the Bender Test suggesting impulsivity. She completed the test within the normal time limits but drew much more than was required in this time. Both the rapid drawing and the excessive number of drawings are frequently found among brain injured children. Rosalie used one sheet of paper to draw all nine Bender designs, but she turned the paper to a horizontal position which represents a type of expansiveness and is often associated with negativism and impulsiveness. *Both the use of time and space suggest possible brain injury.*

Summary of diagnosing brain injury (p. 104): *Rosalie's very poor Bender score, the large number of highly significant indicators of brain injury on her Bender record, her impulsive method of drawing the designs and her use of the paper, all indicate that Rosalie is probably a child with neurological impairment.*

Mental retardation (p. 107): The large discrepancy between Rosalie's chronological age and her level of visual-motor perception suggests that *Rosalie is probably a retarded child.* But since there are indications of brain injury, additional testing is necessary to determine to what extent Rosalie's poor Bender score reflects overall retardation and how much is the result of specific neurological impairment.

Emotional indicators (p. 125): Serious malfunctioning in visual-motor perception reflects a high degree of vulnerability. Rosalie may be expected therefore, to be very vulnerable and likely to develop emotional problems. The following emotional indicators (p. 126) were found on Rosalie's Bender record:

I., Confused Order, indicating poor planning ability and mental confusion. II., Wavy Line on Figure 1 and 2 reflecting emotional instability. IV., Increasing Size on Figure 2 suggesting low frustration tolerance and explosiveness. VIII., Overwork or Reinforced Line on Figure 4 revealing impulsive, acting out behavior and aggressiveness. IX., Second Attempt at Drawing Figures 4 and 6 seems to be associated primarily with impulsiveness in Rosalie's case. She also showed a tendency toward expansiveness by turning the paper to a horizontal position. This has been associated with negativism and acting out behavior.

Thus it appeared that *Rosalie was a vulnerable child with low frustration tolerance who was emotionally unstable, mentally somewhat confused, impulsive, and explosive. She also showed a tendency toward acting out and aggressive behavior. The presence of five emotional indicators and the tendency toward expansiveness showed that Rosalie was a seriously disturbed child who needed psychiatric help.*

Summary of Bender analysis: Rosalie appeared to be a brain injured child of low mental ability with serious malfunctioning in visual-motor perception and with learning problems. She also seemed to be an emotionally disturbed child who required psychiatric help.

The diagnosis of brain injury was supported by Rosalie's medical history. She was apparently a full term, normal baby. But at age 7 months Rosalie became ill with pneumonia and developed high fever with convulsions. Thereafter she became fussy and restless. It is quite probable that Rosalie suffered brain injury as a result of her illness. On the WISC Rosalie was found to be of borderline intelligence. Her Verbal IQ score was 79, her Performance IQ was 75, and her Full Scale IQ was also 75. It appeared therefore, that Rosalie's perceptual problems were even greater than her general retardation. It was also quite probable that Rosalie's brain lesions effected her behavior to a considerable degree and accounted for much of her restlessness, impulsiveness, and explosiveness.

On the Human Figure Drawing Test, Rosalie also revealed borderline intelligence, neurological impairment and signs of emotional disturbance. Rosalie's grade placement on the Wide Range Acheivement Test was 1.6 in reading and 1.7 in spelling. Because of both emotional and neurological problems it seemed that Rosalie would benefit from placement in a special class for children with emotional problems and brain injury.

10. Case History: George

George, a 10 year 8 months old Mongoloid child, was attending a special class for trainable retarded children. He was referred for routine psychological evaluation since he had not been tested in more than three years. George was a friendly, cheerful little fellow who reflected a good home environment where he received much love and attention. During the testing session he was very cooperative and affectionate. George seemed eager to please the examiner and enjoyed all tasks presented to him. He expressed much fondness for his teacher and for school. *Plate 37* shows George's Bender Test record. The following is an analysis of his Bender protocol:

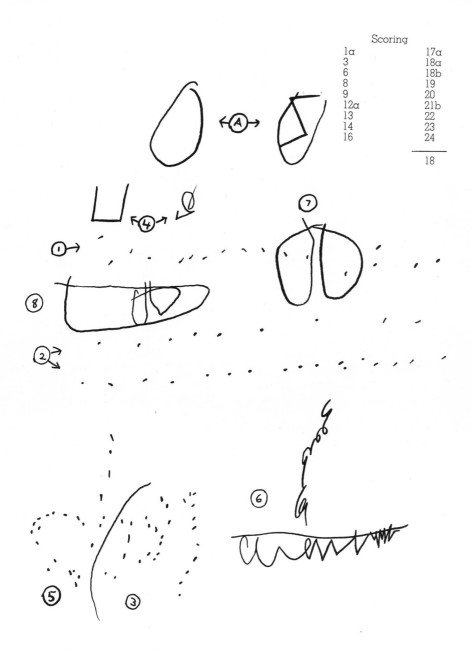

Scoring

1a	17a
3	18a
6	18b
8	19
9	20
12a	21b
13	22
14	23
16	24
	——
	18

Plate 37. George, C. A. 10-8.

Scoring of Bender record (p. 16): Figure A:1a. Distortion of circle into egg shape while the square is unrecognizable. 3. Failure to join circle and square.

Figure 1:6. Perseveration since George drew 17 dots instead of 12.

Figure 2:8. Omission of third row of circles. 9. Perseveration since George drew 17 dots instead of 11 circles in a row.

Figure 3:12a. Distortion of Gestalt of arrowhead; the shape of the design is lost.

Figure 4:13. Rotation of curve by 45°. 14. Failure to join box and curve. Figure 5:16. Rotation of arc by more than 45°. 17a. Gestalt of design is lost since the extension is joined to the end of the arc.

Figure 6:18a. Angles are substituted for curves on both lines. 18b. A straight line without any curves is added. 19. Failure to cross lines. 20. Perseveration on both lines, i.e., more than six sinusoidal curves on both lines.

Figure 7:21b. Distortion of hexagons; both hexagons resemble eggs. 22. Rotation of left hand hexagon by 45°; the two hexagons are parallel instead of at an angle. 23. Failure to overlap hexagons.

Figure 8:24. Incorrect number of angles on hexagon and diamond.

Total Bender score: 18.

Interpretation of Bender score (Table 6, p. 188): George's Bender score of 18 is almost 8 standard deviations below the normative score for his age group. *His grossly defective visual-motor perception is on the maturation level of a four year old child in nursery school.*

Intellectual evaluation (p. 45): At the time of testing George was 10 years 8 months old. His level of maturation in visual-motor perception was 4 years. This indicates that George is a severely retarded child with an IQ of about 40.

School readiness (p. 52): George's perceptual maturity resembles that of nursery school children. He is not yet ready to begin with formal school training even on the pre-primer level.

Diagnosing brain injury (p. 75): Since George is a Mongoloid child it is known that his brain has not fully developed and cortical malfunctioning is expected. A diagnosis of brain injury is not necessary. However, it is interesting to examine how George's impairment reveals itself on his Bender record. His extremely poor Bender score resembles that of brain injured children. An analysis of individual scoring items (*Table 19,* p. 189) shows six deviations on George's Bender record which are found *almost exclusively* on the Bender protocols of ten year old children with brain injury. They include: 6, 8, 9, 13, 18b, and 20. Eleven other scoring items occur more often but not exclusively on the Bender records of ten year old brain injured children. These include: 1a, 3, 12a, 14, 16, 18a, 19, 21b, 22, 23, and 24.

Time and space used to complete Bender Test (p. 100): Both the time and the space used by George to finish the Bender Test are within the normal limits for his age group. George completed the test in 4 minutes 29 seconds and used one sheet of paper.

Summary of diagnosing brain injury (p. 104): Being a Mongoloid child George is known to suffer from cortical malfunctioning. This *malfunctioning is clearly reflected in his extremely poor Bender score and in the unusually high incidence of individual indicators of neurological impairment on his Bender record.*

Mental retardation (p. 107): *The very large discrepancy between George's chronological age of 10 years 8 months and his perceptual maturity level of 4 years indicates serious mental retardation.* It was stated earlier that his IQ level is probably in the 40's.

Emotional indicators (p. 125): A child with extremely poor visual-motor perception tends to be a vulnerable child and may be expected to have emotional problems. An analysis of George's Bender record for individual emotional indicators (p. 126) shows the presence of: I., Confused Order which reflects poor planning ability and is common among all preschool children. Since George's mental age is on the preschool level, Confused Order of Bender designs is to be expected and cannot be considered a sign of mental confusion or emotional problems. II., Wavy Line on Figures 1 and 2 suggests poor coordination and emotional instability. It is probable that both apply to George. George is undoubtedly a vulnerable and unstable child but *the low incidence of emotional indicators on his Bender record as well as his behavior during the testing session suggest that he does not have serious emotional problems.* It seems that his parents and the school are meeting his needs well and that George feels secure and happy despite his vulnerability. A vulnerable and unstable child is more likely to develop emotional problems when exposed to stresses and strains, but he need not develop emotional problems if stresses and strains are kept to minimum. *George illustrates how a very seriously impaired child can be well adjusted.*

Summary of Bender analysis: George's Bender record indicates that he is a severely retarded child with cortical malfunctioning whose maturity in visual-motor perception is on the level of four year old nursery school children. He is not yet ready to begin formal school training. George appears to be a well adjusted, happy child who shows no signs of serious emotional problems.

These findings were in agreement with additional psychological test data. George obtained a mental age of 4 years 3 months and an IQ of 42 on the Stanford Binet Intelligence Scale, Form L-M. His Human Figure Drawing resembles that of a four year old child. George appears to be well placed in his present class and seems to be functioning as well as can be expected.

APPENDIX

Table 6. Normative Data for the Developmental Bender Scoring
System for Children

Distribution of Bender Mean Scores and Standard Deviation

Age Group	N	Mean Scores	Standard Deviation	Plus/Minus S.D.
5–0 to 5–5	81	13.6	3.61	10.0 to 17.2
5–6 to 5–11	128	9.8	3.72	6.1 to 13.5
6–0 to 6–5	155	8.4	4.12	4.3 to 12.5
6–6 to 6–11	180	6.4	3.76	2.6 to 10.2
7–0 to 7–5	156	4.8	3.61	1.2 to 8.4
7–6 to 7–11	110	4.7	3.34	1.4 to 8.0
8–0 to 8–5	62	3.7	3.60	.1 to 7.3
8–6 to 8–11	60	2.5	3.03	.0 to 5.5
9–0 to 9–5	65	1.7	1.76	.0 to 3.5
9–6 to 9–11	49	1.6	1.69	.0 to 3.3
10–0 to 10–5	27	1.6	1.67	.0 to 3.3
10–6 to 10–11	31	1.5	2.10	.0 to 3.6
Total	1104			

Distribution of Bender Mean Scores by School Grades

Grade Placement Beginning of Year	N	Mean Age	Mean Score	Standard Deviation	Plus/Minus Standard Deviation
Kindergarten	38	5–4	13.5	3.61	9.9 to 17.1
1st Grade	153	6–5	8.1	4.41	4.0 to 12.2
2nd Grade	141	7–5	4.7	3.18	1.5 to 7.9
3rd Grade	40	8–7	2.2	2.03	.2 to 4.2
4th Grade	39	9–8	1.5	1.88	.0 to 3.4

Table 19. Bender Indicators of Brain Injury for Children Age Five to Ten

Extra or missing angles:
　　Figure A—Significantly* more often in BI at all age levels.
　　Figure 7—Common in BI and NBI though more frequently in BI at all age
　　　　　　levels; *no* BI drew correct angles before age 8.
　　Figure 8—Common in BI and NBI through age 6, significant* for BI there-
　　　　　　after.

Angles for curves:
　　Figure 6—Common in BI and NBI but significantly* more often in BI at all
　　　　　　age levels, *all* BI drew angles up to age 7.

Straignt line for curves:
　　Fighre 6—Rare but highly significant** for BI when present.

Disproportion of parts:
　　Figure A—Common in BI and NBI through age 6, significant* for BI there-
　　　　　　after.
　　Figure 7—Common in BI and NBI through age 7, significant* for BI there-
　　　　　　after.

Substitution of five circles for dots:
　　Fighre 1—Present in BI and NBI but significantly* more often in BI at all
　　　　　　ages.
　　Figure 3—Present in BI and NBI through age 6, significant* for BI thereafter.
　　Figure 5—Present in BI and NBI through age 8, significant* for BI thereafter.

Rotation of design by 45°:
　　Figures 1, 4, and 8—Highly significant** for BI at all age levels.
　　Figure A and 5—Significant* for BI at all age levels.
　　Figure 7—Present in BI and NBI through age 6, significant* for BI thereafter.
　　Figure 3—Present in BI and NBI through age 7, significant* for BI thereafter.
　　Figure 2—Present in BI and NBI through age 8, significant* for BI thereafter.

Failure to integrate parts:
　　Figure A and 4—Significant* for BI at all age levels.
　　Figure 6—Rare but significant* for BI when present at all age levels.
　　Figure 7—Common for BI and NBI through age 6, significant* for BI there-
　　　　　　after.

Omission or addition of row of circles:
　　Figure 2—Common in BI and NBI through age 6, highly significant** for BI
　　　　　　thereafter.

Shape of design lost:
　　Figure 3—Present in BI and NBI through age 5, significant* for BI thereafter.
　　Figure 5—Rare and does *not* differentiate between BI and NBI at any age.

Line for series of dots:
　　Figures 3 and 5—Rare but highly significant** for BI at all age levels.

Perseveration:
　　Figure 1, 2, and 6—Common in BI and NBI through age 7, highly significant
　　　　　　for BI thereafter.

　* Significant: Occurring more often but not exclusively in BI group.
　** Highly significant: Occurring almost exclusively in BI group.
　BI: brain injured; NBI: non-brain injured.

REFERENCES

Aaronson, B. S., Nelson, S., and Holt, S.: On a relation between Bender Gestalt recall and Shipley-Hartford scores. J. Clin. Psychol., 9:88, 1953.

Aaronson, B. S.: The Porteus Mazes and Bender Gestalt recall. J. Clin. Psychol., 13:186-187, 1957.

Abramson, H. A., Waxenberg, S. E., Levine, A., Kaufman, M. R., and Korhetsky, C.: Lysergic acid diethylamide (LSD-25) XIII: Effect on Bender Gestalt Test performance. J. Psychol., 40:341-349, 1955.

Armstrong, R. G., and Hauck, P. A. Correlates of the Bender-Gestalt scores in children. J. Psychol. Studies, 11:153-158, 1960.

Baldwin, M. V.: A note regarding the suggested use of the Bender Gestalt Test as a measure of school readiness. J. Clin. Psychol., 6:412, 1950.

Barkley, B.: A note on the development of the Western Reserve Hapto-kinesthetic Gestalt Test. J. Clin. Psychol., 5:179-180, 1949.

Barnes, T. C.: EEG validation of Rorschach, Hunt, and Bender Gestalt Test. Am. Psychol., 5:322, 1950.

Baroff, G.: Bender Gestalt visuo-motor function in mental defectives. Am. J. Ment. Deficiency, 61:753-760, 1957.

Beck, H. S. A comparison of convulsive, non-convulsive organic and non-organic public school children. Am. J. Ment. Deficiency, 63:866, 1959.

Bender, L.: A visual motor Gestalt test and its clinical use. The Am. Orthopsychiat. Ass. Res. Mon., No. 3, 1938.

————: Bender Motor Gestalt Test: Cards and manual of instructions. The Am. Orthopsychiat. Assoc., Inc., 1946.

Bensberg, G. J.: Performance of brain injured and familial mental defectives on the Bender Gestalt Test. J. Consult. Psychol., 16:61-64, 1952.

Billingslea, F.: The Bender-Gestalt: An objective scoring method and validating data. J. Clin. Psychol., 4:1-27, 1948.

Brenner, A.: Nature and meaning of readiness for school. Merrill-Palmer Quarterly, 3:114-135, 1957.

————: A New Gestalt Test for measuring readiness for school. Merrill-Palmer Quarterly, 6:27, 1959.

Byrd, E.: The clinical validity of the Bender Gestalt Test with children: a developmental comparison of children in need of psychotherapy and children judged well adjusted. J. Proj. Tech., 20:127-136, 1956.

Chorost, S. B., Spivack, G., and Levine, M. Bender-Gestalt rotations and EEG abnormalities in children. J. Consult. Psychol., 23:559, 1959.

Clark, R. The relative contribution of six techniques of evaluating first grade problem children. Paper read at Amer. Assoc. Psychiat. Clinics for Children, Los Angeles, March, 1962.

Clawson, A.: The Bender Visual Motor Gestalt Test as an index of emotional disturbance in children. J. Proj. Tech., 23:198-206, 1959.

————: The Bender Visual Motor Gestalt for children. A manual. Beverly Hills, Western Psychological Services, 1962.

Corotto, L. V. and Curnutt, R. H.: The Effectiveness of the Bender-Gestalt in differentiating a flight group from an aggressive group of adolescents. J. Consult. Psychol., 24:368-369, 1960.

De Hirsch, K.: Specific dyslexia or strephosymbolia. Int. J. Phoniatry, 4:231-248, 1952.

De Hirsch, K.: Tests designed to discover potential reading difficulties at the six-year-old level. Am. J. Orthopsychiat., 27:566-576, 1957.

Eber, M.: A Bender Gestalt validity study: The performance of mentally retarded children. Dissert. Abstr., 18:296, 1958.

Feldman, I.: Psychological differences among moron and borderline mental defectives as a function of etiology. I Visual-Motor functioning. Amer. J. Ment. Deficiency, 57:484-494, 1953.

Gallagher, J.: A comparison of brain-injured and non-brain-injured mentally retarded children on several psychological variables. Child Development, 22, No. 2, 1957.

Garrison, M.: A comparison of psychological measures in mentally retarded boys over a three year period as a function of etiology. Train. Sch. Bull., 55:54-57, 1958.

Gobetz, W.: A quantification, standardization and validation of the Bender-Gestalt Test on normal and neurotic adults. Psycho. Mono., 67:6, N.356, 1953.

Goldberg, F.: The performance of schizophrenic, retarded and normal children on the Bender Gestalt Test. Amer. J. Ment. Deficiency, 61:548-555, 1957.

Goldberg, L. R.: The effectiveness of clinician's judgments: The diagnosis of organic brain damage from the Bender Gestalt Test. J. Consult. Psychol., 23:25-33, 1959.

Greenbaum, R.: A note on the use of the Word Association Test as an aid to interpreting the Bender. J. Proj. Tech., 19:27-29, 1955.

Halpern, F.: The Bender Gestalt Test. In Anderson, H. H. and Anderson, G. L. (Eds.). An Introduction to Projective Techniques, New York, Prentice Hall, 1951, pp. 324-340.

Halpin, V. G. Rotation errors made by brain-injured and familial children on two visual motor tests. Amer. J. Ment. Deficiency, 59:485-489, 1955.

Hanvick, L.: A note on rotation in the Bender Gestalt Test as predictors of EEG abnormalities in children. J. Clin. Psychol., 9:399, 1953.

Harriman, M. and Harriman, P.: The Bender-Gestalt as a measure of school readiness. J. Clin. Psychol., 6:175-177, 1950.

Henig, M. S.: Predictive value of a reading readiness test and of teacher's forecast. Elem. Sch. J., 50:41-46, 1949.

Hildreth, G.: Metropolitan Achievement Test, Primary I Battery: Form R. Yonkers-on-Hudson, World Book Co., 1946.

Hildreth, G. and Griffith, N. L.: Metropolitan Readiness Test. Yonkers-on-Hudson, World Book Co., 1949.

Hirschenfang, S.: A comparison of Bender Gestalt reproductions of right and left hemiplegic patients. J. Clin. Psychol., 16:439, 1960.

Hutt, M.: Tests of personality: picture and drawing techniques C: Revised Bender Visual-Motor Gestalt Test. In Weider, A. (Ed.) Contributions toward Medical Psychology. New York, Ronald Press, 1950.

Hutt, M. and Briskin, G. J.: The Clinical Use of the Revised Bender-Gestalt Test. New York, Grune & Stratton, Inc., 1960.

Jastak, J.: Wide Range Achievement Test, Wilmington, Del., C. L. Story Co., 1946.

Keller, J.: The use of a Bender-Gestalt maturation level scoring system with mentally handicapped children. Am. J. Orthopsychiat., 25:563, 1955.

Keogh, B. and Smith, C.: Group techniques and proposed scoring system for the Bender Gestalt Test with children. J. Clin. Psychol., 17:172-175, 1961.

Kitay, J.: The Bender-Gestalt Test as a projective technique. J. Clin. Psychol., 6:170-174, 1950.

Knoblauch, H. and Pasamanik, B.: Some thoughts on the inheritance of intelligence. Am. J. Orthopsychiat., 31:454-471, 1961.

Koppitz, E. M.: The Bender Gestalt Test and learning disturbances in young children. J. Clin. Psychol., 14, 292-295, 1958.

————: Relationships between the Bender Gestalt Test and the Wechsler Intelligence Scale for Children. J. Clin. Psychol., 14:413-416, 1958.

Koppitz, E. M., Sullivan, J., Blyth, D., and Shelton, J.: Prediction of first grade school achievement with the Bender Gestalt Test and Human Figure Drawings. J. Clin. Psychol., 15:164-168, 1959.

Koppitz, E. M.: Teacher's attitude and children's performance on the Bender Gestalt Test and Human Figure Drawings. J. Clin. Psychol., 16:204-208, 1960.

————: The Bender Gestalt Test for Children: A normative study. J. Clin. Psychol., 16:432-435, 1960.

Koppitz, E. M., Mardis, V., and Stephens, T.: A note on screening school beginners with the Bender Gestalt Test. J. Educ. Psychol., 52:80-81, 1961.

Koppitz, E. M.: The Bender Gestalt Test with the Human Figure Drawing Test for Young School Children. Columbus, Ohio Dept. of Education, 1962.

Koppitz, E. M.: Diagnosing brain damage in young children with the Bender Gestalt Test. J. Consult. Psychol., 26:541-546, 1962.

Lachman, F. M. Perceptual-motor development in children retarded in reading ability. J. Consult. Psychol., 24, 427-431.

Lee, J. M. and Clark, W. W.: Lee-Clark Reading Readiness Test. Los Angeles, California Test Bureau, 1951.

McGuire, F.: A comparison of the Bender-Gestalt and Flicker Fusion as indicators of Central Nervous System involvement. J. Clin. Psychol., 16:276, 1960.

Mehlman, B. and Vatovec, E.: A validation study of the Bender-Gestalt Test. J. Consult. Psychol., 20:71-74, 1956.

Miller, L. C., Loewenfeld, R., Lindner, R., and Turner, J.: Reliability of Koppitz' scoring system for the Bender Gestalt. J. Clin. Psychol., 19:2111, 1963.

Murray, E. and Roberts, F.: The Bender Gestalt Test in a patient passing through a brief manic-depressive cycle. U.S. Armed Forces Med. J., 7:1206, 1956.

Nadler, E. B., Fink, S. L., Shantz, F. C., and Brink, R. W. Objective vs. clinical evaluation of the Bender Gestalt Test. J. Clin. Psychol., 15:39-41, 1959.

Niebuhr, H. and Cohen, D.: The effect of psychopathology on visual discrimination. J. Abn. & Social Psychol., 53:173-177, 1956.

Olin, T. D. and Reznikoff, M.: A comparison of copied and recalled reproductions of the Bender Gestalt designs. J. Proj. Tech., 22:320-327, 1958.

Pasamanik, B.: The epidemiology of behavior disorders of childhood. Paper read at Assoc. Res. in Nervous and Mental Disease, New York, 1954.

Pascal, G. and Suttell, B. The Bender-Gestalt Test. New York, Grune & Stratton, 1951.

Peek, R. M. and Quast, W.: A scoring system for the Bender Gestalt Test. Minneapolis, Minn., 1951.

Peek, R. M. and Olson, G.: The Bender-Gestalt recall as an index of intellectual functioning. J. Clin. Psychol., 11:185-188, 1955.

Peek, R. M. and Storms, L.: Judging intellectual status from the Bender Gestalt Test. J. Clin. Psychol., 14:296-299, 1958.

Ravens, J. C.: Progressive Matrices. London, Lewis & Co., 1949.

Shapiro, M. B., Field, J., and Post, F.: An inquiry into the determinants of a differentiation between elderly "organic" and "non-organic" psychiatric patients on the Bender Gestalt Test. J. Ment. Sc., 103:364-374, 1957.

Shaw, M. C. and Cruickshank, W. M.: The use of the Bender Gestalt Test with epileptic children. J. Clin. Psychol., 12:192-193, 1956.

Siegel, S.: Nonparametric statistics. New York, McGraw-Hill Book Co., 1956.

Simpson, W. H.: A study of some factors in the Bender Gestalt reproduction of normal and disturbed children. Dissert. Abstr., 19:1120, 1958.

Smith, C. and Keogh, B.: The Group Bender-Gestalt as a reading readiness screening instrument. Percept. Motor Skills, in press.

Stewart, H. and Cunningham, S.: A note on scoring recalled figures of the Bender Gestalt Test using psychotic, non-psychotic, and controls. J. Clin. Psychol., 14:207-208, 1958.

Strauss, A. A. and Lehtinen, L. E.: Psychopathology and education of the brain-injured child. New York, Grune & Stratton, 1947.

Sullivan, J., Blyth, D., and Koppitz, E. M.: Correlations between early and later achievement in the elementary school. Unpublished manuscript.

Sullivan, J. and Blyth, D.: Prediction of later achievement patterns from early administration of the Bender Gestalt Test. Unpublished manuscript.

Sundberg, N. D.: The practice of psychological testing in clinical services in the United States. Am. Psychol., 16:79-83, 1961.

Terman, L. and Merrill, M.: Revised Stanford-Binet Intelligence Scale. Boston, Houghton Mifflin, 1937.

Tucker, J. and Spielberg, M.: Bender Gestalt Test correlates of emotional depression. J. Consult. Psychol., 22:56, 1958.

Wechsler, D. Weschler Intelligence Scale for Children. New York, The Psychological Corporation, 1949.

Wertheimer, W. Studies in the theory of Gestalt Psychology. Psychol. Forsch., 4, 1923.

Wewetzer, K.-H. Bender-Gestalt-Test bei Kindern: Auswertungsmethode und differential diagnostische Möglichkeiten. Z. diagnost. Psychol., 4:174, 1956.

Wewetzer, K.-H. Das Hirngeschädigte Kind. Stuttgart, Georg Thieme Verlag, 1959.

Index

k
l
m
n
7 o
8 p
9 q
0 r
1 s
82 t